The Deep Green Pool

The life, work and legacy of
Patricia Mulholland

Joyce Ann MacCafferty

GUILDHALL PRESS

First published in May 2007

Guildhall Press
Ráth Mór Business Park
Bligh's Lane
Derry BT48 0LZ
T: (028) 7136 4413 F: (028) 7137 2949
info@ghpress.com www.ghpress.com

The author asserts her moral rights in this work in accordance with
the Copyright, Designs and Patents Act 1998.

Photographs copyright of original owners as indicated in
Acknowledgements.

Design by Kevin Hippsley
Copyright © Joyce Ann MacCafferty/Guildhall Press
ISBN: 978 1 906271 01 5

We gratefully acknowledge the financial support of the Arts Council of Northern Ireland under
its Multi-Annual Lottery Programme.

All rights reserved. No part of this publication may be reproduced or transmitted in any form
or by any means, electronic or mechanical, including photocopy, recording, or any information
storage or retrieval system, without permission in writing from the publisher. The book is sold
subject to the condition that it shall not, by way of trade or otherwise, be lent, resold or otherwise
circulated without the publisher's prior consent in any form of binding or cover other than that
in which it is published and without a similar condition this condition being imposed on the
subsequent purchaser.

Acknowledgements

I would like to thank all the people who helped me in this endeavour, whether with photographs, reminiscences or encouragement, or all three, especially: Leslie Baird, David Bigger, Gertie Brady, Máire Bunting, Kevin Campbell, Yvonne Canavan, Maureen Coyne, Dominic Graham, Edmund Henry, Bronagh Hinds, Moya Hinds, Gerry Hobbs, Marie Huston, Pat MacCafferty, Peter MacCafferty, Carmel McGovern, Brenda McKee, Noel Mallon, Enid Minnis, Joyce Murphy, Eileen O'Connor, Kathy O'Connor, Sharon O'Donnell, Gerry O'Hare, Oonagh Pim, Éamon Phoenix, Kevin Rafferty, Carolyn Revie, Sheila Ringland, Frankie Roddy, who is sadly no longer with us, Roma Tomelty, Mary Turley and Loretto Watson.

A particular thank you is also due to Brian Barry for all the information about his uncle Peadar O'Rafferty, and to Jean Brown who improved the structure of the book.

I am deeply indebted to Margot Brown, Brendan Carson and Valerie Hamill who cheerfully handed over their albums to me; these proved a rich source of material. Ciarán Hinds, Norman Maternaghan, Yvonne McKinley, Sheelagh McRandal and Audrey Walker took the time and trouble to provide me with photographs, programmes and other documents. Their recollections form a vital part of the story.

Stella Logan, Maeve McGahan and Frank O'Neill were most obliging with pictures from the family album and information about their Aunt Patricia's background.

Grainne Gilmore is owed a special acknowledgement for her generous offer of financial assistance.

My task would have been more difficult without the practical help of Brian Bunting, Ciarán O'Somacháin and my son James. Brian also supplied many of the photographs.

The moral support and helpful advice of my husband Shay were indispensable; in fact, he can probably be held responsible for the original idea.

I also wish to thank the Honourable the Irish Society for their financial help.

And then there are two men whose company was as entertaining as it was enlightening, and who, unfortunately, died before publication: Reggie McClure, stalwart of the ballets and supporter of festival dancing to the end, was a mine of information and a valuable and generous source of photographs. Dr James Hawthorne CBE, husband of the late Patricia King, was most helpful and encouraging. His wit and hospitality will not be forgotten.

My appreciation also to Paul Hippsley, Declan Carlin, Kevin Hippsley and Joe McAllister at Guildhall Press for their professional input, and the Arts Council of Northern Ireland for supporting this publication.

None, I think, equalled in beauty and delight the appearances of the Irish Ballet . . . that tribute still stands to these young artists and their gifted founder.
Sam Hanna Bell

Contents

Foreword – Ciarán Hinds	6
Four-Bar Intro	7
First Step	11
Advance and Retire	23
The Lead Up	39
Thread the Needle	53
Promenade: 1953–59	67
Figure of Eight: 1961–68	99
Cast Off: 1971–91	125
Sidestep – Mulholland Dancers on Tour	141
Recall and Awards	163
Hook and Chain – Festival Dancing	185
Bibliography	202

Foreword

I was delighted when Joyce Ann MacCafferty asked me to write a short foreword to this account of Patricia Mulholland and the Irish Ballet Company. All of us, at some time, either pay silent homage to, or recognise publicly, people who have had a profound influence over our lives and I am very glad to have the opportunity to do so now in *The Deep Green Pool*.

Patricia Mulholland was a remarkable woman, a vital force in the cultural life of the North of Ireland from the 1950s to the 1980s. To be a teacher of Irish dance, to have the patience and dedication to pass on our traditional steps to generation after generation, is one thing – to then weave these steps and dances into a narrative through which the great Irish legends were recounted, stories of Oisín, of Cúchulainn, of Fionn MacCool and the Children of Lir, was something unique.

With the support of the Northern Ireland Arts Council, she created her own company, known as the Patricia Mulholland Irish Ballet, which travelled the length and breadth of the province and beyond, sharing these epic stories with audiences who, year after year, packed out theatres, town halls and school assemblies whenever they played.

Her creative talents lay in not only the direction and choreography of the company; she was also a supreme violinist, classically trained, but who devoted her musical skills to the accompaniment of the ballets, the scores of which resounded in a variety of jigs, reels, slow airs and laments.

With so much creativity and devotion to her projects, Patricia Mulholland was an inspiration to all who came in contact with her – you could round up a posse of O'Neills and Campbells, Dohertys and Raffertys, Gilligans and Tansleys, Sturdys and Henrys, Toners and Tomeltys, Mooneys and Rooneys, McCollums, McBrides and McLaughlins, Bailies, Byrnes and Bells, and a few hundred others and not hear a dissenting voice.

My own professional life has been greatly influenced by the fourteen years I spent dancing with the company – the precision, the presentation, the absolute necessity of teamwork, the endless hours of practice . . . and so much FUN! So many, many, wonderful memories of that time, and I'd like to salute Joyce Ann for bearing witness to this extraordinary woman.

Ciarán Hinds

Four-Bar Intro

'So I hear you're writing a book. What's it about?'
 'It's about my old dancing teacher.'
 'Really? Who's that?'
 'Patricia Mulholland.'
 'I vaguely remember the name. What kind of dancing did she teach?'
 'Irish . . .'
 'Oh, dear . . . glitter and tack.'
 'No, my kind of dancing doesn't do bouncing ringlets and that sort of thing.'
 'But surely when you've seen one Irish dancer, you've seen 'em all?'
 'On the contrary, festival dancers are different from the "caricature" Irish dancer in several ways. They look different, they dance differently and they even have different religions.'
 'You'll be telling me next, it's a Protestant dance for a Protestant people!'
 'Half right. It's a Catholic dance for a Catholic people – or for anyone who's interested. Festival dancers concern themselves with good dancing, not worrying about identity. You will find a greater mix of dancers and teachers in festival dancing than in the "traditional" associations. For example, you can go to a festival in the middle of Belvoir Park Estate, surrounded by Union flags, and find very traditional Irish dancing and music of a very high standard. Festival dancing has been taught on the Garvaghy Road in Portadown. The dancing festival in Ballymoney is held in the Protestant Hall – not that anyone is taking any account of religion, yet it illustrates a cross-community aspect of Irish dancing that mightn't otherwise spring to mind.'
 'How come I haven't heard of this?'
 'Before now, you mean? There you have it: one good reason for writing this book, to put on record the sterling work done by many teachers, past and present, in bringing together people of all kinds in a common, worthwhile pursuit; and most of all, one teacher in particular – Patricia Mulholland, who contributed so much to the cultural history of this province.'

I have had this sort of discourse, if not this actual conversation, with many friends and acquaintances.

In the last few years, Irish dancing has attracted enormous amounts of unprecedented attention. Entertainments based on Irish dance can be seen all over the world; books and television documentaries have been produced, explaining or exploiting the art form (some very scholarly works, some not at all). But it is curious that even the most thorough account leaves out any but the most cursory mention of the form of Irish dancing, referred to in this book for the sake of convenience, as festival dancing.

Festival dancing deserves to be better known on two counts: first, on a purely artistic level, it has more to offer even the random observer than other forms of Irish dancing, in my opinion; second, festival dancing has always been a witness to cross-community involvement since its beginnings.

And I have not been able to find one source that acknowledges this crucial genre, so it was this serious omission that prompted action on my part. As for the Patricia Mulholland Irish Ballet Company, it also seems to have been air-brushed out of the annals.

Even Helen Brennan (an alumna of Queen's University, Belfast – the same university that conferred an honorary MA on Miss Mulholland), who advised the producers of *Riverdance,* states in her book *The Story Of Irish Dance* that in this show 'appeared a TOTALLY NEW DANCE PHENOMENON' (my capitals). Now, perhaps she'd never heard of Patricia Mulholland, but anyone who has, knows that while the athleticism and technique of *Riverdance*'s first exponents might have been new, the staging of a romantic *pas-de-deux* and a powerful chorus line executed in an Irish idiom had been seen many years before and on many occasions.

Frank Whelan, in his *The Complete Guide To Irish Dance* (published in 2000), singles out a Belfast teacher whose figure-dance team in the '60s and '70s was 'very much sought-after for big events, concerts and television performances.' At last, one thinks, a reference to Patricia Mulholland. But no, it's a description of another person entirely! Mind you, he goes on to suggest that Irish dancing in Ulster collapsed due to the Troubles. The many burgeoning dancing schools, whether Coimisiún, Comhdháil or Festival, which have entertained audiences all over the North and further afield, would be surprised, to say the least, at that remark.

The silence that surrounds the Mulholland name in all accounts of Irish dancing has been broken only by one author that I can find, and then only as a nod in passing. Dr John Cullinane has written extensively on several themes concerning mainstream Irish dancing and mentions Patricia Mulholland as being very innovative, particularly in her imaginative set dances such as *The Deep Green Pool.* He singles out Mulholland protégées Maureen McCann, Yvonne Hood and Sheila Fitzpatrick as great dancers – all champions in their day.

Musician and academic Mícheál Ó Súilleabháin's acclaimed television music series devoted one programme to the dance tradition of Ireland and was, of necessity, constrained to a limited account. But elsewhere, he has stated that 'Patricia Mulholland's work is an essential part of the story of Irish dance in our time.'

It is strange that such a talent as Patricia Mulholland's and its resultant output can be virtually unknown, at best – and ignored, at worst – in the lexicon of Irish dance history until now. This book is meant to go a little way towards remedying that deficiency. In researching it, I have spent the best part of two years talking to friends and relatives of Patricia Mulholland and to ex-Mulholland dancers (indeed, I myself danced for her for seventeen years) in an effort to trace the influences that brought about this phenomenon.

Significantly, everyone whom I asked for help (with only one exception) gave of his/her time readily. Moreover, the enthusiasm with which they recalled their association with Miss Mulholland is evidence of another facet of this extraordinary woman's energy – she could generate a lot of fun!

The last will and testament of Patricia Mulholland states her occupation to have been that of choreographer, which is defined by the Oxford English Dictionary as 'a composer of the sequence of steps and moves for a ballet or other performance of dance.' Choreographer she certainly was, leaving behind a body of work that included over twenty full-length ballets, several divertissements, many original team and set dances and countless new settings of traditional Irish dances. But she was much more than just a "composer of steps and moves".

This book is simply an attempt to capture something of her achievements as a musician, teacher and visionary, and, as the latter suggests, an artist ahead of her time.

Joyce Ann MacCafferty

First Step

Music is my life. **Patricia Mulholland**

I first met Patricia Mulholland when I was about four and a half years old.

My mother took me down the Ormeau Road from Ballynafeigh to Donegall Pass, travelling through an area that some wits now call the "Liberated Ormeau". We climbed onto the number 77 Waterworks bus, which crossed town through Durham, Albert, Northumberland and Manor streets – and then into North Belfast. I enjoyed this and subsequent journeys, looking out of the bus window.

But I didn't realise just how quickly we would pass from Catholic enclave to Protestant stronghold. This led to some confusion in my mind: as I saw NO TAIGS ADMITTED on a wall very close to the Falls Road, and knowing at least that the Falls was generally Catholic, I believed for years that "taigs" were "prods". It was years later, when I used to go along to St Matthew's vestry in Ballymacarrett in East Belfast with my grandmother for her weekly Apostolic Work meetings – Grandma was vice president of the organisation for over fifty years from its foundation in 1923 – that fellow apostolic worker Julie Bradley clarified matters for me. It is probably no surprise that Julie became a teacher, rescuing others from their ignorance as she had saved me.

When we arrived at Newington Street, a woman wearing glasses, who, I later discovered, was Mrs Mulholland, opened the door and ushered us in. Patricia herself came into the room and my first thought was what a pretty lady she was, with her blue eyes and curly, black hair.

She explained to my mother that she was reluctant to take such a young child. I learned later that she felt there was a danger that very young children could become too "dried up", as she put it, if they started too soon or practised too often during their early years. There was positively no chance of that happening to me: she needn't have worried, I was always lazy.

But my mother insisted and so I ran about the room "catching butterflies" – an exercise from ballet class. I must have done something else, but what it was, I don't remember. The butterfly catching must have done the trick, for I was taken upstairs to the practice room, and, then and there, was taught the first step of the light double jig. This was the start of my Irish dancing career, including a long stint in what I would come to know as the Irish Ballets, the start of my relationship with Patricia Mulholland, and the beginning of friendships that are still going strong.

On the way back to the bus stop, we called into a shop on the corner of Newington Street. This was a real find for a thirsty dancer, because you could buy a shot of lemonade for a penny. The shopkeeper had a tray of glasses on the counter and poured brown lemonade into them from a big bottle; he had larger glasses, too, for the even thirstier at twopence a go. The Health and Safety rules of today didn't apply then and we weren't too worried about that sort of thing in any case.

This was sometime in late 1951 and Patricia Mulholland was well-established at this time. But how had it all begun?

The early decades of the twentieth century were a particularly busy time for British shipyards, including Harland and Wolff in Belfast. It steadily became the biggest employer in the city, eventually giving work to 14,000 men in 1914. The yard brought in more and more work, securing orders from the White Star Line, for example, to build their ocean liners *Olympic* and *Titanic*. These were the largest and most luxurious ships ever seen then, requiring a very high standard of workmanship. Not all the craftsmen could be found locally, up to and including this time, and so, expert, skilled labour had to be brought in from England and Scotland.

This was how William Mulholland, an English master joiner, came to be in Belfast. He was born and reared in Barrow-in-Furness, where his family had long links with the shipyard. His father James worked as a joiner for Vickers. His mother, née Annie Fielding, had relations who were in similar employment with the same firm.

William came to the city along with many others to work in the shipyard. Here he met a Lisburn girl, Mary (Minnie) O'Hare, and fell in love and married her. Though William's generation was from Barrow-in-Furness, his family was originally from County Derry. (A branch of the Mulholland clan is associated with Loughinisholin, not far from the ancestral home of my own family.)

But the early part of their married life was spent in Barrow-in-Furness, where their first child Stella was born. Just as work had brought him back to England, so it meant a return to Belfast in 1910. This was a feature of the Mulholland household for many years, the toing and froing between England and Ireland, neither father nor mother being entirely happy in each other's homeland but having to follow the work.

In Belfast, he was employed as a cabinet-maker on the *Titanic* and the *Olympic*. He was initially a sort of enigma to his workmates in the yard, for here was this Englishman with none of the outward signs of being a Catholic but who was nonetheless RC, at least nominally.

Apparently there were three grades of joiner in the yard – joiner, carpenter and cabinet-maker – the last being the best qualified. This distinction was a matter of some pride to William, for when Patricia was beginning to make a name for herself, his son-in-law made a jocose remark about it, saying that such-and-such was some achievement for a joiner's daughter, and William would insist that he was no mere joiner but a cabinet-maker.

The family was still living in Belfast, in Mileriver Street, when Patricia was born on 3 January 1915. She was deliberately vague about this date throughout her life, even in hospital, and sometimes even celebrated on the wrong day. Apart from a sort of female vanity that believes a lady should not disclose her age, she was afraid that parents would not send their children to a middle-aged teacher, and she warned her nieces never to allow newspapers to publish their ages under photographs.

She could get away with pretending to be younger than she was, because she never seemed to age. In all the years that I knew her, from 1951 until she died in 1992, she did not seem to change at all in appearance.

Four years after Patricia's birth, Frank, the only son, was born in Belfast, but this settled period was not to last: the family moved back across the Irish Sea in pursuit of William's employment.

Durham was home to the young family for a number of years, and although Patricia had sentimental memories of the great cathedral, she detested their house there, as it was dank and uncomfortable.

William had a lifelong interest in brass band music, in keeping with his northern English upbringing, and even in later years, when he was deaf (might this have been an occupational hazard?), he loved to listen to the bands in Alexandra Park, straining to hear the music. His nieces, Stella and Maeve, remember him listening to the wireless with the volume turned up full and his ear pressed to its side.

Patricia Mulholland on her mother Minnie's knee with sister Stella.

After a few moves around the general Limestone Road area, the family settled in Newington Street in the house which saw so many people through its doors over the years.

There was a hallstand in the entrance, over which the dancers threw their coats, scarves and schoolbags. This was made by William Mulholland. The mantelpiece and fireplace in the living room were his work also. They were decorated with ornate carving. Some would trace the intricacy of Miss Mulholland's dances to an inherited love of embellishment, evident in her father's work. They also shared a painstaking attitude to a task – he was very particular in his craft, never using nails, always mortise or dovetail joints. He was also creative and built a special cradle for his daughter Stella's twins. The family still have samples of his handiwork.

Minnie's dressmaking augmented the family income: she made outfits for her daughters, including their dancing costumes.

It says a lot for Minnie and Billy that their children were sent to music and dancing classes and that they took tap and Scottish lessons as well as Irish, even though money was tight at times.

The first violin in the house was bought at an auction, originally for Stella, but she didn't like it and Patricia, who was several years younger than Stella, asked her mother to keep it for her.

Stella as a Highland dancer.

Irish Colleen, Patricia.

Patricia was an accomplished tap dancer.

Patricia's first music teacher was Sally McGifford, who played with the Belfast Philharmonic; she later had lessons from John Crowther, a well-known Belfast musician at the time.

From an early age, Patricia showed a determination to succeed, a characteristic that was to see her through many a crisis later when ill health threatened but never stopped her career.

If festivals became important to Patricia in later years, they certainly played a part in giving her a good start. Then, as now, several festivals offered bursaries to prize-winners to encourage them in their field. Larne offered a bursary for the top instrumentalist at a time when Patricia was really just starting to come to grips with the violin. Mrs Mulholland knew that if Patricia could win it, this would make a difference to their budget, and so she encouraged her to practise for the competition. She later confided to my mother that she was afraid Patricia was taking it far too seriously, because she practised for hours at a time, until the perspiration ran down her face and, on occasion, Mrs Mulholland thought the fiddle might break from overuse!

This hard work paid off in the end, because Patricia won the bursary – much to her delight and the relief of her mother.

She won senior violin competitions regularly, scoring 90 out of 100 as often as not.

A Carrickfergus adjudicator's comments read: 'This young lady played the Vivaldi with great sensitiveness and with a beautiful, poetic conception of the music.

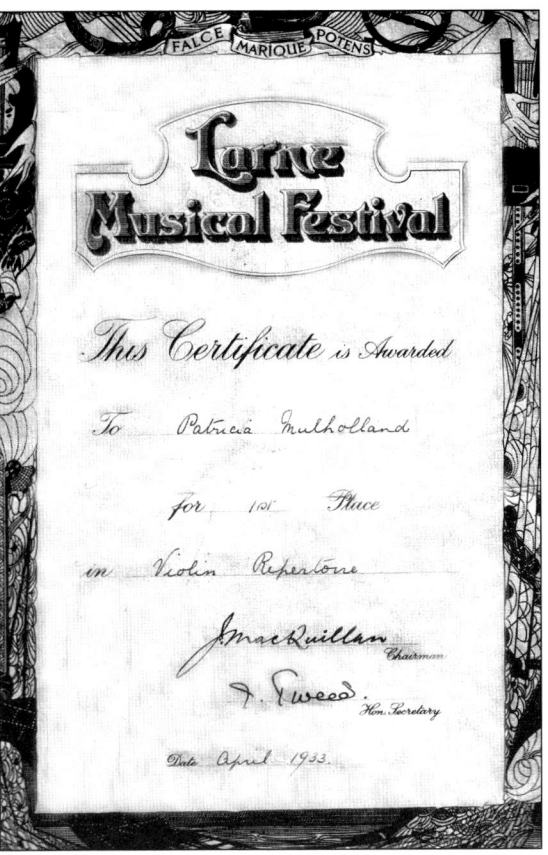

Patricia continued to compete successfully at festivals, as this Larne certificate demonstrates.

Excellent rhythm and fluent phrasing. She has a fine sense of style. The adagio was finely drawn but the playing of the whole sonata showed first-rate musicianship. She felt the music and so did we.' This adjudicator, David T Yacamini, who was a self-professed Scot, despite the name, was obviously impressed by the young girl, for Mrs Mulholland told the story of how he asked Patricia to show him her hands and how he turned them over in his and examined them carefully before telling her that she certainly had the physical attributes to become a professional violinist. It may have been this man who was so impressed by her playing that he later gave her a Josef Klotz violin. This instrument had a very warm tone, being between a violin and a viola in size.

The violin was never far away from Patricia; it became a sort of extension of her personality. The only time she was parted from it was when she sent it away to have a new fingerboard fitted. It was fascinating to see how her playing wore grooves under the strings, so much was it in use.

William's deafness was cruelly frustrating, not just for him, a man who loved music and who possessed a fine tenor voice, but also for the family as communications became more and more difficult. Relationships had often been fraught from time to time with disagreements about where the family should live and about the practice of religion.

Both Minnie and William were Catholic, but Minnie was decidedly more pious than her husband, and his less ardent approach was a bone of contention. His health, too, must have played a part in family tensions, because the poor man was always complaining. His niece remembers going to the shop regularly to get two Askit powders and ten Park Drive cigarettes. It was only after he'd been taken into hospital at the end of his life that it was discovered he had a tumour on the spine.

Stella, the elder sister, had always been a good dancer and she took up the teaching of Irish dancing. She claimed that Patricia was the better dancer; however, several people dispute this and some who knew them as young women have said that Stella was definitely the more gifted dancer and Patricia the better teacher. Apparently, Patricia had poor carriage when she danced.

Stella built up her classes and in a short time had pupils in Belfast, Larne, Lisburn and Portadown who competed at festivals at home and at Coleraine and Derry. Nobody had a car in those days, so it meant that she had to take the train, or, in some cases, walk, even in the snow, to ensure that she reached her classes. One gets the impression that it might have been easier to walk to and from Lisburn – even in the snow – than to have to explain to Mrs Mulholland why there were no fees from the pupils that week.

Stella was an accomplished pianist and she and her sister were accustomed to playing duets at musical soirées. At first, Patricia's repertoire was entirely classical and she admitted to 'looking down her nose' at traditional music, but Stella taught her some dance tunes so that she could play for her dancers one night when she, Stella, was unavailable. And so, from a sort of accidental beginning, came a gradual love for Irish music. Eventually, Patricia became an avid collector of Irish music, a composer, and an almost unrivalled exponent of the slow air.

Many years later, when the Patricia Mulholland Irish Ballet Company was in full swing, Stella used to accompany Patricia when Gertie Brady, the official accompanist, was unavailable, or when the performance was not one officially sponsored by the Arts Council, say, a charity night. The dancers loved her playing; she did have a background in dance, but it was rather her lovely touch on the piano that enlivened the music and the chemistry between the two sisters that enhanced their performance.

Meanwhile, Patricia was on track to a solo career as a concert performer, but as she grew older, she began to have doubts about this direction. It was not that she loved music any less, or that she was afraid of hard work; no, it was simply that she could not cope with stage fright.

Anyone who ever heard her play in her heyday could never doubt her virtuosity, but she became too nervous before a performance to give of her best, and as she matured, so did the problem. This was not a case of the ordinary nervousness that adds an edge to a performance, but one that had an almost crippling effect. Although she was hugely talented, she was not secure in herself and this insecurity would never leave her throughout her career. She could play brilliantly, in any venue, as long as she was accompanying dancers, but would never perform solo if she could avoid it at all. Even at a very casual level – in class, say – if her pupils prevailed on her to play something other than the usual dance tunes, she would start, then break off in the middle, saying, 'That's enough of that,' or 'I can't remember any more.' As children, we had a curious liking for her rendition on the fiddle of an imitation of badly played bagpipes – she would occasionally delight us with this cacophony on request.

Norman Maternaghan, the choreographer, tells the story of when the company went to the Eisteddfod in Wales in 1950 and she was invited to play and couldn't refuse. Well, she nearly went to pieces before the performance and asked Norman to stand beside her for reassurance. He was one of her principal dancers at this time and one can only imagine what the other dancers thought of this arrangement. Any bad feeling among his colleagues would have been compounded by the fact that she then asked him to accompany her to hear Vittoria de Los Angeles. She asked him first what kind of music he liked. He answered that he loved the Hollywood musicals. Indeed, it was an interest in this genre that had attracted him to dancing. However, she informed him that it was time he heard some different sorts of music and produced the tickets for the operatic concert. This did not go down at all well with some of the other dancers, who had expected to be going somewhere else with Norman that evening.

L-R: Patricia King, Patricia Mulholland and Madeleine Mackey at the 1950 Eisteddfod.

Later, when Patricia Mulholland was at the height of her powers, a novice member of the stage crew discovered her performance nervousness to his cost. During the ballet *The Children Of Lir*, Miss Mulholland was accustomed to play *The Coulin* during an *entr'acte* while the men changed their shoes, and on this occasion, the unfortunate technician decided to shine a large spotlight on Patricia as she played, wondering why nobody else had thought of this brilliant idea. Well, she nearly lost her nerve and he nearly lost his job!

Things in the Mulholland household were on an even keel for a while. And then Stella fell in love. Mrs Mulholland did not rush to give her blessing to her daughter. Perhaps she was afraid that the balance of their lives would be upset. Perhaps she did not relish the thought of losing the income generated by the dancing classes. Maybe she just thought that marriage was a risky business, judging by her own experience. But the ultimate result of Stella's marrying was that Patricia became a dancing teacher.

Stella's husband, Joseph O'Neill, was a butcher with a very successful business in Duncairn Gardens. He was also a very generous man.

Mrs Mulholland, Mr and Mrs O'Neill, Mrs Canavan and Mrs and Mr Coyne.

My grandfather, who belonged to a Catholic organisation called The Knights Of Saint Columbanus (in fact he was a founding member), used to talk about a meeting that this group held in the Carlton Restaurant in Belfast about raising money for some charity. There were a couple of dozen men present at this meeting and they all had tea and something to eat. When it came to sorting out the bill, it was discovered that Mr O'Neill, Stella's husband, had paid for the entire group.

The O'Neills used to take a house during the summer in Kilclief in County Down and Stella and Patricia used to play at musical evenings there. Peter, Eugene and Joseph Tomelty used to attend these evenings, crossing Strangford Lough in a boat from Portaferry. They were obviously just as good sailors as singers!

These nights gave Mr O'Neill the idea of using the same personnel in concerts that were more formal to raise money for various charities. Kevin Campbell, later a principal dancer, was fortunate enough to hear Patricia playing a movement from the Mendelssohn violin concerto at just such a concert in the Newington Hall.

Patricia continued her sister's classes in places like Portadown and Larne until some of the senior dancers could take over. When one thinks of it, Miss Mulholland must have been incredibly busy, even in the early part of her career, what with her children's classes in Belfast and further afield, and adult classes for The Belfast Folk Dancing Society, which she taught from the mid-1930s. Her dancers also often performed at charity events.

She also gave extra tuition to those who showed promise and who seemed to merit the attention. Both Maureen McCann and Yvonne Hood remember going to Belfast for extra classes and staying with Miss Mulholland in Newington Street if they missed the last train home. Norman Maternaghan had private lessons, one night a week for a year, before he was invited to join the adult class.

Here, a young team entertains patients in Belfast's Mater Hospital in the 1940s. Patricia's niece Stella is third from right, facing camera.

However, busy and all as she was, Patricia still found time for a social and personal life. She, too, fell in love and became engaged to be married. The couple spent a lot of time together, naturally, even going to Mass and confession together! But it was not all religious practice. Miss Mulholland herself told the story of a visit to the seaside. She'd been looking forward to a swim, as she had a new swimsuit she was dying to try out; she'd knitted it herself. Everything was fine until she went into the sea: the wool absorbed a lot of water and its weight pulled the suit right down past the limits of decency!

The engagement did not lead to a wedding. Patricia thought long and hard about this decision to break her engagement. Devotion to her career may not have been the only consideration, though an obviously important one. Her own parents' marriage was not made in heaven, and her sister had met with opposition to hers. Add to these that she was devoted to her mother right up to the end of her life, even coping with Minnie's dementia, rarely getting a night's sleep towards the end. Whatever the reason, she felt so confused about which road to take that she went to Lough Derg, that famous place of pilgrimage, to pray for guidance to make the right decision.

It was surely the right decision, for it would be hard to imagine Patricia Mulholland immersed in domesticity and/or raising children. Her training and leanings were towards the artistic rather than the domestic. Carmel McGovern recalls that she claimed she had been too busy practising the violin to learn about ordinary household affairs; so when anyone came into the house, they had to make the tea.

She would probably have suffocated as a housewife if she'd given up her teaching, and she felt that if she had continued her career alongside coping with family duties, then her marriage would have suffered.

In reality, she was already married to her career. She told journalist Judith Rosenfeld, 'I did not think it would be fair to the man. I believe marriage is a career, and if you want to make a success of it, you have to put it first. And I could not have done that.'

Gradually, the family home in Newington Street became the only centre for all the dancing classes. The house must have been extremely sturdily built, because the floor in the upstairs front room took a regular pounding from the feet of dancers of all sizes.

It seems incredible, now, to think that adults had their lessons here, not only small children. The room was about thirteen feet square, at most, with a small bay window and alcoves either side of the fireplace. This fireplace assumed special importance, as Kevin Campbell recalled, because whenever a team dance was performed at a feis or concert, the first question was *Where's the fireplace?* as it was the point of orientation for all the teams – we didn't seem to bother with the more technical "top couple" or "heads".

There were benches arranged round the room, one of which was in one of the alcoves. This was where the "bold boys" usually sat, as it was behind Miss Mulholland (she sat on a high stool to play, on the other side) and therefore out of her line of sight, so they could sit ensconced, and could make faces at those dancing, or exchange stink bombs etc with impunity. Boldness in those days was pretty tame by comparison with these days!

She always seemed to attract large numbers of boy dancers until latterly. It may just have been coincidence at the start – perhaps brothers were sent along with sisters – but once there was a group of boys at the class, it was easier to keep them there when they had made friends of the same sex.

The ballets, too, had a considerable male corps during the first three decades of their existence. Her approach to obtaining the services of men was simple: if they had any kind of appearance at all, she would use them; it didn't matter to her if they weren't too expert at the dancing, because she knew that she could teach them that.

A cousin of mine, who was staying with us while his parents were away on holiday, came along to rehearsal one Saturday (I think my mother may have chased him out of the house) and suddenly found himself a member of The Patricia Mulholland Irish Ballet Company.

While the dancing went on upstairs, Mrs Mulholland entertained the mothers downstairs. The business of buying second-hand pumps and costumes was transacted in the living room. We were always encouraged to avoid placing shoes on the table because of the superstition that it preceded a fight; but to do otherwise was virtually impossible in the circumstances.

Patricia Mulholland, right, in Newington Street with her fiancé in fashionable plus-fours and her sister Stella, in the mid-1940s.

The serious gossip sessions, meanwhile, went on in the front sitting room. For anyone given to this sort of thing, it must have been fascinating, because most of Belfast passed through with their offspring. Thus, Mrs Mulholland knew the news of the world – everything from which school insisted on every pupil using the same kind of pen (was it Osmiroid?) to the shaky state of family relationships – and she enjoyed sharing all this knowledge. Mind you, it must have been difficult to leave when your child came down the stairs, without being afraid that you would be the next topic for discussion.

Around Christmas-time, there was always a crib beside the fireplace, and it was the first place I ever saw the Three Wise Men "travelling" towards the stable during Advent until they arrived on the feast of Christmas Star. The three little figures started off near the door and we looked in to see the progress they'd made in the weeks coming up to the holiday.

My grandmother, especially, and my mother enjoyed all the chat, particularly Mrs Mulholland's candour about her husband, to whom she referred disparagingly as "Mulholland", and even "oul' Mulholland" on occasion.

Le tout Belfast passed through the doors of Newington Street. Adherents of every kind of Christian religion – and none – danced there. It seems this mix happened by accident, at least at first. Patricia's classes were mixed, right from the beginning, but, of course, the influence of the Belfast Folk Dancing Society (BFDS) and the Guides cannot be overestimated. Parents who had danced with the BFDS naturally sent their children to the teacher who had taught them, and the same thing can be said for the Guides.

This was an extremely important aspect of Miss Mulholland's influence, another facet of her approach to life in which she was ahead of her time.

It was inconceivable that anyone's religion was taken into account, except, that is, for Sunday mornings. Kevin Campbell has happy memories of how everyone enjoyed going off to feiseanna at weekends in places like Newry, Derry, Dundalk and Portstewart. On arrival at the guesthouse, the first task was to find out the times of all the Sunday services: Anglican, Methodist, Presbyterian or Catholic. And on Sunday morning, all were dispatched to their respective service (whether they wanted to go or not). If a church of a particular persuasion could not be found, then the dancer concerned would go to the nearest to his way of thinking. Then they all came together afterwards for lunch or a walk on the beach or whatever else had been organised.

When they were on the continent, where there might be only a Catholic service available, then everyone went to that. In 1964, when the company was in the Bordeaux region of France, one local newspaper commented on the fact that on the Sunday morning, a piper piped the dancers into two churches – one Catholic and one Protestant.

Everyone could worship God in his or her own way on a Sunday, but it never, ever interfered with dancing or with friendship.

Newry Feis seems to have been a favourite venue for a lot of dancers. Sheila Fitzpatrick loved going there and staying in a hotel with her mother. The feis continued during the war years, and, one night, Sheila and her mother and several other Mulholland dancers from Larne were just settling down for the night when the sirens sounded and everyone had to shelter under the stairs. Mrs Fitzpatrick started the rosary and everyone joined in, as far as they were able, including the Protestants from Larne.

One dancer, who was about ten at the time, was asked by her clergyman if there were Catholics at her dancing class. She answered that indeed there were. He asked her if she had to hold hands with them and she said that yes, she did have to hold their hands in some dances. He told her that this was dangerous and must not continue. It's not clear what he was so afraid of, but she thought his advice was so silly that she never went back to his church.

Most of the time, the make-up of the corps of dancers varied between fifty-fifty and sixty-forty per cent, Catholic to Protestant.

Patricia Mulholland was a devout Catholic all her life (as was her mother), but she never let religion interfere where it did not belong. Her influence on her dancers in this respect was enormous. We learned religious tolerance along with our dancing steps without even realising it.

Lifelong friendships were forged that would otherwise not have existed between Catholics and Protestants.

Education for Mutual Understanding is now part of the school curriculum. From the 1930s, Mulholland dancers were doing practicals in this throughout their dancing careers.

It is ironic and sad to note that Newington Street, where we learned so much about mutual understanding, has so often been the scene of bigotry and its resultant violence.

Advance and Retire

Quite a lot of people felt that Irish dancing was all right as it was and that any attempt to introduce a more relaxed interpretation of a traditional art form was tantamount to heresy. **Patricia Mulholland**

Mention Irish dancing to people and most of them probably think straightaway of fantastically decorated dresses, curly wigs and thick, white ankle socks. Certainly, at feiseanna, that is the norm (for female dancers at any rate). But fear not, there is another kind of Irish dancing, the exponents of which look a little different and whose experience of Irish dancing and competition is very different from that of the average feis dancer.

There are obvious similarities in the two kinds of dancing and the two branches do stem from the same original tree, but the development of each has happened in its own distinctive manner.

Picture the scene: a teenager has practised her reel, slip-jig, hornpipe and set dances, and arrives, nervously, perhaps, at a feis. The musicians – a fiddler, pianist and maybe accordionist – set up at the side of the stage, ready to play for all the entrants in the intermediate reel, say. She receives her number and will dance a lead-round, sidestep and possibly one or two steps on the stage along with one or two others before the adjudicator rings a bell to indicate that he/she has seen enough.

Another girl of the same age has also practised her dances and arrives at a festival. The musicians set up in the same way to play, possibly even the same tune, and the adjudicator will "ring her off" after giving her a mark.

The two occasions might seem different only in location, but even a cursory examination will reveal differences – the name of the event, for a start. Some dancers compete at festivals, others at feiseanna. The word *feis* (plural, *feiseanna*) roughly means festival in English, although the purists would insist that a feis is a celebration of several disciplines, not just one; for example, Feis Dhoire Cholmcille is to be considered a real feis because there are competitions in singing, instrumental music, poetry, Irish language storytelling etc, not just Irish dancing. But in common parlance, to most people, a feis would mean a competition for singers or Irish dancers.

Some dancers consider themselves Irish through and through and view their dancing as an extension of their nationality. Their parents will have chosen to send their offspring to Irish dance classes as a natural expression of their culture, and the teachers to whom they send their children will have passed an examination qualifying them in various aspects of Irish traditional dance, including a rudimentary knowledge of the Irish language.

Some consider themselves no less Irish than the first group, but see their dancing as another accomplishment, comparable with playing a musical instrument or reciting verse. Northern Irish residents are fortunate in the availability of reasonable, sometimes free, and competent tuition in all sorts of cultural endeavour, partly through the work of the schools and partly that of the education area boards.

Then there is another group for whom Irish dancing is a desirable pursuit and perfectly compatible with their Britishness. This is not a new phenomenon. My own great-grandfather, a man called John Wilson from Draperstown (and buried in the Church of Ireland graveyard at its centre), was famous for a jig danced in his stocking soles. Now, just how common a practice this was I have no idea; perhaps it was simply a personal eccentricity of his, but someone must have taught him.

Go to any mainstream Irish dancing championship, such as the All-Ireland, and you could be forgiven for thinking that the dancers are cloned from one model, so uniform is the appearance (especially of the girls), achieved by means of curly wigs and highly decorated dresses with stiff skirts; and so similar is the choreography, with its emphasis on vertical movement. Moreover, the background and life-experience of the dancers is similar too – generally working-class and Catholic.

However, there is another form of Irish dancing that has co-existed in the North of Ireland for several decades, which brings together all sorts of people, and that is festival dancing – so-called because the competitions in which the dancers take part are at festivals that belong, in some cases, to the British Federation of Music Festivals. Dancing competitions are held in Portadown, Holywood, Ballymoney, Ballymena, Limavady, Newtownards, Larne, Ballyclare, to give but a sample; these are names that do not resonate with "Irishness".

The introduction of Irish dancing to local music festivals can be traced back to the 1920s and the influence of people like Peadar O'Rafferty. (Naturally, Irish dancing had often been included also in earlier feiseanna like Feis na nGleann, but it was not seen at festivals until this time.)

Patricia Mulholland and pupils of hers, such as Maureen McCann, continued this development in and around Belfast in the 1950s. Jean Tennent later brought Irish dancing competitions to Ballymoney and Limavady.

When Mulholland dancers were denied entry to Gaelic League competitions, it was an obvious alternative to compete at other festivals. Several festivals already had Irish dancing sections, like Larne. Most pre-1950s festivals had competitions in singing, instrumental music, speech and drama and ballet, but they expanded to offer Irish dancing competitions also. Indeed, many a festival is kept afloat nowadays by the large numbers of Irish dancers taking part.

But even when Patricia Mulholland was still "within the pale" of the Gaelic League, her dancers reflected a great mixture of backgrounds, as is evidenced by Larne woman Betty Lewis winning a championship while serving in the Women's Auxiliary Air Force as a radio operator. Betty was also a high achiever in other fields: she won the silver medal in the Guildhall Elocution Exams of 1941. Clear enunciation was vitally important in radio work – 'roger, wilco and out,' etc. Betty came to be known later as Gillian Claus and her husband was CO of an RAF station in Cyprus where my father was Senior Medical Officer.

When she discovered that I had been with Miss Mulholland, she immediately danced a few steps of a slip-jig, very gracefully, too. She managed to involve me in a plan to fly the dancers over to Akrotiri to perform in the old Roman theatre in Curium, but, unfortunately, it never came to fruition. She was rather given to flights of fancy, which I didn't realise until much later.

Geography would, of necessity, have played a part in this mix, for there are considerably more people of Scots/English descent in the northeast of Ulster than, say, in Mayo, but there was always a choice. What made a parent send a child to Miss Mulholland rather than Miss McAleer? Convenience might naturally dictate this choice, but there is no doubt that Miss Mulholland attracted all sorts of people from all over Belfast and beyond; some pupils even came to her from Dundalk.

In my own case, I was brought to audition in Newington Street (Miss Mulholland's own home then and location of her junior classes) after my mother saw Mulholland dancers on a Pathé newsreel in the cinema showing events at the 1951 Festival of Britain. She was struck by the grace and artistry of the display, which seemed very different from the usual type of Irish dancing at that time. I was already having ballet lessons from Lena King (as did Margot Bell around the same time), but once I was introduced to the more relaxed delights of a dancing class that had lots of rowdy boys, I soon lost interest in the more formal world of butter-muslin hair-bands and examinations where you had to remember to curtsey to the accompanist.

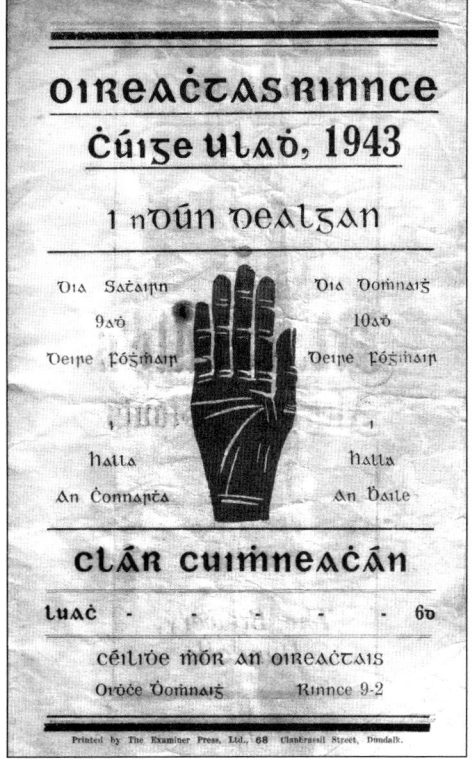

Dundalk Feis book for the 1943 Ulster Championships.

Now, the question is, why did Mulholland dancers start competing exclusively at festivals rather than feiseanna? They had been very successful at Ulster and Ireland championships, particularly in the 1940s: their teams were famous at the time and at most competitions carried all before them; what's more, they really enjoyed attending these events, making a weekend of it in places like Newry and Derry. So what happened to sever this association?

At this point, it is necessary to say a little about the Gaelic League (Conradh na Gaeilge), which was established in 1893 to foster the Irish language. It was founded, as Pádraig Ó Snodaigh puts it, by a Glens Catholic and a Connacht Protestant. He also tells us that the first Belfast branch grew out of the Belfast Naturalists' Field Club (of which FJ Biggar was a member) and that the Shankill boasted an early branch. I do not intend to detail the history of the organisation; there are many works that do that better than I ever could, but it is essential to understand just how strong a stranglehold the dancing section of the league – An Coimisiún le Rincí Gaelacha – had, and indeed has, on dancing teachers. In 1939, Art Mac Ganna stated in the foreword to *Ár Rinncidhe Foirne* (the *vade mecum* for all team dancers), '. . . from the social point of view, it may be said that Irish dancing has been the spearhead of the struggle for the re-establishment of a distinct Gaelic culture and civilisation. It follows, therefore, that the propagation of Irish dancing is a matter of great moment and its regulation and control secondary only in importance to the revival of the language itself.'

Northern teachers were never entirely happy with what they saw as interference from Dublin and its local representatives. This dissatisfaction is understandable, especially if one considers some of the more restrictive (if short-lived) rules; for example, as many items of the dancer's costume as possible should be of Irish manufacture or origin. But even today, the Commission prescribes particular skirt lengths and denier of tights.

One of the hoops that Irish dancers had to jump through before they competed in major championships in the late 1940s was that they had to learn some Irish. And this applied to dancers as well as teachers. I can't imagine this going down any better with today's Commission dancers than it did with, say, Norman Maternaghan, who remembers a half-hour or so, before each class, being devoted to the Irish language. If it was good enough for the Abbey actors, I suppose the thinking went, it was good enough for Irish dancers. In 1939, when Frank O'Connor was ousted from his position as director of the Abbey Theatre, more or less by government officials, the Gaelic League put pressure on its actors to learn Gaelic. Later, actor Peter O'Toole was not accepted by the Abbey because of his lack of a *cúpla focail*.

Most Mulholland dancers felt that this ploy was aimed less at fostering knowledge of the Irish tongue than at placing an obstacle in the way of Northern Protestants. (This notion in itself suggests an ignorance of the history of the development of the Irish language, considering the work of Presbyterians et al.)

An insistence on minor details is mildly annoying, especially if it's hard to see how one's dancing is going to be improved by such. But unfortunately, in at least two cases, individuals' livelihoods were affected because local managers carried their authority so far as to interfere with the taking up of permanent posts.

A well-known Bangor teacher had her dancing class simply taken over by a member of the Irish Dancing Commission only to regain it after his initial enthusiasm petered out. By that time, she'd lost several months' income. Eventually, this teacher was expelled from the Commission for exposing herself to "contamination" from British influence; the fact that she took her classes in a British Legion hall did not go down well. Add to this that some of her pupils were members of the Girls' Brigade and that, worst of all, they danced in places where the English national anthem might be played.

In another case, a very well-known dancing teacher was advised that if she took up a post in a Belfast grammar school, her pupils would be refused a platform for competition. You may ask what connection there is between ordinary school and dancing school that would interfere with one's eligibility to compete at feiseanna. Well, teaching in any school in those days required the individual to take an oath of loyalty to the British monarch, a requirement up until the 1970s. And this was anathema, at least in theory, to the ultra-Irish of the Commission.

Strange to relate, some of the same people who had stood in her way had no difficulty at all in combining their own jobs, which had required the taking of an oath, with their membership of the Gaelic League. This was the anomaly in the application of the all-important rules. On some occasions, they seemed to be used as weapons rather than guidance. And then, of course, there are the rules within rules that only the inner lodge seems to know about and the ordinary members only find out about when they run up against an obstacle. I'm thinking here of the dancing teachers who pay their dues for many years, thinking they're full members, and then discover that, in fact, they're only associate members without a full vote in certain matters.

Some Commission dancers had no difficulty in explaining their attendance at "British" festivals by claiming that they appeared on the days when the English anthem was not played. Until recently, I could not find anyone who could remember this anthem, or any other, for that matter, being played at any dancing festival. But Dominic Graham remembers it being played at Portstewart, Ballymena and Ballymoney on the last night. However, it seems to me that the rules did not apply to everyone with the same rigidity.

George Leonard presenting prizes to Máire Bunting, left, and two Bangor dancers at Portadown Festival, 1956.

In any case, in the early 1930s, around thirty women and a few men were registered with An Coimisiún le Rincí Gaelacha, the Gaelic League association for Irish dance teachers, but it wasn't until 1941 that the first adjudicator examination became a prerequisite of judging competitions. On the first examining panel was George Leonard, who adjudicated at festivals for decades.

The same panel examined the first candidates for the teaching certificate in 1943. Anna McCoy was present at Dundalk Feis when the first Scrúdú Teastas Mhúinteora Choimisiún le Rincí Gaelacha (TCRG) – the Irish dancing teacher certificate – was awarded. She remembers honorary certificates being presented to Leo Madden and Peadar O'Rafferty, who were well-enough established at that time to warrant receiving the award without having to sit an exam.

Peadar O'Rafferty was Miss Mulholland's dancing teacher and an author of books on Irish dancing; unfortunately, I found it impossible to obtain a copy of any of them. He also had a disagreement with the Commission but was eventually reconciled with them. He held an adjudicating certificate, the forerunner of today's Scrúdú Teastas Mholtóra Choimisiún le Rincí Gaelacha (ADCRG).

Relations between the ruling body of the Commission and its members were always bedevilled by arguments and hostilities of one kind or another, and so it was really no surprise that anyone with a mind of her own should part company with them, especially as an alternative platform could be provided in the festivals and other avenues that were opening up.

MR. PEADAR O'RAFFERTY. L.I.F.D.S.
(Oireactas Certificate 1915.)
THE ESTABLISHED & PRACTICAL TEACHER OF AUTHENTIC IRISH DANCES.

43. ST. JAMES PARK,
BELFAST.

Peadar O'Rafferty's business card.

As has been pointed out, Patricia Mulholland was not the only individual to have a run-in with the Commission. In fact, dissatisfaction with it, felt particularly by Northern teachers, was to keep bubbling up from time to time and led ultimately to the split in 1969/70 and the breaking away from the Commission of An Comhdháil, an association of several schools of Irish dancing who valued their autonomy more than the link with the Dublin-based umbrella organisation. This association runs its own feiseanna. In 2003, for example, the Comhdháil na Múinteorí le Gaelacha ran its All-Ireland and International championships over eight days in Ennis, catering for hundreds of dancers from all over the British Isles.

Miss Mulholland had attracted enough attention to herself – her prize-winning pupils with their revolutionary style and particularly her "extra-mural" activities – to provoke the wrath of the Irish Dancing Commission. It is difficult to imagine now, but teachers and dancers in the 1940s and '50s were expected to ask permission to perform at anything outside the usual feiseanna. Anyone who has even a passing knowledge of Patricia Mulholland's character would recognise that this would not go down well. And while some individuals might have danced or adjudicated here or there without permission and have gone unnoticed, the Mulholland dancers were appearing at prestigious, public and widely reported events, so the powers-that-were could not but hear about them.

Mulholland Champions
All-Ireland

1942 – Betty Lewis; Junior – Sheila Fitzpatrick
1943 – Sheila Fitzpatrick; Junior – Yvonne Hood
1944 – Sheila Fitzpatrick
1945 – Maureen McCann
1946 – Yvonne Hood, Brian Coleman
1947 – Sheila Fitzpatrick
1949 – Junior – Patricia King

Patricia King with All-Ireland cup, 1949.

Mulholland Champions
Ulster
1943 – Sheila Fitzpatrick
1944 – Maureen McCann
1946 – Brian Coleman
1946 – Runner-up – Yvonne Hood
1948 – Patricia King
1949 – Yvonne Hood
1949 – Runner-up – Norman Maternaghan
1949 – Junior – Isobel Begley

Sheila also has two gold medals from the Father Matthew Feis.

At her first All-Ireland in the Mansion House in Dublin, Sheila won the reel and slip-jig, and a girl, whom she'd nicknamed Donegal Kate, complained because she said she'd never have won if Patricia Mulholland hadn't been playing for her. The committee actually took this complaint

Sheila Fitzpatrick's championship medals – three All-Ireland and one Ulster.

seriously and told Patricia that she could not play for Sheila, and so she had to dance to the music of the "two old biddies" who provided the accompaniment for everyone else. She was a bit worried about this, but Miss Mulholland told her just to ask for *Bonnie Kate* for her next reel. Well, she waited during the introduction, but she couldn't distinguish where the eight bars finished. Eventually, she asked the two accompanists to try *Bonnie Kate*. They answered that that was what they were playing.

This was in 1943, during the war and when there was no ice cream in the North, and Sheila overdosed on this luxury in O'Connell Street, with the result that she was terribly sick. Her mother told her not to bother with dancing in the championship, but she said no, that if she didn't, Donegal Kate would only think she was afraid. So she steeled herself to go on, and each time she came off, Brendan somebody (she thinks he may have been a Johnston dancer who later became a pharmacist) more or less carried her to the lavatory. In spite of this handicap, she won the championship. Sheila gives the impression that these events were all very friendly (for the most part) and that all the dancers looked forward to them, as much for the camaraderie as the dancing. Indeed, dancers from different schools were expected to join forces at Sligo Feis to dance team-dances together such as the *Three Tunes*.

Once, her mother had ordered shoes from Dublin especially, but Sheila didn't find enough support in them and borrowed Anna McCoy's. Anna then used to banter her about winning in borrowed shoes. She remembers Anna's mother as being beautifully dressed at the All-Irelands, except for one item of clothing – a scruffy old fox-fur. They used to wonder why she made do with this old thing, but it turned out that she was using the object as a cover for smuggling, taking tea and sugar across the border in either direction. (This was quite adventurous, as the penalty for such activity could be imprisonment!)

Various reasons have been suggested for Patricia Mulholland's departure/expulsion from the Gaelic League, some so ridiculous as to be patently untrue. It has been said, for example, that her dancers wore the Union flag on their backs. Other reasons are so anodyne as to fail to explain the split. It is quite difficult to separate fact from the fiction that surrounds the event.

When I asked Dr John Cullinane, official archivist of An Coimisiún le Rincí Gaelacha, why Patricia Mulholland parted company from the association, he suggested that she simply preferred to dance at festivals, some of which are affiliated to the British Federation, as mentioned above. But others did this without incurring the wrath of the Gaelic League.

Others have quoted a post-war victory celebration in Bangor as the cause of the parting of the ways. At this event, fireworks concluded the spectacle, spelling out *God Save The King*. This may have been confused with a later event when Maureen McCann's pupils were involved in an entertainment for a visiting ship.

Yet another theory alluded to a folklore festival, possibly in Nice in 1952, when Mulholland dancers were alleged to have walked behind the Union flag. Patricia Mulholland had already left the Commission by then. It is a question if Mulholland dancers were at this festival; certainly, a group of Newry dancers attended. However, Mulholland participants at an earlier event in a Spanish bullring in Pamplona can remember their team making a flag specially for the occasion, with a background of "St Patrick's blue" with a cross in the centre. On another occasion, on the island of Majorca, when the Mulholland dancers made their entry into an arena along with all the other participants, they did so to the tune of *The Last Rose Of Summer*.

Festivals of folk music and dance were popular all over Europe after the Second World War and were viewed as a means of bringing people together. Indeed, this practice continues. The organisers would have tried to ensure that all of the countries represented at the festival had their flag flying at public events. There is no doubt that Mulholland and other dancers could be said to have danced under a Union flag. But they also performed under the French, Spanish, Greek and Italian flags. You can begin to see the picture. The Mulholland dancers were not the only group of Irish dancers who travelled to take part in these, but while some narrow-minded, poor souls used the opportunity to criticise their country woman for allegedly walking behind or dancing before a British flag, Patricia Mulholland was open to the experiences there, storing away all the different approaches to dance for future reference.

Many people feel that it was the occasion of the Festival of Britain that sealed Patricia's fate when she brought a team of Guides to dance in London. These were British Guides, not Irish Guides. Enough said! However, Mulholland dancers had disappeared from feiseanna before 1951.

There is a common theme emerging from these accusations, well-founded or not. Mulholland dancers might have been Irish, but they just weren't Irish enough, in that they were not dissociating themselves sufficiently from all things British. Moreover, it is on this point that the Commission was departing from the founding principles of the whole Irish revival. In applying oneself to a national art form, be it literary, dramatic or in terms of dance, it is obvious that one should not stray too far from one's roots or one loses focus and dilutes the product too much. Nevertheless, if one stays too focussed on a single aspect, then the approach is too narrow to allow development and encourages the kind of internecine strife that bedevils so much of Irish dancing.

Dancers entertaining a deputation of international visitors in the City Hall, Belfast, in the early 1960s. Back row, L-R: Reggie McClure, Seamus Agnew, Hilda Holden, Patricia Mulholland, Lord Mayor, Olive Melville, Gráinne Agnew, Brian Bunting, Jim Rooney. Front row, L-R: Patricia O'Neill, Sheelagh McDade, Lynne Maxwell, Marlene Bailie, Dermott Brooks, Anne McManus, Stella O'Neill, Margot Bell.

Patricia was always willing to provide a platform for her dancers, no matter who asked for them and no matter what the venue. And her dancers, in their turn, just loved to perform, no matter what the audience.

It is difficult to pinpoint one particular incident that triggered Patricia Mulholland's departure from the constriction of the Commission, but certainly, politics played a major part. In this, she was in good company, as Douglas Hyde, co-founder of the Gaelic League, was abandoned by them in 1915 when he refused to allow politics to influence the executive of the League. Politics brought him back when he was appointed the first President of Ireland in 1938.

Perhaps it was more of an accumulation of misdemeanours and confrontation that paved her exit path, not to mention jealousy, but several observers agree that a defining moment in this episode was a concert in what used to be the Ritz cinema, now the site of Jury's Inn in Belfast.

Among others at this midnight matinee were James Young and the actress Diana Dors, as were the Mulholland dancers who performed *The Lace Collar* – one of Patricia's pictorial dances. According to one witness, this brought the house down. Anyway, at the end of the concert, all the artistes were invited on stage for a final bow and the orchestra struck up *God Save The King*. Everyone on stage sang along with most of the audience.

Anyone over a certain age will remember the playing of the *King* or *Queen* as a permanent feature of theatrical events, even film showings. In England, few people bothered waiting for the anthem in cinemas, but, of course, everything is different in Northern Ireland and, depending where you were, it could be quite awkward to either stay or go. One group was always offended by the playing of the anthem whereas another would be just as offended by its omission.

Anthems in Northern Ireland tend to be used as identifiers by one community of the other, rather than any dignified expression of genuine loyalty to any regime. The history of theatrical events is littered with anecdotes about this song, none of which suggest any great loyalty to a British monarch, rather a sort of bloody-minded reminder of who's in charge.

In 1942, impresario Carl Clopet brought five plays to Derry's Guildhall. As the *Derry Standard* of the day put it, 'James MacCafferty's quartet supplies the music which is selected with happy taste in keeping with the spirit of the play being presented each evening and is executed with skill and sympathetic interpretation.' On the first night, before the curtain opened on *They Walk Alone*, the quartet struck up *God Save The King*. Predictably enough, the audience made its feelings plain (there was a minor riot) so Mr Clopet decided to dispense with the anthem the following night, when *Rebecca* was on the programme. On the third evening, as the musicians were assembling before *White Cargo*, Lady Dudley McCorkell (wife of an ex-mayor of Derry) approached James and expressed a devout wish that the musicians would not be 'pandering to the ruffian element' by refraining from their duty, as she saw it. James responded that he would do just whatever the director told him to, that it didn't matter to him what tune he played, *God Save The King* or *Yes, We Have No Bananas* – both were in three-four time and in the key of G. Lady McCorkell was a bit put out by his remark, though whether it was because of his lack of enthusiasm for the anthem or his coupling of it with *Yes, We Have No Bananas* is not clear. Ten years earlier, a group of protesting workers, both Protestant and Catholic, needed a marching tune that wouldn't offend either sect and so their band played *Yes, We Have No Bananas* – a rare example of cross-community co-operation in a street protest.

The Guildhall was also the scene of another contretemps about the same tune in the 1960s. The Arts Council was putting on one of Brian Friel's early plays and the hall was packed. The stage crew looked down at the audience, sensing that air of anticipation and were just about to dim the lights when the recently appointed director of the Arts Council of the day, who had accompanied the play to Derry and was obviously full of zeal for doing things by the book, insisted that they had to play the *Queen* (according to Arts Council rules). Despite all the best efforts of those more experienced hands around, he could not be prevented from putting on the record in the wings. During the playing of the anthem, those on stage could hear scrambling noises, and as the record came to a halt, another wee "duke" through the curtain revealed an empty auditorium.

Curiously enough, visiting English productions only had to play the *Queen* on the first and last night, though the locals were obliged to play it every night. At least nowadays, there isn't the same problem with anthems at concerts and films – we like to think we're more enlightened. Intransigence is not the sole prerogative of one side. George Bernard Shaw is reputed to have taken his nationalism so seriously that he refused to remove his hat or stand for *God Save The King* until the Irish Free State came into being in 1922.

However, in 1949, the year after Ireland left the Commonwealth, the same year that the British government passed the Ireland Act, which stated that Northern Ireland would not cease to be part of His Majesty's dominions without the consent of the parliament of Northern Ireland, feelings ran high, and the Commission for Irish Dancing called Patricia Mulholland to account. It was not the first time she'd had to explain her actions. She'd already been suspended for three months in 1947 for bringing a team of Guides to dance at the then Princess Elizabeth's birthday celebration. She pointed out to her inquisitors that it was only polite to stand for the *King* in King George's England. However, it was the last time she was going to submit to the ruling body of the Commission.

The final confrontation took place in Derry, and the regional panel of the Ulster Council of the Irish Dancing Commission was well within its rights to criticise her dancers for standing for the *King*, according to their lights. Sheila Fitzpatrick remembers that at some time in the late '40s, word came from Dublin that no member should be involved in "foreign" games (so you couldn't play hockey or soccer; indeed, spectating at "garrison" sports was enough to warrant expulsion) nor should they go anywhere where the *King* might be played. It was at this time, too, that dancers were told they had to do some Irish language along with their dancing. Sheila was not at all keen on this suggestion, as Irish had not been her favourite subject at St Dominic's.

Miss Mulholland felt that the Commission was trying to take her living away from her, and told them so. Her most profitable outings (both in financial and propaganda terms – bringing Irish dancing to audiences previously unfamiliar with it) were in places where it was possible that the *King* might indeed be played. This particular disagreement seems to have marked the end of her association with the Gaelic League.

Frankie Roddy, legendary dancer from Derry, remembered being in St Columb's Hall in the city when it was announced from the stage that Mulholland dancers would no longer be taking part in feiseanna. He recalled the buzz that went round the hall as everyone

Certificate from Lisburn Feis, 1946, for first place for a Mulholland Three-Hand.

discussed the news. Some people were sorry, but many were relieved in a way, because, for one thing, it meant that other dancers would have more opportunities to win prizes.

My next door neighbour Molly O'Hara, who danced for Nellie Sweeney, remembers the impact of a three-hand reel danced by Maureen McCann, Brian Coleman and Sheila Fitzpatrick, which she found elegant and different from the usual, because the dancers stretched out their arms when holding hands, instead of making sure that their elbows touched as was, and is, common practice for Commission dancers.

This simple but telling change to an accepted form is an example of Miss Mulholland's eye for the graceful. She was not afraid to experiment, but this unorthodox approach could be interpreted as iconoclasm. Add to this that she had firm ideas about what she wanted, and that she was unafraid to express her opinion, and it is not difficult to understand how she might attract criticism, maybe even jealousy or resentment, from those who felt that they had the guardianship of "traditional" Irish dance. Teachers, particularly, who felt their own position threatened by her creativity, may just have decided that it was safer to exile her rather than have to raise their own game.

Later, in 1959, Martin Wallace described her approach to Irish dancing as 'broad-minded' and 'flexible.' He continued, 'She has helped to liberate Irish dancing from its too close association with nationalism, so that all sections of the community can enjoy and participate in it. Similarly, she has freed its techniques from inhibiting tradition so that there is a growing audience for it here and throughout Europe.'

It is noticeable that all the so-called traditional dancers have managed to adapt and modernise their choreography and dress since the '50s without feeling that they have sold out. A once rigid objection to anything other than what they held to be traditional seems to have given way to an acceptance of all sorts of influences from all sorts of places, including the USA and – oh, horror! – England. Classical ballet has been liberally borrowed from, and steps like *entrechats* and dancing *en pointe* (high toes) are now routinely seen on feis platforms; everyone now waits during their introductory music, in fifth position – hardly traditional steps, but then the word "traditional" itself brings its own problems.

I am reminded of my Uncle Basil's assertion that the only reference to anything like Irish dancing in the literature of the Ulster Cycle or elsewhere of similar antiquity is an incident when Muircheartach of the Leather Cloaks and his men are described jumping up and down on a mountainside to keep warm! Cynicism aside, the roots of Irish dancing can't be traced to anything in ancient Irish literature. It is difficult to link the sun rituals of Bealtaine, say, with the modern canon of Irish dance. Hugh Murray's thesis on Traditional Dance Forms is informative on this subject. Certainly, by the time of Elizabeth I, Irish dancing was recognised as a distinct form.

Ironically, festival dancers (especially females) now look more traditional than feis dancers: their skirts are fluid and follow the line of the leg rather than bouncing stiffly against it; and black tights for the seniors give a more streamlined look than the thick, ankle-hiding "poodle" socks so loved by the tanned-leg brigade. Many people, teachers and observers alike, consider festival dancers as the natural inheritors of Irish traditional dancing, seeing them as being less influenced by American innovation.

Peadar O'Rafferty once stated that it would be ironic if the development of truly traditional Irish dancing were to be left in the hands of Protestants. Many feel that festival dancing is a more authentic form of inherited Irish dance.

Festival dancers, never in the past, and rarely now, have an individual costume for championship and they wear their dancing-school costume for both solo and team work. Rules have been brought in recently to curb tendencies in the use of coronets and sparkle.

All the changes in costume, choreography, the English and American influences and lack of objection to erstwhile-despised venues, suggest that change in itself is not a problem for the Irish dancing establishment. It just took them a little longer to engage with change in the '40s and '50s than it seems to now. Perhaps they're more at ease with themselves. It is unimaginable that the Commission would interfere today with its dancers who perform in *Riverdance* because they have appeared before a British monarch.

However, the list of rules still gives an impression of rigidity, with its instructions covering aspects of competition like appropriate fees, the numbers of competitors to be recalled, music speeds, types of permitted footwear and – a particular favourite – 'An Coimisiún may issue guidelines as required which shall be binding . . . these may relate to any other matter or aspect An Coimisiún may consider desirable.'

Lest an impression be given that all Commission personnel were against Patricia Mulholland and what she stood for, it is only fair to point out that dancers like Tom Farrelly were saddened by the split; subsequently, Brendan de Glin asked her to consider returning to the fold and, after the setting up of An Comhdháil in 1970, she was asked by some of its members to join their ranks, but, of course, by that time, she was busier than ever and unlikely to take on anything more, even if she'd been so inclined. However, only George Leonard actually took the step of leaving the Commission along with her. Despite the Mulholland break from the League, which meant that her dancers now competed exclusively at festivals, Commission adjudicators continued to judge dancing at these festivals all over Northern Ireland without attracting condemnation. Mona Scully went so far as to say of Mulholland teams in 1951, 'We've nothing like them in the South. You could send them anywhere and be proud of them.'

Eugene O'Donnell also came to festivals to judge the dancing, as did Frankie Roddy and Gerry Hobbs, among others. But apparently there was a way round the problem of appearing at these "British" events. This is where the rules of the Commission assume an Alice-in-Wonderland quality and mean just whatever you want them to mean. You might be a qualified teacher or adjudicator, but as long as you weren't actually registered, then British festivals were not off limits!

This mark sheet from Portstewart Festival in 1956, seven years after Miss Mulholland's break from An Coimisiún, illustrates how well-known and respected personnel from the Gaelic League had no difficulty in adjudicating at festivals; moreover, the extravagant praise shows that this adjudicator really enjoyed the dancing. It is also evidence of the excellent dancing of Grainne Agnew and Margot Bell, with their 'nice hands' and the 'beautiful opening' of their couples, not to mention their 99 marks out of 100. Derryman Eugene O'Donnell was an All-Ireland champion dancer in his day; he was also a wonderful violinist who lived and worked in the

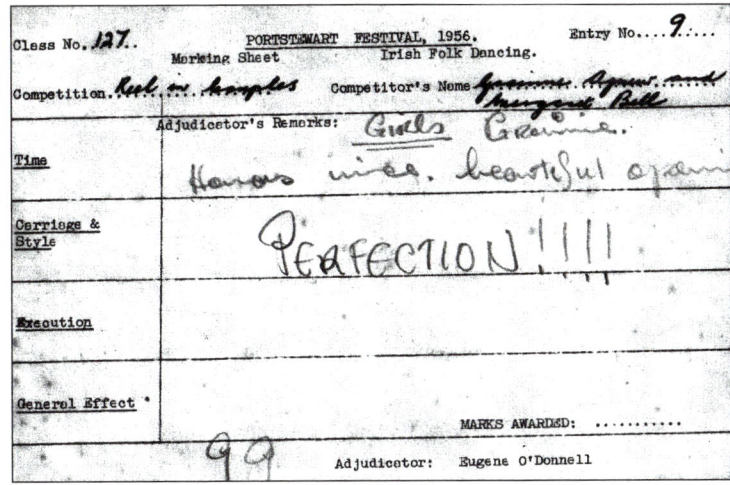

Adjudicator's "perfection" mark sheet for Grainne Agnew and Margot Bell, Portstewart Festival, 1956.

States for many years before coming back to Derry in the '90s. He was not a *registered* teacher, so he would not have fallen foul of any Commission rules in taking part in an unauthorised competition.

Mona Scully mark sheet from Portadown, 1956.

John Cullinane, archivist of An Coimisiún, has described Patricia Mulholland as a fantastic teacher, ahead of her time and one held in highest regard by all.

But it has been impossible to gain access to any record of the meeting at which Patricia Mulholland was expelled, if such exists. The only place where I met a blank wall in all my research was Commission headquarters in Dublin. Perhaps no record remains of this event. At any rate, nobody from the Commission was prepared to volunteer any relevant information. There is, as yet, no official archive of the Irish Dancing Commission. Dr John Cullinane is working on this and I hope all will be revealed in the near future.

Interestingly enough, one of the approved set dances for Commission competitions in 2004 was *The Deep Green Pool*, a composition of Miss Mulholland's (both dance and music) which was never published. Someone somewhere must have liked it so much that they listened intently and wrote it down.

Whether the ruling council of the Commission or their Northern representatives objected to her perceived Britishness, or just her way of doing things, there is no doubt that she herself saw their attitude as a threat to her livelihood. And whether she jumped or was pushed was no longer relevant as she realised that she could plough her own furrow.

Freedom from the Irish dancing establishment certainly allowed Miss Mulholland to develop as she pleased, and indirectly opened the way for her to inaugurate her Irish Ballet Company.

The Lead Up

As far as I was concerned, arms poker-rigid beneath an expressionless face had little attraction. I wanted to inject more feeling and, in the process, let Irish dancing come into contact with the widest possible audience. **Patricia Mulholland**

Peadar O'Rafferty, who was Miss Mulholland's teacher, has rightly been called the "father of Irish dance" in the North.

In 1912, the year after he won the Ulster Championship, he was charged by the Irish Dancing Commission with improving standards in Ulster. Not only did he carry out this mission with enthusiasm and positive results, he also introduced Irish dancing into quarters not previously familiar with it to any great extent. He is remembered with affection by all who knew him, including his pupil, Patricia Mulholland, as her letter of condolence (*over*) to his family shows. (This was written shortly after she moved house.)

His mother was from the Donegal Gaeltacht. Her proudest boast was that she had met Roger Casement in Ardglass when he was the guest of Joseph Biggar. Mrs O'Rafferty used to take a house in the town for the seasonal workers who followed the herring harvest. Many of these girls were from Donegal and were native Irish speakers. During my childhood holidays, they could still be seen gutting the fish on the quayside and packing them into barrels, and my Uncle Basil, always a keen Gaeilgeoir, used to chat to them.

Peadar O'Rafferty and Maire McStocker in 1911.

Peadar and his wife Winnie, pupil of Carl Hardibeck.

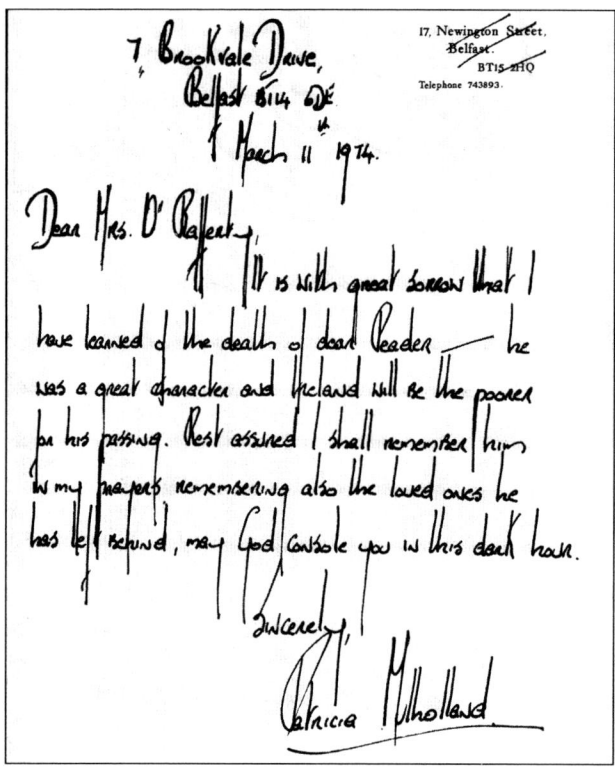

Letter of condolence from Patricia Mulholland to the widow of her dancing teacher.

Peadar always had a great love and huge enthusiasm for Irish culture and taught Irish dancing from 1906, initially after finishing his day's work at Murray's Tobacco Factory. But from 1912, he was able to devote himself entirely to his dancing classes.

In the early 1920s, he and his pupils appeared regularly at concerts all over Belfast including the Ulster Hall, the Plaza and the Hippodrome. After one St Patrick's Day carnival in the Plaza, the *Northern Whig* commented: 'Mr P O'Rafferty and Miss Nellie Fluke, who secured first prize at Larne Musical Festival on Saturday for senior solo dancing, were heartily encored for the Munster Jig and the Hornpipe.'

Besides taking ordinary dancing classes for children of all ages, he was also involved with instructing the Guides. At this time, there had been a revival of interest in folk dancing in England and Wales, and there was a feeling that the Guides in Northern Ireland should learn something about the dances of their own country. Peadar was engaged to instruct the Belfast Cadets and this activity received great encouragement from Lady Baden-Powell, as the letter (*right*) to him from the Duchess of Abercorn illustrates.

Up to that time, the Ulster Scouts and Guides did not have a national dance to perform at their international outings. It's all very well being British to the backbone, but it's actually quite difficult to demonstrate "Britishness" as a nationality as distinct from a category of passport. A Scotsman does not have the same problem in demonstrating his Scottishness, nor the Welshman his Welshness, while retaining his Britishness. So the Ulster Scouts had to work up something Irish for their "turn" at jamborees.

I am reminded of my cousin's husband, an Englishman, who worked for a Japanese car company and who found himself at a meeting of high-powered executives where a local representative sang a Japanese song after dinner. The cousin-in-law was volunteered by his boss to keep up their end and sing a song. He was no singer and couldn't really think of any song until at Sir's insistence, and in a blinding flash of inspiration, he performed what he could remember of his wife's party piece – *Ard Tí Chuain*. It conjures up a lovely picture: an Englishman singing an Irish song in Japan. Face was saved.

But I digress.

```
THE GIRL GUIDES
(PROVINCE OF ULSTER).

DEPUTY CHIEF COMMISSIONER FOR ULSTER—
    HER GRACE THE DUCHESS OF ABERCORN.          Secretary—Miss I. H. PATTERSON.
PRESIDENT OF COUNCIL. ...  MRS. J. C. WHITE, J.P.
                                                Headquarters for Ulster :
            12th November 1925.                 50 UPPER ARTHUR STREET,
                                                        BELFAST.

Mr Padre O'Rafferty.
    28. Walnut Street.
        off Donegal Pass.
            Belfast.

    Dear Mr O'Rafferty,
            I would like to offer you my best thanks
    for your very generous assistance you gave to the Belfast
    Cadets, in teaching them the Irish Reels, which they performed
    so delightfully, at the Welcome to the Chief Guide last week.
            It was extremely kind of you to take so much trouble
    in the matter and Lady Baden-Powell was very pleased with
    their performance, and in her Address urged all Guides to
    keep up the Irish Folk dancing in their Companies.
            Again thanking you,
                Yours truly,

                    Rosalind Pierson

                    Deputy Chief Commissioner for Ulster.
```

The Duchess of Abercorn conveys encouragement from Lady Baden-Powell to Peadar O'Rafferty and his pupils.

In 1925, the Lambeg Folk Dance Society was founded on a rising tide of interest in all things Irish. Several members of this group were also members of the Society of Friends (Quakers) from Lisburn. It is perhaps no accident that the Quakers were in the vanguard of promoting Irish dancing, believing, as writer Ulick O'Connor put it, 'in good works and integrity rather than superstition and the coloured sash.' This group, taught by Peadar, seems to have been the only adult Irish dancing team at that time, and they appeared regularly at concerts and competitions.

Music festivals decided to introduce Folk Dance sections into their competitions, and again, Peadar was the man responsible for teaching Irish dancing to new classes – in Larne, for example. This town started its Irish dancing section in 1927; Ballymena and Dungannon followed suit shortly after.

He was also active in teaching in girls' clubs, like the Social Services Club, which drew members from places like the Shankill, and encouraged others to give up their time to help in this sort of work. These girls' clubs, the Lambeg Folk Dance Society and the 28th Rangers' Company, all featured in the prize-winners' list at the very first Northern Irish Dance Festival in 1929, as did the Peadar O'Rafferty Academy dancers and indeed, the Mulholland dancers (taught by Stella) and Miss Mulholland herself.

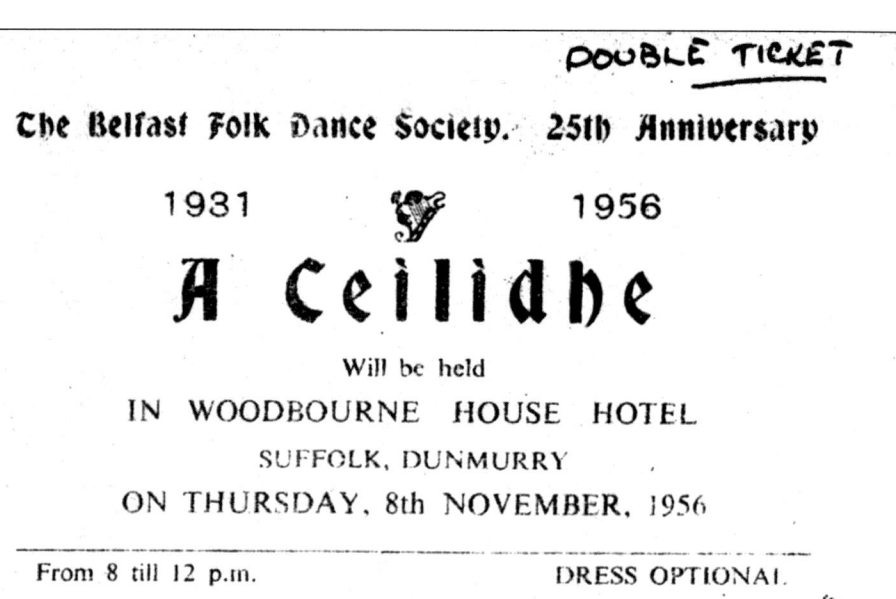

The Belfast Folk Dance Society, established in 1931, continued into the 1960s. Here is a ticket for a céilí in 1956.

Peadar also taught Irish dancing at Stranmillis Training College from 1921 to 1935.

The Belfast Folk Dancing Society was founded in 1931, and during this same year at the Dungannon Festival, Peadar suggested that every school should teach Irish dancing, because, as he pointed out, student teachers were learning the art at both Stranmillis and St Mary's training colleges.

The BFDS and the Lambeg Folk Dance Society competed successfully at festivals and performed often at concerts. At Ballymena Festival in 1932, the BFDS team came first; runners-up were the LFDS.

Peadar taught in some Belfast schools, including St Anthony's Cross and Passion in Willowfield, where Gertie Brady and her sister Marie used to accompany him when his wife, Winnie, was unable to.

These two were quite experienced performers for their years, being used to playing duets on violin and piano in the family pub and their own parlour for visiting dignitaries. The girls enjoyed playing for the dancing classes in their school; and after a while, they were asked to accompany Peadar's lessons in the training college. Gertie particularly enjoyed this association, because not only was she paid for her work (she was only about twelve at the start of the venture), she also remembers, with relish, the lovely tea and buns that Flo Irwin provided for them at Stran. Florence Irwin had a wonderful column in the *Northern Whig* during the war years with headlines like *Pigs' Feet Can Be Nice As Well As Nourishing* and *Soapless Washing Of Dirty Dishcloths*. Peadar O'Rafferty's good work was to be continued, for very shortly after she took over her sister's classes, Patricia was invited to tutor the Belfast Folk Dance Society. This was a step towards the most

Mulholland dancers with their teacher at a concert in the Whitla Hall, Belfast, in the early 1950s. Gertie Brady is middle row, centre, in polka-dot dress.

creative part of her life, although she might not have realised it at the time. Peadar had done the groundwork in encouraging a broadly based clientele enthusiastic about Irish dance. Patricia would increase attendance at this society and, through her inspirational teaching, would attract even more attention.

Patricia Mulholland was very much the product of her upbringing. As has been mentioned already, her father was English and the family had to go to live in England a number of times, staying in several of the shipbuilding cities of the North before they finally settled in Belfast.

On one occasion, at least, her father's nationality was a cause for comment when a Belfast dancing teacher was heard to remark to her neighbour at a concert in Armagh, 'You know, of course, her father's English. So what could you expect!'

I doubt if the same critic would have attached any blame to Pádraic Pearse, Cathal Brugha et al, who were the offspring of an English parent. Mulholland, after all, is an old Irish name belonging to the family who used to look after St Patrick's bell.

Although this notion that she was an outsider persisted in some Irish dancing quarters, and "outsider" she was – not in any pejorative sense – in that she was uniquely qualified to do what she did. Nor was she prepared to genuflect in the direction of the Irish dancing authority if it did not suit her.

Her experiences and training were diverse and different from those of an average teacher of Irish dancing. First, she did not aim for a career in this field; it was almost by accident that it came about. What a happy accident!

This difference in background, training and experience separates her from most, if not all, other Irish dancing teachers. Her greatest gift, in the view of those who knew her, was a huge talent for choreography. Her musical training was obviously an excellent companion to her skill in interpreting music in choreography. When Michael Revie, son of Carolyn MacMaster, was starting out on his dancing career, which has taken him all over the world, Merle Park advised him to go to Patricia Mulholland to develop his musicality. Yet it was not simply the putting together of learned steps with learned rhythms, she was wonderfully creative, with a strong visual sense; as the artist Kevin Rafferty put it – she could paint pictures with dances and dancers. This talent, which had already found expression in her team dances and specially composed set dances, was to come to fruition in her Irish Ballets.

She was not confined by the often narrow-minded, limited vision of some Irish enthusiasts. Her artistic soul was engaged by new ideas and the challenge of putting them into practice.

However, when it comes to the setting up of the Patricia Mulholland Irish Ballet Company, the achievement of which she was rightly most proud, we must look at a chain of events that include being in the right place at the right time and also having the right contacts. Synchronicity brought Patricia Mulholland and her dancers to the Festival of Britain in 1951 and led directly to the creation of her Irish Ballets.

A network of acquaintances and friends provided the spur to advance her artistic ideas about dance. These same contacts also provided support for the new venture. People who had been impressed by her artistic ability were not only useful to her career but also became lifelong friends, appearing at important moments and offering continuing support.

Before any performance of the Irish Ballet, there was a lot of activity behind the curtain and in the dressing rooms, as one might imagine.

For long periods, the stage crew and wardrobe mistresses would remain the same personnel, but there were often willing helpers who appeared now and then to assist with make-up etc. Some of the senior dancers would help make up the little ones; for instance, during one period, I loved having my face done by Valerie Canavan (her sister Yvonne and I were in the same class at secondary school, where Valerie had been ahead of us and I thought she was the bee's knees). Leslie Baird remembers Frances Tomelty doing his make-up for him for his first part in the ballets – the monkey in *The Oul' Lammas Fair*.

Costume designer Mercy Hunter would always attend big performances in Belfast, helping to apply make-up and checking that nobody got too carried away with their own ideas. My own preference for strange-coloured eyeliner and unsuitable jewellery, as she saw it, met with her disapproval more than once.

Alfred Arnold, composer and arranger, came to lots of venues when the company was touring and helped the men with their make-up. He always wore a blue and white striped butcher's apron when working with the greasepaint. Some of the dancers would choose to travel in his convertible rather than the bus. Some of us would simply not have given up our place in the back of the bus, for it provided a sort of alternative education to all who travelled in it. It was the first place I ever heard pop songs, rude songs and general, good-natured rowdiness. Romances were started and ended there. My contemporaries and I were quite bewildered when Miss Mulholland told us that, during the later tours, the back of the bus was quiet!

And then there were the visiting dignitaries who called in backstage to wish Miss Mulholland good luck.

It was in these circumstances that most of us would have met, for the first time, two ladies – Miss Hogg and Miss Jackson. Miss Mulholland always emphasised, when mentioning these two, that they were her very good friends. But it is only when you discover the history of their friendship that you realise just how good a friend Miss Hogg was and how important she was to Patricia Mulholland and the Irish Ballet Company.

It was through Miss Hogg that Patricia came to be involved with the Belfast Folk Dancing Society, which, in turn, meant that she taught lots of dancers who came to love Irish dancing and who would not normally have been expected to be interested in such a pursuit. These enthusiasts then sent their children to Miss Mulholland. And it was indirectly through Miss Hogg that the first Irish Ballet came to be staged.

There can be many reasons for individuals to take up Irish dancing, but there is no doubt in my mind that the combination of Patricia Mulholland and Lillian Renshaw Hogg must be considered a key point in the development of a cross-community interest in Irish dance in Belfast at a certain period and which continues to the present day.

Miss Hogg, as everyone called her, was originally from the Saintfield area of County Down. Her middle name, Renshaw, is the same Renshaw of the commercial school that used to occupy premises in University Street (now commemorated only in name by a bar in the same block). It is just possible that she was related to the photographer AR Hogg, as he was from the same part of the country.

She graduated from Liverpool Training College in 1924 with a first-class diploma in physical training and taught in Scotland before finding a post in a Bangor school.

She was appointed to the inspectorate in 1945, along with her great friend Rhona Jackson, becoming the first PE inspector in Northern Ireland.

These two ladies taught European dance as part of a three-year intensive gymnastics course, which qualified the participants in teaching, based at the Central Presbyterian Assembly Hall in Belfast (usually called the Assembly Buildings). Miss Hogg saw no reason why European dance should not also encompass Irish dance. Accordingly, around late 1936 or early 1937, she invited Miss Mulholland to take charge of the Irish dance class, taught up to almost this time by Peadar O'Rafferty.

These classes attracted not just serious students; they provided a pastime for anyone with an interest in an active hobby or keeping fit, which was becoming very fashionable at this time. One class member was Pat McTavish, who became the first lady umpire at Wimbledon. Enid Minnis went to the gymnastics course, having been encouraged by Miss Hogg to keep fit, and became an enthusiastic Irish dancer. The lessons were advertised largely by word of mouth and attracted hundreds!

Gertie Brady remembers a well-dressed, well-spoken lady (Miss Hogg) arriving at her door in The Mount to ask her if she'd like to come and accompany Miss Mulholland at the BFDS. This partnership continued into playing at competitions and for the ballets and survived nearly forty years.

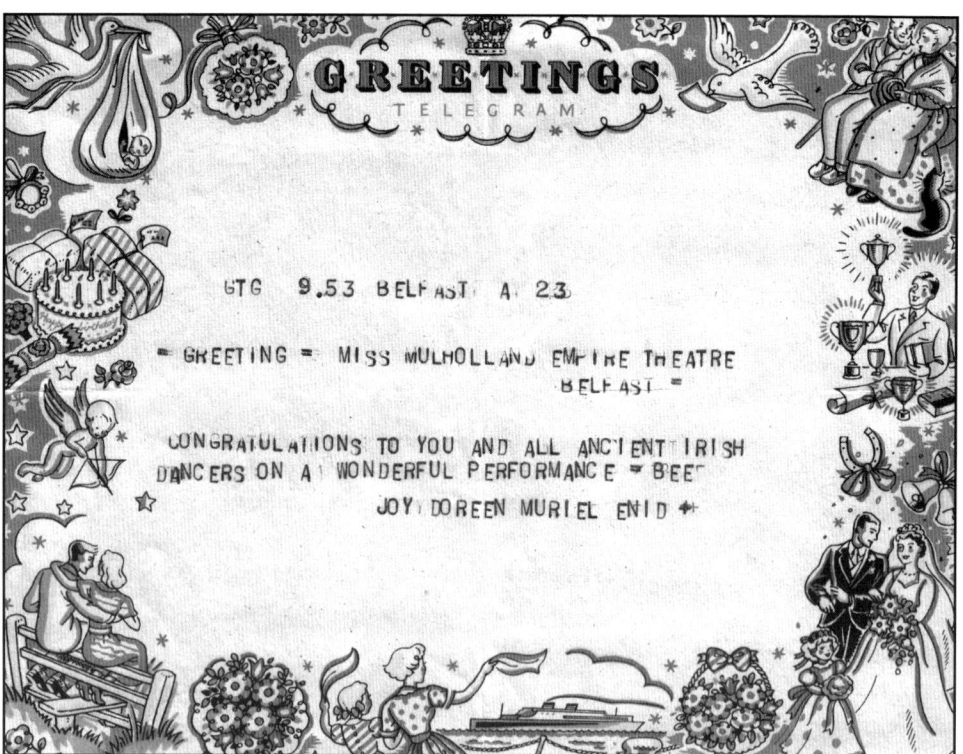

Congratulatory telegram to Miss Mulholland from Enid Minnis and friends after her first major ballet, Cúchulainn, *1953.*

Group of Guides with leaders and Miss Mulholland. Audrey Clarke is fourth from right.

The Second World War interrupted the classes, as personnel were occupied with matters that were more serious, and some BFDS members, like Rita Hogg (Lillian's sister) and her colleague Enid Minnis, were evacuated to Portballintrae, accompanying their pupils, junior boarders from Victoria College, where many of the dancing classes were conducted at different periods.

Out of her association with the BFDS came Miss Mulholland's attendance at British establishment gatherings in England. Several of the BFDS dancers were Girl Guides (as they were called then), who saw a way of combining their two interests. Patricia was asked to train them in some team dances and a group was invited to perform at the twenty-first birthday party of the then Princess Elizabeth in 1947. This, in fact, led to a three-month suspension from the Gaelic League for Miss Mulholland's own dancers.

Two dancers from the BFDS, Eithne Bamford and Lily Kennedy, were active Guiders and they knew that Guides from all over the United Kingdom were preparing different displays in many varied disciplines for the forthcoming Festival of Britain. They thought it would be a good idea if the Northern Irish Guides could come up with an exhibition of folk dancing in London. These two enterprising ladies asked Miss Mulholland to train a Guide team for the festival, which she did throughout the winter of 1950.

Two other members of that team were Patricia King and Audrey Clarke, who were later on to become principal dancers in the ballets. Patricia was Emer in *Cúchulainn* and Audrey was Sava in *The Mother Of Oisín*. Patricia also won the Ulster Championship in 1948 and also the All-Ireland in 1949.

Among Audrey's favourite recollections of her fortnight in London is her memory of standing on the stage of the Festival Hall, arranged for the start of the *Bonfire* dance, and the curtain going back to huge applause from the audience.

Miss Hogg, at that time, was a valuable contact for Miss Mulholland, because without her invitation, Patricia would not have been involved with the BFDS nor have all these dancers from right across Belfast society and beyond. Without the BFDS, her contact with the Guides would not have existed, and it is unlikely that the same doors would have opened for Mulholland dancers or their teacher.

In the autumn of 1953, Patricia Mulholland was asked to teach a course of Irish dancing in the new Ulster College of Physical Training. The college building was as yet unfinished, and so the course was held in the Fisherwick Church Hall, Belfast. The appointment would have been confirmed, on the advice of Inspector Lillian Hogg, by the then Ministry of Education. As Dr Oonagh Pim (the college's first principal) has said, the course was a great success with such a dynamic teacher who showed such commitment to her work.

But most of all, it was Lillian Hogg's position on a CEMA committee which paved the way for Miss Mulholland's association with the Arts Council and the financing of the Patricia Mulholland Irish Ballet Company. CEMA – Council for the Encouragement of Music and the Arts – was the forerunner of the Arts Council.

The combination of Patricia's experience and associations made the creation of the ballets almost inevitable. Her childhood training, outlook, and, of course, innate ability, meant that once the occasion demanded it, she was uniquely placed to produce just what was required by CEMA in 1951.

Miss Mulholland had seen at least one folk ballet on the continent in the course of bringing her dancers to European festivals. I believe she was unaware of the existence of the fledgling Irish group Ceol Chumann who produced two dance dramas, *Peter Street* and *Casadh An tSúgáin*, in the late 1930s. Certainly, she never saw their work. Several newspaper reports mentioned this group in connection with her company's performance in Dublin in the St Francis Xavier Hall in 1960. Gabriel Fallon wrote in the *Evening Press* that he had 'regularly mourned the death of Ceol Chumann and its effort to establish something approximating to a Gaelic dance drama', and described Patricia as 'seemingly taking up where Ceol Chumann left off.' The *Irish Times* critic was generous in his praise, apart from a quibble about Patricia Mulholland's claim in the programme that she was the first to devise and produce an Irish folk ballet. However, there can be no questioning the fact that she was the originator of this kind of folk ballet, 'so peculiarly our own', and that she had the drive to keep it going for forty years.

Yet there is another curious connection that may have played a part in lighting the fuse, as it were.

In the 1940s, the Scouts' Gang Show did not come to Belfast, so local Scout troupes produced their own end-of-term entertainment.

Reggie McClure had been involved in Scouting all his life, and for one of these shows he wrote a skit on a Maurice Walsh novel and called it *The Tinker's Bride*. He wrote to Walsh to ask permission. And it tells us something of the author's nature that he recommended that Reggie read and adapt his novel, which contained an eye-witness account of a traveller's wedding. Reggie wanted some dancing in the piece and it was naturally to Miss

Mulholland that he turned, knowing of her work with the Guides, some of whom were joining the Scouts for this performance. Is it stretching a point to suggest that this might have been an embryonic Irish Ballet?

Incidentally, this was how Reggie came to dance for Miss Mulholland, because after *The Tinker's Bride*, she asked him to return the favour, as it were, and so he became a stalwart of the company. His first major role was as Ferdia in *Cúchulainn*.

Patricia Mulholland followed in the footsteps of her master, Peadar O'Rafferty, in teaching student teachers and in training Guides and Scouts, but circumstances led her in a different direction. Her involvement with British dancers and British celebrations certainly brought down censure from some quarters, but it undoubtedly led her into avenues of expression that might never have been explored if she had been content to comply with the wishes of the Irish Dancing Commission.

It was already evident that she was a good choreographer. Even at that stage, her team dances reflected this ability to marry steps with music and movement coupled with visual suggestion. This was a God-given ability, but it was to be presented with a chance to really flower by the law of supply and demand, or, to put it another way, cometh the hour, cometh the woman.

The Council for the Encouragement of the Arts (CEMA) felt that Northern Ireland should really have its own ballet company, or, at least, some kind of local dance company to celebrate the forthcoming Festival of Britain in 1951.

It is difficult now to imagine how people felt at that time. The Second World War was well over, but the United Kingdom was still recovering from the deprivations of the conflict. Common foodstuffs, which we take for granted, were in relatively short supply, and so families were only allowed to buy certain allotted amounts. In this self-indulgent era of instant gratification, those who are too young to remember rationing would not really see the point of the celebration of the availability of different foods, textiles and other products. But back then, the nation was looking to the future, and the purpose of the festival was to demonstrate that life could and would be better. Not everyone thought it was an entirely good idea – Churchill was a strong opponent, seeing it as socialist propaganda. Most Tories viewed it as a profligate socialist enterprise, with its £12million budget. However, anyone involved with it – especially architects, who saw the sweeping away of dingy streets for the new buildings as an optimistic start to an age with a social conscience (if only) – remembers the period as a happy one. The festival attracted six million visitors and lasted five months.

Whether all the visitors went home with an altered view of their own lifestyles is debatable. Nonetheless, an impact was made on the leaders of the artistic life of Northern Ireland in the run-up to the event and they were anxious to be a part of this showcase, representing their home place with the best they could find in drama, art (Mercy Hunter's husband George McCann sculpted a statue of St Columba, now in Derry's Guildhall), music and, conveniently for Miss Mulholland, in dance. The indefatigable Dame Dehra Parker, president of CEMA, lent her energies to the task.

Composer Howard Ferguson had written a ballet, but it had no relation to Ulster, and the music committee of CEMA had expressed an opinion in 1949 that any proposed ballet should have an Ulster theme or be based on Ulster music.

> **FOLK SONGS AND DANCES**
>
> ## An Irish ballet
>
> (By Our Music Critic)
>
> The first performance of an Irish ballet was the outstanding feature of last night's concert of folk song and dances in the Ulster Hall. The concert was sponsored by C.E.M.A.
>
> Both in mime and dance the Mulholland team of dancers gave a most expressive interpretation of this new ballet, which is based on Joseph Campbell's poem, "The Dancer." The choreography by Patricia Mulholland is set to traditional airs and dances, which were played last night by the B.B.C. Northern Ireland Light Orchestra, conducted by David Curry, and a "country fiddler" on the stage. The lighting and décor were arranged by the Belfast Arts Theatre. Miss Babs Heaghey, who spoke the poem, gave us the most enchanting item of the ballet in her solo slip jig. The dancing was superb and the grouping and miming were most effective, but all would have been enhanced with fuller lighting effects.
>
> The programme also included several folk songs delightfully sung by Patrick Shuldham-Shaw (tenor), several orchestral items, Irish folk dances, and "The Tara Brooch," a beautiful dance created by Miss Patricia Mulholland, who shared a well-deserved ovation with her dancers at the close of the concert.

Newspaper report from 1951 of the first performance of a Mulholland ballet, The Dancer.

In 1950, nothing had been resolved and three people on the CEMA committee, among them Miss LR Hogg, were charged with co-opting anyone they felt could give specialised assistance in promoting Ulster folk song and dance. Miss Mulholland and Miss Hogg were old friends by this time.

By October 1950, four concerts had been arranged and the possibility was being considered of creating an Irish Ballet accompanied by an orchestra of Irish fiddlers; curiously, the folk songs and dances were now to be advertised as "Irish" rather than "Ulster".

Arrangements for dance, including Irish dance, were henceforth to become the province of the Drama Committee of CEMA; Alfred Arnold was chairman of this committee until 1952. He was also the Controller of the Festival of Britain Committee for Northern Ireland, had been a member of the Cambridge Footlights Club, and was a talented musician – later to receive a papal knighthood for his services to sacred music. (Many people felt he should have been made director of the Arts Council, but it wasn't to be and he retired to Gozo, where he became involved with Church music.) He formed a long-lasting relationship with Patricia Mulholland, composing music for her, designing and applying make-up for the cast of the ballets and throwing some great *après-theatre* parties into the bargain!

So it came about that the first Patricia Mulholland Irish Ballet was presented as the finale of the third concert in this series of four arranged by CEMA. It was called *The Dancer* and based on a poem by Joseph Campbell.

The Dancer, with Brian Coleman in the title role, presented in 1951 in the Ulster Hall, Belfast.

Brian Coleman, one of Miss Mulholland's champions, took the principal part. The first verse ends:

'In his feet music,
And on his face death.'

Hugh Murray interpreted this as the curious juxtaposition of exquisite footwork with a mask-like face, devoid of expression, so often found in Irish dancers. Their feet and legs can be animated in the extreme; and yet the top half of their bodies is totally unused. The poem finishes:

'Clay in his thoughts,
And lightning in his tread.'

In a way, Patricia was laying out her *apologia pro arte sua*, perhaps without realising it, for, thirty years later, she said to journalist Terry McLaughlin, with regard to the antagonism between different viewpoints on Irish dancing, 'All I wanted to get across was that Irish dancing should convey the essential character of the Irish. It was as simple as that. As far as I was concerned, arms poker-rigid beneath an expressionless face had little attraction. I wanted to inject more feeling and, in the process, let Irish dancing come into contact with the widest possible audience.'

The ballet was a great success and left an indelible mark on at least one young member of the audience in the Ulster Hall. Kevin Campbell has a vivid memory of the music of David Curry's orchestra and the dramatic stage effects. So inspired was he that he went on to become a mainstay of the company himself.

Roma and Frances Tomelty came to Miss Mulholland as a direct result of the impression made by this first ballet on their mother Lena.

If Patricia Mulholland had not been invited to teach the BFDS, she would not have been asked by the Guides to dance at the Festival of Britain. And she might never have met Alfred Arnold.

Yet most importantly, if she had not enjoyed the friendship of Lillian Hogg, she might not have had the same *entrée* to CEMA, later the Arts Council, which funded her company for the best part of three decades. Nor would she have been asked to create her first Irish Ballet in 1951. The Patricia Mulholland Irish Ballet Company might never have happened.

Thread the Needle

Irish dancing is not fossilised: I deplore the image which has given rise to this feeling.
Patricia Mulholland

Patricia Mulholland's first vocation was not to teach, but, once embarked on this career, she gave it all her energy. For two decades, she taught in a fairly orthodox manner. She was a gifted teacher, able to develop the potential of her pupils. Norman Maternaghan, for example, is said to have come to her in a pretty raw state, but within a year, she had taught him enough to win every major competition he entered. Of course, it wouldn't have worked if he had lacked the industry and ambition to put into practice what he was taught. He had already had lessons from Sally McCarly, a pupil of Marjorie Andrews, but was interested in the steps that he saw Sadie McKernaghan dancing and decided that he wanted to learn similar steps. So he changed to Sadie's teacher – Miss Mulholland. (Sadie Bell, née McKernaghan, went on to found the Ballymena school Seven Towers, which is still producing excellent dancers.)

Young McCarly team at Coleraine Festival in the 1930s.

It's interesting that Carolyn MacMaster was also enticed to go to Miss Mulholland by the quality of her choreography. Although quite young, she could see a difference in the steps she was learning and steps she recognised as superior. Like Norman, she made it her business to join Miss Mulholland's class and to put to good use what she learned there. She remembers practising all the way home to Bangor on the train. She became a principal in the ballets and her three children are professional dancers.

Mulholland champions dancing The Tara Brooch.

Patricia's dancers, in the 1940s particularly, excelled at winning prizes in competitions, including Ulster and All-Ireland championships. Sheila Fitzpatrick, Maureen McCann, Yvonne Hood, Betty Lewis, Brian Coleman, Patricia King and Isobel Begley are all remembered as outstanding champions in their day.

But Patricia Mulholland was never entirely satisfied with what she saw as the rigidity of most Irish dancing. She disliked the stiffness of carriage associated with it and was always interested in introducing slightly new ways of doing things. This was not change for change's sake, but the result of an active mind exploring and experimenting with new steps or new ways of doing old ones.

For example, at one stage, she devised a new setting of *The Hunt*, using double drumming to suggest horses' hooves. This in itself was nothing new, but she required the drumming to be done with the feet side by side, rather than crossed, thus emphasising the effect. This innovation was too much for one adjudicator, who missed the point entirely and who suggested the dancer performing *The Hunt* should practise crossing her feet neatly in the execution of this step. It was obvious that the dancer in question was capable of placing her feet anywhere she liked.

This happened in the 1970s at Feis Dhoire Cholmcille, bastion of Coimisiún dancing, when the feis secretary, Father Kevin Mullan, himself an ex-Kerrigan pupil, bravely invited Patricia Mulholland to send a couple of dancers to the competitions. Ever one to oblige, where possible, she did. The abiding memory of the two girls who went was the sound of the other competitors practising their heavy dances in the wings while dancers were on stage and the synchronised action of competitors as they bowed after their dance. Ex-Mulholland dancer Sheila Ringland (née Fitzpatrick) was one of the adjudicators that year. Two pupils of Jean Tennent – also festival dancers, and gifted, at that – also went along and won some prizes, but rumour has it that when their teacher expressed surprise that neither Dominic Graham nor his partner had been mentioned in the championship, she was told in no uncertain terms that no championship was in any danger of going outside Derry. The experiment did not continue.

Patricia Mulholland was extraordinarily gifted in her capacity to fit footwork to music. This, in my view, is the key to the Mulholland phenomenon. She had the musical training to understand rhythm well and also had the dancing experience to select a movement that would exactly complement a phrase in any tempo. Her childhood lessons in various kinds of dance were no hindrance, rather an extension to the traditional repertoire of Irish steps.

Anyone who ever saw her or heard her playing the violin could only draw the conclusion from the music she produced that it came from deep inside her. I believe that it was her musicality that developed the Mulholland style and that brought the Mulholland Irish Ballet to birth.

Add to this the fact that she never stood, sat or walked without poise. And yet, curiously, those who saw her actually dance – as distinct from demonstrating a step to pupils – say that her carriage was less than perfect. She always looked elegant, even when it was not easy for her to appear so. Her indifferent health over the years must have cost her real effort at times, and yet she still managed to convey an impression of elegance and grace. I remember one occasion, in April 1958, when she came straight from hospital to a performance in the Ulster Hall: although she was strapped up and in pain, she played for two hours and acknowledged the applause of the audience as if nothing were wrong at all. Then she was presented to Governor and Lady Wakehurst before she returned to hospital. The show had gone on. The Wakehursts were fans of the Patricia Mulholland Irish Ballet Company and apparently used to take cine-film of performances. What an interesting archive that would be!

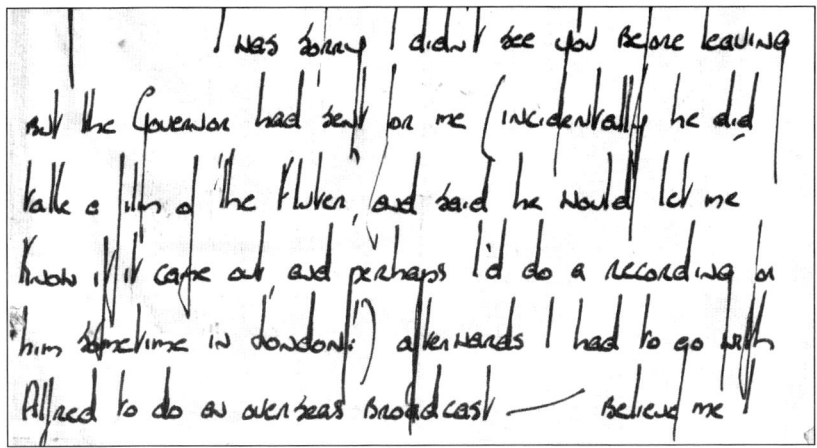

Extract from Patricia Mulholland's letter to Fergus Gilligan, mentioning Lord Wakehurst's filming of a ballet.

The marrying of her musical and choreographic talents found its fullest expression in composing set dances for particular individuals. *The Deep Green Pool, The Reaper (Of Glanree), The Spinning Wheel* and *The Whirlpool* are examples of musical compositions that stand on their own merit as evocative, wistful airs, conveying different emotions, from vague regret to menace. An arrangement of *The Whirlpool* was used to great effect as the theme for a production of Jo Tomelty's *All Souls' Night* at the Lyric Theatre in Belfast.

> **players theatre**
>
> *Opening Thursday, October 3rd 1991*
>
> ## ALL SOULS NIGHT
>
> by
>
> **JOSEPH TOMELTY**
>
> BARBARA ADAIR   BRENDAN COYLE
> GERARD CROSSAN   MARTIN DEMPSEY
> WALTER MCMONAGLE   JOHN O'TOOLE
> ALI WHITE
>
> **Director**
> ROMA TOMELTY
>
> **Designer**   **Lighting Designer**
> SHEILA GODBOLT   COLIN CARNEGIE
>
> **Music**
> JOHN COYLE
>
> Theme: *The Whirlpool* by Patrica Mulholland
> (By kind permission of Patricia Mulholland)
>
> Arranged, performed and recorded by John Coyle
>
> **THE TAKING OF PHOTOGRAPHS IS NOT PERMITTED IN THE AUDITORIUM**

Lyric Theatre Programme.

But when you add Mulholland choreography to these blissful accompaniments, it is indeed a match made in heaven.

But what exactly is a set dance? The answer depends on whether one is considering the music alone or as an accompaniment. What dancers call set dances are what traditional musicians probably call slow airs and, in some places, long dances. Another answer depends on whether one is a feis or festival dancer.

In general terms, a set dance is a heavy dance, that is, one danced in heavy shoes. It can be in jig or hornpipe tempo. The first step is interchangeable with any ordinary jig or hornpipe step, but the second step or "set" is longer by at least half as many bars than the first. Feis dancers do the right and left foot of the first step (eight bars each) and then the right foot only of the set.

Up to very recently, festival dancers learned right and left foot of the first step, right and left of the set and then right and left of the third (and last) step. Pressure of time at competitions often limited their performance to going as far as the right foot of the set, but every dancer knew that he/she might have to do the whole dance, depending on the adjudicator and their performance. Sometimes, an adjudicator would want to see the complete dance if he had been impressed by the soloist. There was always a third step choreographed, even if it weren't seen, unlike at feiseanna, where the third step no longer exists. For festival championships, the third step is still required in theory and still has to be choreographed, but is never now seen on the competition platform.

It's taken for granted here that the reader knows that all Irish solo dances have a step lasting eight bars of music – eight bars for the right foot, then eight bars for the left. Either step has the same movements but reversed for each foot. The right foot is in front of the left in a certain move during the first eight bars, then it's reversed for the next eight. In a reel, say, after the lead round (which might last eight bars or sixteen) there is a sidestep to the right, sidestep to the left, first step on the right foot, first step on the left, second step on the right, second step on the left and so on.

The music for set dances includes some of the most beautiful slow airs in the traditional repertoire, such as *A Piper Through The Meadow Straying* (elsewhere, *A Piper In The*

Meadow Straying), Youghal Harbour, The Blackbird, The Three Sea Captains and *Planxty Irwin* (slightly different musically). Some of these names are allegorical. *The Blackbird*, for example, is said to commemorate Charles Stuart, the Young Pretender. Jo Tomelty always believed the *Piper* symbolised Death. *Sean O'Guire Of The Glens* represents a vanquished Ireland and dates from Cromwellian times.

In other cases, the names of the set dances reflect the period during which the tunes were composed: *Bonaparte's Retreat (*originally a French tune, *Ça Ira,* that switched sides*) Madame Bonaparte* and *Rodney's Glory.*

Others can be deceptive, such as *The Princess Royal*. It has nothing to do with any monarch's daughter but was composed by Turlough O'Carolan circa 1725 in honour of the daughter of his patron, McDermott Roe.

These dances are the most demanding for the performer, as he/she is expected to dance in time and to execute crisp beats as usual, but also to interpret the music. Shoes worn for heavy dancing, which look like orthopaedic supports with built-up soles and protuberances sticking out from the heels and which require extra straps to hold them onto the feet, detract immeasurably from any performance.

In a championship, a dancer is required to perform his/her best light dance, a jig or a hornpipe and a set dance. Another difference between feis and festival dancers is that festival men, as a general rule, wear pumps for light dances; feis men wear an ordinary court shoe with leather soles, considerably lighter than those they wear for heavy dancing,

In bigger competitions, like the Northern Ireland Championships, he will need to have at least four set dances, polished and ready for performance; two in 2/4 time and two in 6/8 (hornpipe and jig). He will expect to dance one of each, usually chosen by the adjudicator. Festival dancers tend to build up their set dances to a climax, with the heaviest beating in the last step, but, as a general rule, feis dancers go at it hammer and tong from the start.

The overall effect of any set dance depends on the choreography in the first place, and it was in the devising, and indeed composing, of set dances that Patricia Mulholland excelled. A newspaper critic once described how the sound of the dancer's feet was '. . . effectively used to convey menace in the scolding crone's dance' in *The Black Rogue*. Another magic ingredient was the fact that she could design these dances specifically for individuals, knowing their strengths and particular styles.

The Deep Green Pool – the name conjures up an image of a calm, smooth surface, hiding who-knows-what depths below – was composed, music and dance, for Yvonne Hood, who was an extremely graceful, controlled dancer. *The Reaper (Of Glanree)* was another composition specially set for Yvonne, and the opening of the first step conveyed the sweeping of a scythe through a meadow. Yvonne won the Ulster Championship with this set dance in 1949. It was the first time the Ulsters had been held in Derry and the last time that Mulholland dancers ever took part in a feis.

Youghal Harbour was choreographed for Norman Maternaghan, an exceptional dancer. The set was particularly stirring when Miss Mulholland would "let herself go".

Water was always a favourite inspiration (she told me once that she loved to feel rain again after a spell of good weather or a trip abroad) and provided the theme again in the 1980s, when *The Whirlpool* was composed for Kathy O'Connor, a skilled exponent of the smooth turn.

The Spinning Wheel was another composed for Kathy. The devising of this one brought Miss Mulholland to a museum to learn exactly how the machine worked. She was never afraid of hard work and always spent time on preparation, so that by the time she actually taught a dance, she had a very clear idea of what she wanted.

Norman Maternaghan recalls how she used to choreograph steps by first sitting, playing the fiddle and moving her feet. Audrey Clarke says she used to spend her sleepless nights coming up with new ideas.

This business of choreographing "to order" might be considered a disadvantage for other dancers if one looks at the experience of one adjudicator, Frankie Roddy, who taught all over the North. He was adjudicating at Bangor Festival one year, and during one competition sat through a performance of *The Reaper*. The girl who had danced this thought she'd done a good job and was rather disappointed when she didn't secure first place. Mr Roddy went up on stage to make his remarks after the competition and to give the results. He explained that he thought the only person capable of doing justice to *The Reaper* was the dancer for whom it had been choreographed. You see, he had enjoyed Yvonne Hood's performance of this dance at an Ulster championship and anything after that was just an anticlimax.

So the combination of music, choreography and individual ability could produce a wonderfully satisfying result, but it could equally be a pitfall for the unwary if an audience or adjudicator had an ideal performance in mind.

The Mulholland slip-jig is another example of this sort of thing: the slip-jig has a curious tempo – 9/8 time. The emphasis, in this case, is definitely not on the jig. Patricia Mulholland composed music for several slip-jigs and refined this dance into one requiring enormous control, sophistication and grace. It is just possible that she was influenced very early in her teaching career by Cork dancers by the name of McTaggert, who did a high-stepping, graceful slip-jig. In her hands, it became quite balletic in places, with the use of steps that resemble *glissades* and *frappés*. A departure of this nature brought inevitable criticism from some traditionalists. In an interview in 1981 with Terry McLaughlin, Patricia pointed out that her approach to Irish dancing was not universally welcomed: 'To be quite honest, the reaction at first in some quarters was extremely hostile. Quite a lot of people felt that Irish dancing was quite all right as it was and that any attempt to introduce a more relaxed interpretation of a traditional art form was tantamount to heresy.' But this was nothing new; in 1937, at Feis Dhoire Cholmcille, the adjudicator Brian Cosgrove declared that Irish dance done without grace was simply horseplay. He denied that a graceful approach to Irish dancing was a copying of ballet – as some seemed to claim – but a first requisite of any kind of dancing. He was right.

Now, a Mulholland slip-jig, when attempted by anyone less than expert in the three requirements mentioned above, looks simply ridiculous and gauche; it can be rightly dismissed as "walking about the stage", or even worse, calling to mind the "ministry of silly walks".

Solo dances were not the only dances based on traditional forms that received the Mulholland treatment. Her team dances were greatly appreciated, inspiring admiration from even the least likely of audiences. Some of the inspiration for these came from her readiness to see opportunities in the most mundane.

A chocolate box she received from a Dundalk pupil, possibly Isobel Begley, at a time when sweets were rationed, had a picture of a Tara brooch on the cover and the team dance inspired by this formed part of the Mulholland repertoire for fifty years. It can still be seen as danced by the Kathy O'Connor dancers.

The opening of the dance *The Tara Brooch* cast its own spell, as the straight line of men who formed the "pin" moved round the stationary circle of women to the tune of *The Misty Marsh*. Hugh Murray, in his thesis on Irish dance, gives us to understand that the straight lines in Irish dance represent masculinity, while circles and curves, appropriately enough, symbolise femininity.

Once, when Patricia was leaving George Leonard to the GNR station (now the Europa) for his journey home to Dublin, she noticed the emblem on the engine of the train: it was a shield portraying the four provinces of Ireland. This resulted in the team dance *Erin*, in which the dancers sketched the symbols of the Hand, the Crowns, the Harp, and the Eagle and Dagger, finishing with the spelling out of the word ERIN.

Casadh An tSúgáin or *The Twisting Of The Rope* is a traditional tune based on a traditional activity, which could still be seen in country areas up until fairly recently. There is an ancient Irish poem based on it. It is also the name of the first Irish language play performed in the Gaiety Theatre in Dublin in 1903, written by Douglas Hyde and which he brought to a close with a four-hand reel. A short-lived Dublin group, An Cheol Chumainn presented a dance drama on this theme, but the Mulholland dance version of the idea was evidence of the ease with which Patricia could deal with a complicated concept to produce an intercurvilinear piece of art in terpsichorean terms, seeming to tie everyone in knots, only to release them again, suddenly, with almost magic effect, always winning applause from the audience at that point.

The Twisting Of The Rope.

The Woven Shawl was an early Mulholland team dance which included complicated arm movements. Patricia brought her team along to the BFDS for an exhibition one night, but somebody's concentration lapsed and the dance turned out a complete mess. Sheila Fitzpatrick, who was a member of the team along with Madeleine Mackey, John

McErlain and Norman Maternaghan, was afraid that they were going to be "killed".

When it came to her Irish Ballets, Patricia Mulholland had free rein to develop Irish dancing in a very new way and to teach her dancers to use their arms and bodies, not just their feet. She herself said once, 'It strikes me as the right thing to do. Irish dancing is not fossilised – I deplore the image which has given rise to this feeling and it is something I always fought against. I have tried in the Irish Ballet Company to develop it logically and apply it to a variety of situations.'

Apparently, Kurt Joos had tried something along the lines of Irish dance drama in the 1930s in Dublin. The *Irish Times* critic, writing in February 1960, felt that Patricia Mulholland should not have claimed that she was the innovator of this dance medium. The same critic appreciated her achievement and was enthusiastic in his praise for the work of her company. He was even more appreciative of her musical talent: 'Without detracting in any way from the Irish Ballet Company, who appeared in the St Francis Xavier Hall last night, I feel that when the dancing is forgotten, the music will stay in the mind. Patricia Mulholland, the director and inspirer of the company, has a fine taste in Irish folk music, and plays it so beautifully on the violin that it overshadows the dancing to some extent.'

Whether Miss Mulholland was aware of the work of Kurt Joos and/or the Ceol Chumann is impossible to deny or confirm categorically, but it is certainly indisputable that she brought to birth something that simply had not been seen before and that she developed it, in artistic terms, as far as she could. Irish poetry, song and legend were the material she used as a foundation for a new and artistically valid treatment of traditional dance. If you had seen an advertisement for the Irish Ballet and had gone along expecting to see ballet dancing, you would have been disappointed. Patricia Mulholland's ballets were unmistakably based on Irish dancing and could, perhaps, have been more accurately described as folk ballet. Indeed, one critic in 1958 suggested this, precisely to avoid possible confusion. In the same year, an advertisement for the company described the forthcoming performance as 'an impressive display of Irish traditional folk dance, music and mime.' But as time went on, the name Patricia Mulholland became synonymous with her particular blend of Irish dancing and musical storytelling.

The *Encyclopaedia Of Ireland* suggests that Miss Mulholland was incensed when Joan Denise Moriarty started her professional ballet company in 1973 and called it The Irish Ballet Company, but the official title of the amateur Northern company was always The Patricia Mulholland Irish Ballet Company.

The Cork-based company had had several different names in the course of its existence and was composed of exclusively classically trained dancers. Cork Ballet Company 1947–93, was Miss Moriarty's amateur company. Her first professional group was Irish Theatre Ballet, which lasted only five years, running out of money in 1964. The Irish Ballet Company lasted twice as long, 1973–83. It was during this period that they produced the first full-length Moriarty ballet, *The Playboy Of The Western World*, which was accompanied by The Chieftains and which was hugely enjoyable. Her last professional company was the Irish National Ballet (1983–89). The two ladies were similar in some ways, working tirelessly to realise their visions and hampered by financial considerations.

The Northern group were invited by Aloys Fleischman on more than one occasion to be guest entertainers at the Cork Festival and were greeted enthusiastically by Miss Moriarty.

Cork International Choral and Folk Dance Festival

OFFICES 38 MACCURTAIN STREET CORK IRELAND
TELEPHONE CORK 50222!

AF/VR   6th May, 1981

Ms. Patricia Mulholland
7 Brookvale Drive
Belfast BT14 6DE

Dear Ms. Mulholland,

Allow me to say what a great pleasure it was to all of us here to have had your participation in our Festival last week. Your company's delightful contribution to our programmes was tremendously appreciated, and the exceptional versatility of your dancers greatly admired. It id difficult to find an adequate Irish dimension for the dance section of our Festival, as the conventional Irish dancing grows more wearisome every year! So it was a matter of pride for us to be able to show our visitors what Irish dance forms can achieve when they reach the high level which you have set.

Praise from Aloys Fleischman for the Mulholland dancers.

Some of the movements Patricia Mulholland employed are directly borrowed from classical ballet, such as *attitudes* or *arabesques*; some more obviously are from Scottish dancing, for instance arm on hip with the other curved over the head. But many of the movements were of her own devising entirely.

When a female dancer walked or stood on stage, her arms were never to be held down by her sides, as in traditional Irish dance, but a few inches away, if not daintily holding her skirt.

Posing for a poster for the Riverside Theatre, Coleraine.

Feet were to be pointed at all times, out and down. (So inbuilt did this become that it could cause problems for any Mulholland dancer who went on to other forms of dance, like modern or classical ballet, where they had to retrain themselves to use their feet in different ways.) This was most important and the instruction was repeated often. Just how seriously some dancers took this advice is illustrated by the experience of one of the female principals of the '80s who unfortunately fell over a piece of scenery one night on stage. But she sought reassurance afterwards from Miss Mulholland, hoping that she'd noticed that she'd kept her toes beautifully pointed throughout the incident!

Some arm or hand movements were closely associated with particular footwork and became almost second nature whenever you performed the step. For example, if you were doing "rocks" with the feet tightly crossed and rocking from side to side, chances were you'd also cross the hands over the breast or behind the back.

The slip-jig sidestep was often matched with one arm held out to the side, shoulder high, the other crossed over the breast, sort of "hula" style.

While on stage, every member of the company was required to look animated, interested in what was going on. No "dead ducks", as Miss Mulholland called them, were allowed in the chorus.

Sketch showing position of arms for rocks.

This awareness of others became quite routine after a while and carried over into all ensemble work, whether in a ballet or a three-hand reel. Many's a mediocre two-hand was enhanced by the dancers' sense of presentation and their enjoyment in performing for the audience. This was a facility they acquired from their familiarity with the stage through their dancing in the ballets.

On more than one occasion, dances were practised on the train, en route to a festival. If one criticism can be levelled at Miss Mulholland's teaching, it is that she did not spend much time rehearsing teams. Nor did she waste time on anyone who was not prepared to really work; some pupils who would not have been let near the stage by other teachers appeared at festivals. Her comment was that they should have practised more, but their parents may have felt that she should have taught more. While this could add a freshness or spontaneity to a performance, it could be nerve-wracking for those of us who had less dependable memories than Margot Bell, say, who could prod and pull anyone who needed it, out of sight of the adjudicator.

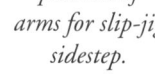

Sketch showing position of arms for slip-jig sidestep.

Dermot Brooks twirls his partners, Patricia and Stella O'Neill.

Some hawk-eyed members at the front of the audience at a Belfast Festival once complained that it wasn't fair for a team that they (the hawk-eyes) considered didn't know their dance to win the competition. The adjudicator, sitting on a dais in the middle of the floor some distance from the stage, could see only the full-frontal presentation and was unaware of the frantic whisperings, pushing and pulling going on in the background. But, as someone pointed out at the time, no other team could have got away with it.

Adjudicators themselves sometimes have to bluff their way out of situations, too. On the last night at Ballymena Festival, there is a tradition that the adjudicator dances for the audience. (I found this out rather suddenly one Easter, but fortunately was able to plead swollen feet as an excuse.) George Leonard was asked to dance one year, during the '50s, at the end of the festival. He first said he had no shoes. That problem was dealt with easily. Then he said he would only dance if Patricia Mulholland played. She was not accompanying, just spectating, and so did not have her beloved fiddle, as George well knew. The feis accompanist offered his. So George took his time, struggling into the borrowed shoes while he tried to remember either *Hurry The Jug* or *The Humours Of Bandon*. Well, he managed to start with the first step of *The Humours*, changed to the set of *Hurry The Jug* and did a right foot *Humours*, left foot *Jug* last step. As he passed, Patricia whispered, 'That's a new one on me – *Hurry The Humours*.' Incidentally, the feis accompanist is reported to have been amazed that his fiddle could sing like he'd never heard it!

The stage experience of the dancers gave them enough confidence to bluff their way out of minor mistakes without giving the game away, and to cope with unexpected contretemps. (Unlike a friend of mine who sang with a local amateur operatic society and who was in the front row of the chorus once at Waterford Festival of Light Opera. As the soprano took her final high note and didn't quite hit it in tune, my friend made a face to show her displeasure!) In 1958, the dancers were part of a charity concert for blood donors in the Wellington Hall. The stage had been extended by means of a set of boxes. One of the boxes slipped and Hugh Murray fell off! The other dancers continued unperturbed, the audience rebuilt the stage and helped Hugh back up where he quickly found his place again.

However, all the self-assurance in the world can't hide a catastrophe. Once, at a Belfast festival, a team went so badly wrong that the only reason Patricia Mulholland continued playing was that the chaotic performance was providing so much amusement for the audience. My brother Edmund was presented with an individual medal for his part in the team's "downfall".

Patricia Mulholland enjoyed a challenge and rose to meet one every time she embarked on a new ballet. There were many ingredients put together that went to make the first Irish Ballet, *The Dancer*, but the leap of faith that it must have required cannot be overestimated. Its creator had to believe, first of all, that she could come up with the required dramatic work and then had to convince good Irish dancers that they were capable of becoming good Irish Ballet dancers – not a foregone conclusion.

This was yet another facet of Patricia's talent, that she could persuade a group of Irish dancers to take to the stage as actors as well as dancers, using mime and hand and arm gestures with which they were unfamiliar. There is a curious ambivalence here, in that she could inspire self-belief in her pupils and yet suffer from insecurities herself.

She taught the steps or directed the scene and then let you get on with it without any interference or last-minute instructions. This applied equally to other fields, in that she would ask her dancers to thank adjudicators with a little speech, or invite ex-dancers to come and adjudicate at her Belfast Festival, encouraging them to do things that they might never have thought of themselves.

She knew that she could teach, for she would take on inexperienced dancers and release them onto the stage, never doubting that they would cope, and yet, there were times when she could not summon that kind of confidence within herself.

The Patricia Mulholland Irish Ballet Company remained amateur in every best sense throughout its existence, but its members achieved a remarkably good standard of performance for most of this time.

In the early '60s, a suggestion came from the Arts Council, possibly through Henry Lynch-Robinson, who designed sets and lighting for the ballets (he was an architect by profession), that the company should turn professional. If it were smaller in number, the argument went, it would be easier to fund and run. The idea was discussed at length by Miss Mulholland and her senior dancers, but it did not come to fruition, largely because most of the principal dancers already had professional careers or were on the point of qualifying for professions, so they felt that the risk wasn't justified. Among the senior dancers at this time were engineers, teachers, doctors, civil servants and psychologists.

If they'd had a little less to lose, who knows what might have happened? This also illustrates the largely middle-class sort of clientele who came to Miss Mulholland. Her fees at this time were probably beyond the pocket of any but the reasonably well paid. (During the early '60s, her fee was two guineas a term.) But she was a generous person and used to adjust her bill or forget to send it every now and then if she saw fit.

This team being presented with a prize by Mrs Graham at Bangor Festival in the late 1950s had members from the Ormeau, Malone, Shankill, Falls and Shore Roads, and from Larne. In the group are: a future teacher, civil engineer, union activist, businesswoman, civil servant, actress, consultant surgeon and a dancing teacher.

However, when all was said and done, no matter how much the dancers loved the ballets or how deeply immersed they were in their dancing, it was still only a hobby for all but a few.

Patricia Mulholland was primarily an artist, not a business woman; she was an innovator in dance but found it impossible to think of her company in business terms – a mental leap that might have led to a very different outcome from the rather sad demise that awaited it in the '80s. If she had brought in a financial manager in the same way that she welcomed a costume or lighting designer, her company might have taken a more professional direction. She was proud of the fact that her company was comprised of amateurs. In an interview with Judith Rosenfeld for the *Irish Press*, she claimed, 'The crowd I have is most enthusiastic and I think they would be spoiled if they became professionals.'

But perhaps this stemmed from the fact that she was reluctant to release her hold on the development of her company – particularly her dancers – rather than an inherent belief in the virtue of amateurism.

Promenade: 1953–59

All I wanted to get across was the essential character of the Irish.
It is as simple as that. **Patricia Mulholland**

The Dancer had been an experiment for Patricia Mulholland and CEMA – a very successful one – so both parties were emboldened to push themselves further and tackle a full-length folk ballet.

As 1953 was the year of the coronation of Queen Elizabeth, CEMA hoped to have an open-air performance of a new ballet in Hazlewood Park, moving to the Floral Hall if it rained. In fact, this plan was never carried out.

Just how much support was provided by CEMA can be judged by the fact that Miss Mulholland was originally offered 150 guineas for the preparation of a new ballet, a sum with which she was not satisfied. Subsequently, a revised fee of £300 was arranged and accepted. (A guinea, for the benefit of any younger reader, was the equivalent of one pound and five pence.) It is always difficult to translate sums of money into modern equivalents, but in the 1950s, one could have bought a reasonable, three-bedroom, semi-detached house for several hundred pounds.

Cúchulainn
First performed: Empire Theatre, Belfast, 1953.

Cúchulainn was probably an obvious choice of subject for the new venture in that he is, of course, an Ulster hero, and many people know parts, if not most, of his story. But Miss Mulholland had a *gae bolga*, as it were, in one of her dancers – Norman Maternaghan. (The *gae bolga* was Cúchulainn's secret weapon with which he was guaranteed to win any battle.) Norman was an ideal Cúchulainn in terms of both dancing virtuosity and dramatic artistry. Patricia King was to play the part of Emer and was a perfect choice; she was lovely looking, graceful and a talented dancer.

This ballet was really a vehicle for Norman Maternaghan, one of the best, if not *the* best, of Miss Mulholland's dancers. She was inspired by him and I think it possible that she was a little in love with him. She did have a tendency to lionise all her principal male dancers. He became a professional choreographer, shortened his surname to Maen, and is, to date, the only recipient from these islands of an Emmy for choreography.

Anyone who ever saw him dance was instantly impressed, with the possible exception of George Leonard, who told Patricia when he saw him first that he would never make a dancer, although Norman learned enough in one year to win practically every competition he entered at a feis.

The new work was a two-act ballet based on most of the famous episodes in the Ulster

Norman Maternaghan/Maen receiving his Emmy from actress Anne Bancroft in 1969 (courtesy of MPTV).

hero's life. The action started with the boy Setanta showing off his athletic prowess and how he became *Cú Chulainn* (Culan's hound). The ballet stopped at the point of celebrating his defeat of Ferdia in a duel.

JJ Campbell wrote a prologue and a narrative which linked the episodes and which was spoken by Alfred Arnold. The idea behind this, I suppose, was to make it as easy as possible for the audience to follow the action, especially those who were not familiar with the tale, or indeed, with balletic drama.

Cúchulainn was another success. All the press reviews of the time were lavish in their praise of the entire company.

The principal dancers, including Hugh Murray, the energetic jester, were singled out for their excellence; the costumes of Mercy Hunter and the lighting effects of Henry Lynch-Robinson also drew praise. David Curry's conducting of the BBC Northern Ireland Light Orchestra in his own arrangements of the traditional airs 'gave full power to a well-knit performance.' The photographs of Patricia and Norman give some idea of their ability, but, naturally, don't convey the full impact of their performance.

Miss Mulholland was given assistance with some aspects of this ballet. John Douglas worked with the principals, especially to improve their miming skills, and he helped her to group the dancers on stage attractively. In several of the contemporary critiques, Patricia King's graceful mime is praised wholeheartedly. One critic described her poise and confidence as that of a professional dancer. And as if that weren't enough, she actually made her costumes with the help of her mother.

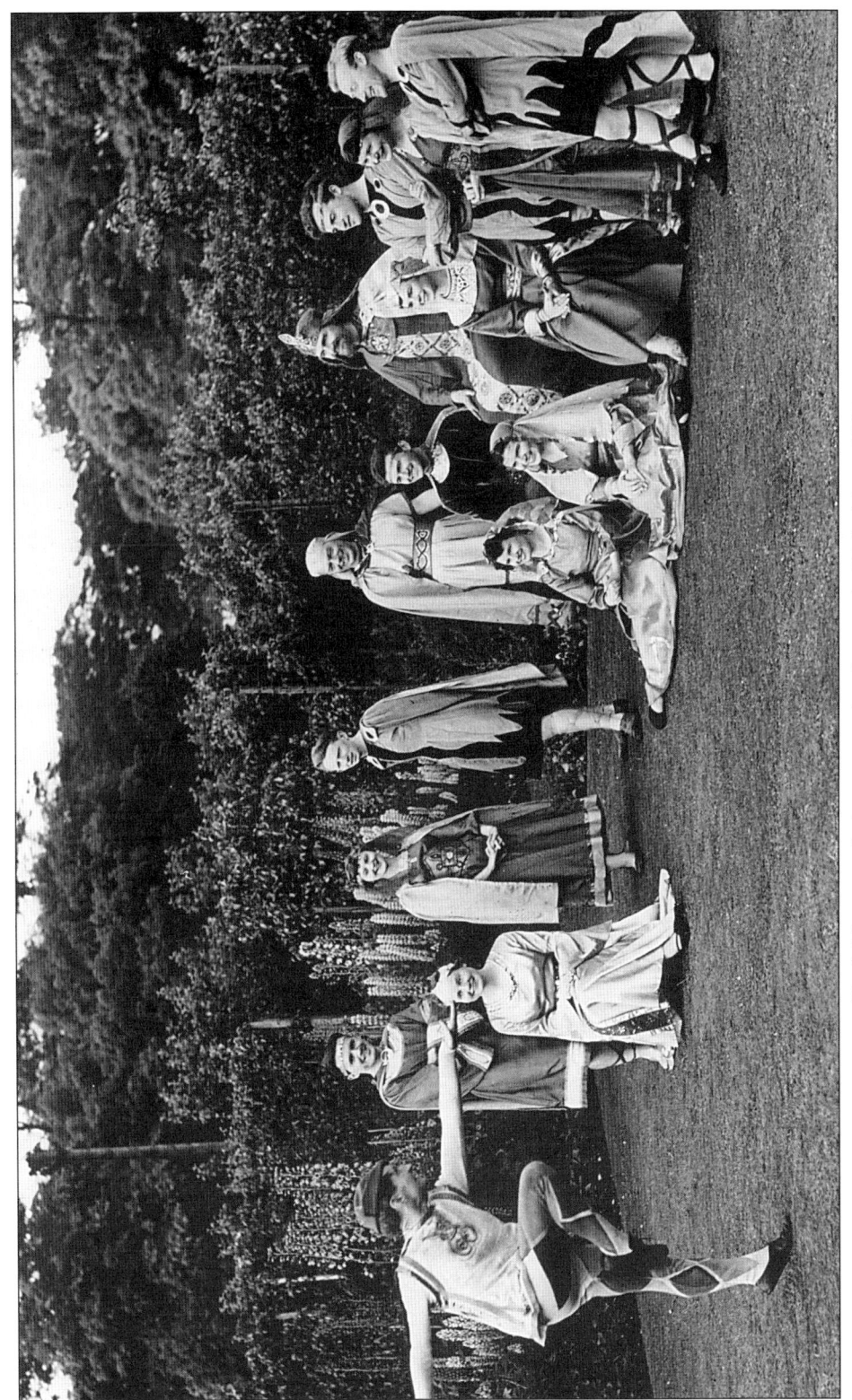

Hugh Murray as the jester entertains the court in Cúchulainn, 1953.

Emer pleads with Cúchulainn.

Norman Maternaghan also has a good artistic eye and his dissatisfaction with the outfit dreamt up for him by Mercy Hunter, the official costume designer, illustrated her approach to designing for dancers. She drew sketches which were attractive enough in themselves – indeed, some were framed, and graced the walls of the Grand Opera House in Belfast – but she knew or cared little about the technical side of dressmaking and rarely, if ever, inquired of Miss Mulholland what was required in terms of facilitating movement.

Miss Mulholland adjusts Patricia King's dress.

At the dress rehearsal for *Cúchulainn*, Norman appeared wearing a tunic, described by one bystander as a demented nightshirt that came down past his knees, and everybody laughed, encouraged by his playing up the impossibility of moving as required. He complained that he couldn't possibly dance in the garment. The company's reaction to his appearance was enough to guarantee that he would be permitted to produce his own costume. The short tunic that he came up with can be seen in the photo opposite; it obviously allowed freedom of movement.

So successful were the first few performances of *Cúchulainn* that it was booked into the Empire Theatre (it used to stand between Victoria Square and Cornmarket) for a week in the April of the following year, 1954, including a matinee on the Saturday.

In the early days of the Mulholland Irish Ballet Company performances, accompaniment was provided by David Curry's BBC Northern Ireland Light Orchestra. This only lasted for *Cúchulainn* and performances of *A Piper* in Armagh and the Empire Theatre. It was a wonderful feeling, dancing on the swell of music that a full orchestra produces. Kevin Campbell and Stella O'Neill found it particularly exhilarating. But of course, not only was this arrangement too expensive to maintain, but it proved somewhat complicated at times.

Empire poster, 1953.

Reggie McClure recalled one performance of *Cúchulainn* that took place in Armagh. The cast and orchestra met outside the BBC building in Ormeau Avenue to get the bus. (This was a tradition that continued for many years.) On this particular occasion, the orchestra had congregated in The Ram's Head, a local hostelry (the owner's son, Kevin Rafferty, later became a principal dancer in the company), and Reggie thought it might have been payday. Anyway, by the time they arrived at the Armagh city hall, the musicians were feeling very mellow. Understandably, there were a few glitches, but a near disaster was averted during the fight at the ford scene in which Cúchulainn fights and kills his friend Ferdia. During the fight, Norman Maternaghan, with his good ear for music, realised that there were sixteen bars missing, but Barry Kinghan was concentrating on his fight as choreographed. Eventually, Norman grabbed him by the throat, forced him to the ground and hissed through clenched teeth, 'Die, for God's sake, we're running out of music!'

With Miss Mulholland accompanying, you could be sure she would always be in the right place with the music and could even disguise your mistakes.

The photographs of scenes from the ballet were taken in the garden of the Canavan family. Valerie and Yvonne Canavan both danced with Miss Mulholland, and their parents were great friends of Patricia and her mother, so it was an ideal location.

Norman Maternaghan left for Canada and greater things just a month after these shots were taken, so there is a bittersweet quality about them, though no real hint of the tears that were shed at the time. Those of us who were children then were quite unaware of the high emotional state of some of the adults.

Reggie McClure, playing the part of Ferdia in Cúchulainn, *is seen here being vanquished in the duel at the ford.*

Row 5, L-R: Colum McBennet and John Garvin. Row 4: Audrey Clarke, a visiting Christian Brother, Pat Traynor, Brian Coleman, Valerie Canavan, John Melville. Row 3: Barry Kinghan, Harper Gourley, Olive Melville, Lynne Maxwell, Sheelagh McDade, Stella O'Neill, Betty Walker, Anne O'Hara, Reggie McClure. Row 2: Margaret Garvin, Patricia King, Mrs Mulholland, Mrs Canavan, Miss Mulholland, Dr Canavan, Norman Maternaghan, Kevin Campbell. Row 1: Paddy McQuitty, Hugh Murray, Yvonne Canavan (with kitten), Evelyn McGrath and Mary O'Reilly.

Armagh Cúchulainn *programme, 1953.*

When he got settled in Canada, Norman started gradually on his professional dancing career and was keen enough to use every available opportunity to travel to classical and modern classes with Alan and Blanche Lund in New York. It was through this contact that he was offered the part of the Leprechaun in *Finian's Rainbow* and received rave reviews. Further work in the Lunds' *TV Spectacular* followed, for, although he was still relatively inexperienced, he had built a good reputation for being industrious and reliable. His talent brought him inevitably to Broadway and Hollywood, first as lead dancer in *Donnybrook*, the musical version of *The Quiet Man*, and to the tutorial skills of Jack Cole. Cole was responsible for choreographing Marilyn Monroe in films like *Gentlemen Prefer Blondes*. Norman worked on Broadway for some years and was about to sign on for another season when he stopped to think. The whole lifestyle seemed very insecure, and coupled with this was the fact that his parents weren't well. So he began to think about coming home.

Just with that, he was contacted by RTÉ, which was in its infancy at that time, and he got the job of staff choreographer, their first and only resident choreographer. He directed the dancing on a weekly show. On one of these, he helped a famous Irish dancing teacher to design a famous couples (dance for two) but could never take the credit. During this time, he learned all about camera shots – a skill that was to stand him in good stead in all his television work in America and England.

Later, in 1981, he directed the Moriarty piece *Reputations*. This was a short ballet, commissioned for television, and many people believe the credit for its success must go to Norman.

Norman Maternaghan/Maen, left, rehearsing in Hollywood.

A Piper
First performed: St Patrick's Parochial Hall, Armagh, January 1955.

After the impressive *Cúchulainn*, Patricia returned to an Irish poem for inspiration for her next ballet: *A Piper*, by Seamus O'Sullivan.

You might imagine that the preparation of a short, light-hearted piece would be less demanding than a major work, but the characters still have to be chosen, in this case, the tradesmen and the 'women with petticoats coloured like flame;' their dances must be sorted out, the music chosen, the staging arranged, etc. Besides all this, Patricia still took normal classes, rehearsals and BFDS classes, never mind the teaching at Jordanstown. Miss Mulholland seems to have had boundless energy.

At the start of this ballet, the company sometimes paraded across the apron of the stage before the curtain opened, following the sound of the music, as it were, and one little girl would trip and a gallant young man would help her to her feet and dust off her dress. In later years, a girl dressed in her green dancing costume would recite the poem beforehand. For some strange reason, the word "gold" in a phrase was changed to "old" on some programmes '. . . went dancing back to the age of gold . . .' and the mistake was never rectified.

The first villager to appear was the artist, complete with smock and palette, and he entered with a great bound. At one venue, the stage was not quite big enough to contain the dancer's athleticism and he cannoned into a piece of scenery and nearly knocked out the musicians. Fortunately, no-one was hurt – well, physically, at any rate.

The baker, schoolmaster, jockey and others entered in turn and the arrival of the ladies introduced a graceful, feminine contrast. Humour was provided by two "eccentric gentlemen", one very strait-laced and carrying a rolled umbrella, the other just his antithesis. Barefoot street urchins danced to *The Soldier's Joy*, a tune that will be familiar to Western film fans.

Choice of music was appropriate throughout, with *An Súisín Bán, Off To Puck Fair* and *Jockey To The Fair* danced to by all the company. During the last piece, the men danced the standard heavy dance while the women provided a light, lyrical counterpoint, moving in and out through the men.

Overhead view of the villagers and the piper.

There was a curious little interlude in the middle where a child asked the piper to play a request and he would eventually come up with the right slip-jig tune, *Sport Of The Chase*; the company then joined in the dance, taking their cue from one individual, then another. One dancer, inspired by the music, would "do her own thing" and the rest would follow her lead.

The ballet opened and closed with a wistfully played air, *A Piper*, possibly one of Patricia's own compositions. At the start, it conveyed the piper's uncertainty as he arrived at a new town, and at the close, it provided a contrast with the bright, busy scenes that preceded it, rather as the poem brings us back to the street after the brief, happy interlude.

A group from a later Piper *performance.*

Some of the costumes changed slightly as time went on. The costume designer for the Irish Ballet Company was Mercy Hunter throughout its history, but at this early stage, some individuals came up with their own ideas. Pat Traynor was the first piper; he wore an outfit reminiscent of a *Pied Piper Of Hamelin* illustration. I remember arriving in the new hall in Armagh and the first person I saw was Pat racing down a corridor, and with his cape flowing out behind him, he struck me as terribly glamorous. Later pipers wore a possibly more accurate, though less attractive, outfit of tweeds with an old, battered hat. The little girls' dresses started out as gingham but were changed to colours of a brighter effect. A still later innovation provided them with white pinafores to wear over their frocks.

This ballet remained in the company's repertoire right until the end, for forty years, and was performed in many towns all round the North of Ireland.

Early on, the children were usually ferried to venues in Gilligans' van; the entire Gilligan family supported Miss Mulholland for many years. Marjorie and her sister Marie had gone to Peadar O'Rafferty's classes at St Anthony's. (Marie showed great promise and was encouraged by Peadar but unfortunately was unable to develop her talent – their mother was a widow and had eight children to rear.) When Marjorie sent her own daughters to Irish dancing, there was absolutely no question but that Patricia

Mulholland was the teacher of choice. Her husband, Fergus, was stage-manager for a long time and his daughters Sheelagh and Patricia both danced as principals in the ballets. Sheelagh also helped with stage management when the arrival of her daughter brought her dancing days to an end. Marjorie was wardrobe mistress for some time.

L-R: *Joyce Ann Henry, Frances Tomelty, John Doherty, Eileen Agnew (kneeling), Frankie McLaughlin, Tom Crangle, Pat Traynor, Tom McDade (just seen), and Brian Bunting.*

Tom Crangle, Frankie McLaughlin and Cardinal d'Alton.

For the very first performance at the opening of the new parochial hall in Armagh in 1955, we were taken, not in Gilligans' van, but in taxis, accompanied by parents or chaperones. It was January and the roads were icy and we didn't get home until about two in the morning, a great adventure. (I wore what was left of my make-up into school the following day!)

Apparently, Miss Mulholland had advised the people who were building the stage to run the planks of wood downstage, rather than across it, which was rare for a parochial hall.

Entertainment at this concert was supplied by David Curry and his orchestra, some singers and the Mulholland dancers. Our taxi-driver greatly enjoyed the singing of a boy soprano; on the way home, he talked of how he loved that one about the pansies and jelly – he was referring to César Franck's *Panis Angelicus*.

One of the other singers that night was Lily Gribben, who was just coming to the height of her powers. Sadly, her career at Sadler's Wells was cut short due to ill health.

One item on the programme was a short, amusing *pas de deux* called *The Irish Washerwoman In Spain*. Bridie Kemp danced a light double-jig to the tune of the title (familiar to radio listeners as the theme of David Curry's *Irish Rhythms*) and Hugh Murray provided the Spanish input in his expert flamenco. The humour of the piece was in the difficulty each had in adapting to the other's dance style. Interestingly enough, Hugh was a serious student of flamenco, spending time in Madrid. He also worked with Helen Lewis and studied at the Laban Centre in London, which led to a Certificate in Contemporary Dance. He was an acknowledged expert in dance in education and later became a graduate in languages. His thesis on Traditional Dance Forms can be found in the Linenhall Library.

The aforementioned Gilligans' van was useful, not just in bringing the children to performances but also in providing an opportunity to swap "intelligence" questions for the "qualifying" or "11-plus" examination. Brendan Campbell proved a reliable source for these. I may actually owe my success in that deplorable exam to his unwitting coaching. His elder brother Kevin was withdrawn from the dancing by his parents during his 11-plus year to allow him to concentrate on preparation for it – much to his disgust. He left his mother in no doubt as to his feelings about this sacrifice, as he saw it, and so, younger Campbells continued their qualifying studies alongside their dancing, luckily for me. In those days, just as now, results of the tests dictated whether one went to grammar school or secondary modern, both of which had pretty different curricula. Nowadays, it seems ridiculous to test for different schools if everyone's being taught to the same syllabus and sitting examinations from the same boards.

Desmond Turner danced the lead in *A Piper* with 'irresistible vivacity' (according to the *Northern Whig* in April 1958) for several years, until a performance in Derry's Guildhall put an end to his dancing career. He hurt his foot on something on stage and bravely tried to dance on, but, unfortunately, he had to be taken off to hospital and never again played a part in the ballets. He went on to teach art at Stranmillis Training College.

During this performance, we used the Minor Hall of the Guildhall as a changing room and I was fascinated by the fact that ships were moored at the quay right behind us. This was long before the port of Derry moved to Lisahally. Little did I think that in future days I would spend so much time in the building when I came to live in the city.

At Pitlochry Festival in Scotland in 1958, the auditorium consisted of a marquee and not much else, and Desmond designed some scenery for the occasion; he continued with this responsibility until he left the company. Kevin Campbell and others borrowed a nearby loft and painted and sawed before they danced on the stage.

Bridie Kemp, Stella O'Neill, Daphne Chestnut, Kevin Campbell, Patricia Mulholland and Colum McBennet leaving the Pitlochry Festival Theatre in Scotland. Inset: Pitlochry programme.

They also used to help to put extensions on stages, arriving before the others, when the company was touring in the early days before the Arts Council took a more professional interest in stage management. Their energies were also required for scene changes during this early period. In fact, it was sympathy for the male dancers that brought Fergus Gilligan into stage management. He was waiting to bring the children home after their performance and could see that the men needed a hand. He obligingly lent his support and, before he knew what was happening, he was stage-manager. He then had to relinquish the driving of the van to Jimmy Campbell, who in turn was co-opted to work in the wings, and the children were henceforth to be put on the bus along with the adults. Several invaluable stagehands and electricians were introduced to the company by Fergus.

From then on, the boys could concentrate on their dancing.

The Dream Of Angus Óg
First performed: 1956.

The Patricia Mulholland Irish Ballet Company used to rehearse in a Scout hall off the Cliftonville Road, close to Solitude, the football ground. My first visit was well timed by chance. I had learned my dance and mime in Newington Street for my part in *A Piper*, but now it was time to attend a full rehearsal with the adults.

As I walked along a stretch of waste ground bordered by a fence of corrugated iron, I could hear a great rattling and banging and occasional strains of a fiddle above the cacophony coming from a large hut-like building. I opened the door and there were all these men brandishing imaginary swords and whirling about. It was the battle scene from *The Dream Of Angus Óg*. To say it made a lasting impression on me is putting it mildly.

Kevin Campbell, as Angus, prepares for battle in The Dream Of Angus Óg.

When Patricia Mulholland had first considered this ballet, JJ Campbell, on whose scenario she based it, expressed doubts. How on earth could she portray a battle on stage between the warriors of Angus and the fairy host? Many others wondered how successful any attempt could be. But she brought it off with great aplomb. Nearly every dancer, male and female, longed to take part in this battle. It was only towards the end of the company's existence, when there were fewer boys in the chorus, that girls got an opportunity, perforce, to fight the Sídhe in the battle scene. Alas, it was long after I had left.

The men marched out on stage, one after another, to *Let Erin Remember*. (A particular Angus led them all over the place on one occasion; he was later presented with a map and compass to improve his sense of direction.) They then formed into ranks for battle formation and "fought" to *Brian Boru's March*. The disciplined lines were maintained as they danced a heavy jig to the music with thrusts and parries of their short swords. Gradually, the dancing became more frenzied as Angus's men sensed victory and they lost only one or two men to their unseen enemy. Rathcol of the *Belfast Telegraph* once described the battle as 'incredibly vivid and magnificently performed.' Geraldine Neeson, in the *Irish Times* of 1978, described the warriors' dance as 'electrifying.'

It was possible to believe at times that Angus's warriors really did take on the fairy host, as experienced at an early Belfast Festival at Queen's in the Whitla Hall in 1964. The platform in this hall, familiar to Queen's graduands, has no proscenium arch, with the result that scenery flats were insecure. Fergus Gilligan, stage-manager, was worried about this, as his letter (*over*) to Noel Mallon (stage electrician) shows.

>
> 16th November, 1964
>
> Dear Noel,
>
> <u>**Irish Ballet.**</u>
>
> **I would very much like you to visit Queen's with me, because we are not going to have the lighting anything like we asked for.** One of the snags is obtaining stands - they say, they cannot get them anywhere. Please 'phone me and we will arrange to meet at Queen's.
>
> Large flats will be provided for the wings, but no braces or weights are available for these. Do you think we could borrow braces, weights and stands from the Opera House, or do you know anywhere else they might be available.
>
> Yours sincerely,

Letter from Fergus Gilligan to Noel Mallon, stage electrician.

During this particular battle, in the middle of blood-red lighting effects, swirling kilts and the battering of men's feet and clattering of swords on shields, one of the flats fell down, raising clouds of dust, putting the fear of God in everyone, but, remarkably, injuring none.

The scene was preceded by Angus dancing *Rodney's Glory* to "psych himself up" for the fight. Mary McGoris in the *Irish Independent*, describing Kevin Campbell's dancing of this in 1958 said, 'In Angus's solo dance in the second scene, there was an almost Spanish touch in the virtuosity with which the controlled sound of the dancer's feet was used to suggest threatening purpose . . .'

Angus was changed by his body servants on stage and armed for the forthcoming fray. They placed a saffron kilt over the skirt-like garment worn previously and were supposed to remove the latter. On one occasion, they were unsuccessful in completely detaching the skirt and, pressed for time, left it under the kilt. It says a lot for the character of the dancer playing Angus Óg that his self-confidence was not dented forever by the slow descent of the undergarment. Another Angus, equally at the mercy of his attendants, had to overcome the fact that his shoes had been placed on the wrong feet, only to hear Miss Mulholland tell him that he'd never danced better!

The Dream Of Angus Óg is one of JJ Campbell's *Legends Of Ireland* (illustrated by Louis de Brocquy); he was friendly with Patricia and adapted the story for her. His son Kevin played the lead for many years, having been the first Angus of all.

As in all her ballets, Miss Mulholland chose music from the traditional repertoire, suiting the tune to the action or, in some cases, the dancer. Several fans came to the ballets to enjoy the music in spite of the dancing. Many of the dancers count this ballet their favourite, largely because of the music.

The choosing of music, suitable in mood, tempo and sometimes title, required a particular skill, not to mention encyclopaedic knowledge of Irish music, which she had in abundance. It was helped by the fact that she enlisted the aid of many friends and acquaintances to keep an eye out for interesting pieces, especially unpublished airs. Among this band were dancer, singer and adjudicator George Leonard, Dubliner Pádraic Cleary, and Belfast woman Clara George (aunt of Margot Bell). She had the added bonus of having Seamus Bunting (father of dancer Brian) and Basil Wilson to translate Gaelic titles for her.

Aficionados of Irish music could have gone to a performance of any of the ballets, or indeed festivals, where she was accompanying, and they would have enjoyed the beauty and appropriateness of the airs and felt they had got their money's worth without ever needing to see the stage. Canon Pádraic Murphy was one such, Seamus Bunting another.

The theme of *Angus Óg* was *Ard Tí Chuain* (elsewhere *Aird A Chumhaing*, that wistful air, the words of which tell of an exile's lament for home, preserved for future generations by the last Gaelic poet of the Glens, John McCambridge). Some have compared this ballet to *Swan Lake*, from the classical repertoire, and it's easy to see why, with its chorus of swan-maidens and their leader. This part was first danced by Stella O'Neill, Miss Mulholland's niece, then by Frances Tomelty when she was only fifteen, much to the chagrin of some older members of the female corps.

Caer, the swan-maiden, appeared to Angus in a dream, dancing a lovely reel to *The Dawning Of The Day*. His servants tried to recall him to reality with *Is The Big Man Within?*

After the exertions of the battle, the warriors and maidens danced together to a feast of different tunes, *The Deep Green Pool*, *The Bold Thady Quill* and *Fanny Power* among them. One unintentionally entertaining aspect of this scene was the view it afforded of the girls' underwear. The material chosen for these slip-like garments, designed by Mercy Hunter, left little to the imagination, as it was quite transparent, revealing the human form of the women. (Perhaps it was deliberate?) It was always a great relief to change into the swan costumes, which required the sticking on of sequins with colourless nail varnish after each outing. The headdresses for this costume were made from white buckram, a stiff material, and they were kept on by means of an elastic band. Valerie Canavan lost hers at an early performance when a floating trail from Audrey Clarke's "wing" caught on it. (There was quite a lot of

Stella O'Neill as Caer in The Dream Of Angus Óg.

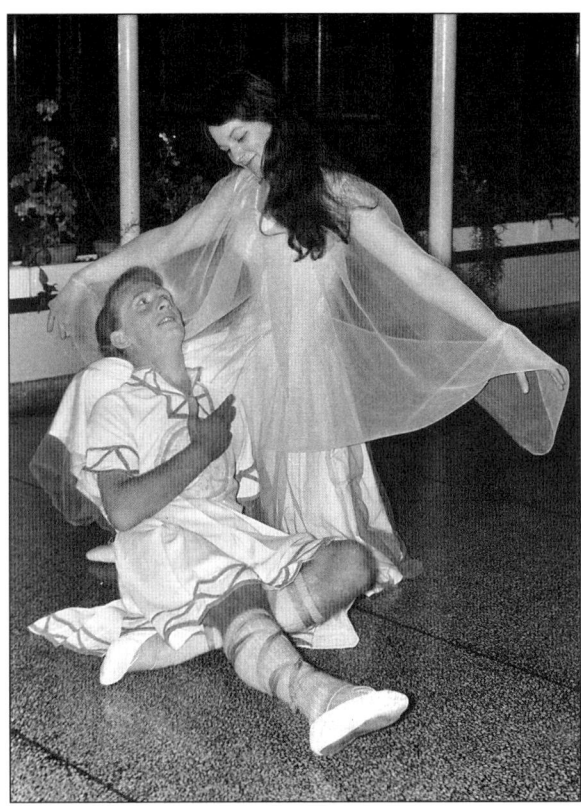

Kevin Campbell and Marlene Bailie as Angus and Caer.

raising of arms and moving them about in the choreography for this scene.) The headgear would not shake off, so Audrey finished the scene with it attached to her "wing" and she and Valerie had great difficulty in hiding their mirth, not at all appropriate for the solemn scene that this was.

The air of magic and enchantment could not have been captured so effectively without the use of that tune we all came to call *The Swans*, possibly another Mulholland original composition. Onto a darkened stage – for it was sunset that brought about their change of shape – came the swans to a slip-jig, cold and aloof, and in their midst, Caer and Angus, who has succumbed to bewitchment for the sake of his love and become a swan like her.

The bittersweet ending was greatly enhanced by the playing of *Willie Taylor,* a fairly ordinary reel tune, but arranged by Miss Mulholland to provide a most evocative accompaniment to the men as they beg the Dagda, in mime, to be allowed to fight for Angus. He refuses them, sadly, and dies, powerless to stop the magic that takes his son away.

The *Belfast Telegraph*'s music critic, Rathcol, in April 1958 made a few justifiable criticisms of *Angus Óg*, suggesting that a little pruning might improve its overall effect. But he continued, 'Nevertheless, Irish Ballet is no longer experimental; it has now proved itself, and has shown that Irish dancing is progressive and therefore alive.'

Follow Me Down To Carlow
First performed: 1956.

Patricia Mulholland took the traditional song *Follow Me Down To Carlow* as the theme for a one-act ballet. Nothing could have been further removed from the magic and mystery of *Angus Óg* or the grandeur of *Cúchulainn*.

A train of characters followed each other on the road: a schoolboy (Michael O'Reilly was the first) bouncing a ball (Hugh Murray), a lady (Valerie Canavan) in her jaunting car who bought ribbons for her pony (Kevin Campbell) from the gypsies, and a bold unbiddable child (Stella O'Neill) with her exasperated mother (Mary O'Reilly).

These and others all came together finally for a team dance to the tune of the title

Early days in TV. Studio 8: some Carlow *characters making an advertisement for the NI Tourist Board. Below right: Bold child Stella O'Neill with candyfloss.*

song. Occasionally, Desmond Turner sang the words of the song as the dancers went through the figures. Sometimes, the company in the team dance would dance off the stage and down through the audience. If the dance were performed at a festival, often the team members would come down and pick up unsuspecting adjudicators and others, dancing all the while and linking arms with the new recruits as they went.

This was a handy piece for the dancers when invited to give a short performance in less formal style.

In the 1960s, the Christian Brothers were celebrating the anniversary of their founder's birth. Brother Beausang, that well-known lover of all things Irish, put on a concert in the Ulster Hall in Belfast, one of several events. The Mulholland dancers presented *Follow Me Down*, which was just right for the occasion, and everyone enjoyed it. Well, nearly everyone, for Brother Beau received complaints! He was asked why he hadn't invited a more suitable act, meaning a group of

Hugh Murray as the Puca in The Black Rogue.

Paddi Lamb and Donna Revie as the fairy woman and Puca in The Black Rogue.

Commission dancers. He was able to reply that he'd started off with "mainstream" schools of dancing and everyone he spoke to hemmed and hawed, not quite sure of dates or availability of individuals. But when he spoke to Miss Mulholland eventually, he was relieved to hear her say, 'Certainly, Brother. When do you want us, and where?'

The Black Rogue
First performed: Empire Theatre, Belfast, April 1959.

The Black Rogue is the name of a tune and also the name of one of the early ballets. Magic featured prominently in it with the appearance of a fairy queen and her retinue.

The action revolves around a poor young piper, his girlfriend and a gander, and how their lives are altered by their involvement with the fairies and the Puca.

The Puca is a mischievous spirit in the same mould as the English Puck and was usually blamed for turning milk sour, withering the blackberries on the bush and generally being a nuisance.

Due to the fact that the piper kills the gander for food, he is spirited away to the Fairy Glen and bewitched by the Puca. On his return to the village, he turns out to be a marvellous musician (after a last prank from the Puca) and wins the hand of his love.

The first Puca was Hugh Murray, an exceptionally gifted character dancer, whose athleticism and mastery of facial expression and gesture set the pattern for subsequent exponents of the role. His niece, Ursula Quinn, took the part later, as did Catherine Gilmore, Noreen McBride, Donna Revie and Alison McKinley, all of whom brought something new to it.

John Garvin was the first young piper, Daphne Chestnut his sweetheart and Brian Bunting the gander. Miss Mulholland was afraid that Brian would outgrow his gander role too quickly and that she would have to find a new one. He would send her postcards while on holiday, telling her how quickly the geese grew on his uncle's farm.

Miss Mulholland with Black Rogue *performers Brian Bunting as the gander, Margot Bell as a fairy, John Melville as the father and Kevin Campbell as a villager.*

Daphne broke her arm and Margot Bell had to learn her part in six days with additional "on-the-job" training during her first actual performance on stage. Margot was not only a quick-study, but could actually retain what she learned.

The fairy queen's solo dance was an unusual piece called *Fragments,* originally performed by the lovely Patricia King. What made this different or unexpected was that it changed tempo intermittently from slip-jig to reel and back, using arm movements to complement the characteristics of the two rhythms – another example of Mulholland inventiveness. Changing rhythm is not entirely unheard of. The *Three Tunes* team dance uses different rhythms – reel, jig and hornpipe – in one dance, though in that case, the tempo changes after eight bars, where there is a natural break. *Fragments* changed after four bars, two bars, or eight.

Mary O'Reilly, Stella O'Neill, Daphne Chestnut and Valerie Canavan.

Lynne Maxwell as the fairy woman in The Black Rogue.

The first chorus of fairies was composed of boys and girls. Grainne Gilmore remembers cutting out her brother's costume round him as he lay on the floor, on top of the material. There were headbands with sequins suspended from threads, inclined to make one squint, or, at least, blink. An attempt was made to match footwear with costumes by dyeing sockettes in various shades of green. (This was before the introduction of pink tights and pumps as standard.) In time, the boys disappeared from this scene, leaving it mainly to teenage girls.

The villagers' costumes were often worn by the dancers instead of their Irish dancing dresses to give a casual impression (see opposite at a performance in Jordanstown).

Back, L-R: Joyce Ann Henry, Patricia Mulholland, Patricia O'Neill, Catherine Gilmore, Ursula Quinn. Front: Margot Bell, Marlene Bailie and Sheelagh Gilligan.

The Mother Of Oisín
First performed: Empire Theatre, Belfast, April 1959.

The Mother Of Oisín was an exceptionally creative work, presenting contrasting scenes of love, cruelty, excitement, magic and sport. It was my favourite Irish Ballet. One would have had to be made of stone not to have been moved by the violent separation of the child Oisín from his mother, Sava, and his subsequent reunion with his father. Kevin Rafferty's portrayal of Oisín was the definitive version for many.

The curtain opened to the Moore's melody *Oh, For The Swords Of Former Time* setting the scene perfectly for Fionn and the Fianna hunting deer. Their dance was a stylised hunt, during which they aimed and threw imaginary spears, the footwork fitting beautifully into the music.

The deer they chase is eventually brought to bay, but Fionn's hounds sense something strange about their quarry and he is persuaded to bring the fawn home to the court at Tara.

Well, the fawn turns out to be a beautiful woman, Sava, under the spell of the black druid whose advances she had rejected.

She will retain her human form only as long as she is under Fionn's protection within Tara. Fionn is called away to fight and the black druid seizes the opportunity afforded by his absence to kidnap Sava. The enactment of the kidnap was violent and very effective. I remember a lighting rehearsal when Henry Lynch-Robinson got all concerned to repeat the action over and over until he got his "green flash op wings" just right, by which time we were exhausted.

Miss Mulholland's scenario for The Mother Of Oisín.

Stella and Patricia O'Neill as Fionn's hounds in The Mother Of Oisín.

Valerie Canavan and Kevin Campbell.

The audience was always brought to a high pitch of excitement as the black druid appeared first in the guise of Fionn (shape changing is a common trick in Irish legend), accompanied by what seem to be his faithful hounds. Sava rushed to greet him, but he flung off his disguise and brutally took her away as the hounds menaced her handmaidens.

This act finished with the anguish of Fionn as the court tried to console him. One Saturday at rehearsal, one of the female "courtiers" was going somewhere special later on and had put rollers in her hair. As she approached Fionn to offer him comfort and he turned her away, Miss Mulholland said, 'Well, now, you could hardly blame him – a vision like that!'

The last act opened on a happy scene with Sava and Oisín (fawn, in Irish) – the result of her love for Fionn – playing happily together. Everyone is nestling in the comfort of this cosy scene when the black druid suddenly reappears to force Sava to his will – his hazel wand ensures that she must submit – and she has to leave her little son behind, unconscious, after bravely defending his mother.

The spirits of the wood appeared and covered Oisín with leaves and branches to protect him. He had to arrange his fall so as to land with his feet in the wings and that his shoes could be changed for his dancing of *The Hurling Boys* in the next scene.

Here, the diaphanous costumes for the wood spirits were very effective from the aesthetic point of view but were revealing, to say the least. To deal with this problem, there were "modesty pieces" attached to the shoulder – three long, scarf-like bits of material, which could be arranged to drape down the front or back. The branches for the young Oisín's protection (often gathered from the Ulster highways en route to performance and, on one occasion, from the Arts Council office garden) caught now and then on bits of costume, including the "jilly-waggles", and one dancer saw one set being shaken off into the wings and thought, *Some poor soul has lost her covering*, then realised it was her and finished the scene without relinquishing her greenery!

PRODUCTION: THE MOTHER OF OISIN																	
LIGHTING	POSITION	FOH		SPOT BAR						Acting Areas		WING P S		FLOODS O P		CYC	Cyc Groundr	
	HEIGHT																	
	REF No (from stage left)	1	2	3	4	5	6	7	8	9	10	11	12	13	14	15	16	17
	TYPE & WATTS																	
	COLOUR REF	53	53	7	5A	7	53	21	53	18	18	2	2	17/6	17/6	32	6	24
Act	Scene	Cue																
1	1	1	1/10	2/10															
		2			3/10	4/10	3/10	6/10	7/10		9/10	10/10	11/10	12/10	13/10	14/10	15/10	—	—
		3	1/6	2/6							9/6	10/6	11/5	12/5	13/5	14/5	15/4	16/10	—
		4	////// BLACKOUT //////																
	2	5					9/10	6/10											
		6(slow)	1/5	2/5	3/10	4/10	5/10	6/10	7/10	8/10	9/5	10/5	11/5	12/5	x				
		7	1/8	2/8												15/10			
		8(slow)	1/5	2/5							9/3	10/3	11/4	12/4					
		9(slow)																16/10	
		10	////// BLACKOUT //////																
	3	11	1/10	2/10	3/10	4/10	5/10	6/10	7/10	8/10	9/10	10/10	11/10	12/10	13/10	14/10	15/10		
		12	1/4	2/4											13/0	14/0			
		13			3/0	4/0	5/0		8/0		9/0	10/0							
		14(slow)											11/0	12/0					
		15(slow)					6/0	7/0	8/6										
		16	////// BLACKOUT //////																
	4	17	1/10	2/10	3/10	4/10	5/10	6/10	7/10	8/10	9/10	10/10	11/10	12/10	—	—	15/10		
		18(slow)	1/0	2/0	3/0	4/0	5/0	6/0	7/0	8/0			11/0	12/0					
		19													13/0	14/10	15/0	16/10	
		20	////// BLACKOUT //////																
	5	21	1/8	2/8	3/10	4/10	5/10	6/10	7/10	8/10	9/7	10/7	11/7	12/7	13/7	14/7	15/7		17/10
		22	1/0	2/0	3/0	4/0	5/0	6/0	7/0		9/0	10/0	11/0	12/0	13/0	14/0			
		23(slow)								8/0									
		24	1/6	2/6	(After curtain)													
	6	25	1/10	2/10	3/10	4/10	5/10	6/10	7/10	8/10	9/10	10/10	11/10	12/10	—	—	15/10	—	—
		26	1/0	2/0							9/5	10/5	11/7	12/7	x				
		27			3/0	4/0	5/0	6/0	7/0	8/0			11/0	12/0	13/10	14/10			
		28													13/0	14/0			
		29(slow)										10/8		14/10					17/8
		30	1/0	2/0	3/0	4/0	5/0	6/0	7/0	8/0	9/10	10/10	11/0	12/0	13/0	14/0		16/8	
		31(slow)													13/10	14/10			
		32(slow)	1/4	2/4							9/4	10/4	11/0	12/0	13/0	14/0			
		33(quick)	1/10	2/10									11/10	12/10	13/10	14/10			
		34	HOUSE LIGHTS															

The Mother Of Oisín *production notes*.

Valerie Canavan, Ciarán Doherty and Desmond Turner.

For the first few performances, the wood spirits had also worn blond wigs of flax, but they were abandoned, as with time the *cheveux de lin* became very smelly.

Just when you thought your emotions had been stretched beyond their limit, the ballet ended as it began, with a hunting scene; but this time, Fionn, his hounds and his men discover Oisín. The little boy pluckily stands up to the Fianna when they tease him, and anyone who hadn't a tear in the eye up to then must surely have been overcome as Fionn and Oisín realise what they must be to each other and sadly remember Sava, their lost love.

The contrasting emotions in the unfolding of this story demonstrated Patricia Mulholland's expert use of drama: how she could involve her audience. She could capture the camaraderie of the Fianna, the restlessness of the hounds, the brutality of the wizard, yet also the joys of love through the medium of dance with mime and music, not forgetting the humour provided by two jesters.

Mercy Hunter's sketch for Oisín *wood nymph.*

Jesters entertain Fionn's court in The Mother Of Oisín.

Henry Lynch-Robinson's lighting and Mercy Hunter's costumes added greatly to the overall effect of the ballet.

Organ grinder Reggie McClure and his monkey entertain the children in The Oul' Lammas Fair.

The Oul' Lammas Fair, 1900
First performed: Empire Theatre, Belfast, April 1959.

Several of the ballets were based on traditional songs, or songs based on traditional events.

The Old Lammas Fair is about 400 years old and is still held in Ballycastle every August (Lammastide), and the chorus of the Percy French song describes the dulse and yellowman, which can still be bought there. Dulse, or dilisk, is edible reddish-brown seaweed and yellowman is brittle yellow toffee.

The Mulholland treatment set the action in 1900, thus affording Mercy Hunter an opportunity to design late-Victorian costumes. Mercy wanted one of the characters to have a pig as a prop, but Patricia put her foot down.

The programme (*right*) lets us see the cast of characters – the stallholders, the young swells, the snobs and the urchins, a soldier hero home on leave, and even an organ grinder and his monkey.

Lord and Lady of the Manor were played first by Audrey Clarke and Desmond Turner. They danced a stiff sort of minuet and arrived back after transacting some business to find their children had "gone native" and become just as dirty and cheeky as the local urchins. With the shock of this, Audrey had to faint into Desmond's arms. She has a special memory of an occasion when Jo Tomelty stood up and clapped her fainting fit.

The Ballycastle locality suggested the use of several airs, including the lovely *Rathlin Isle,* for a ladies' ensemble, lending itself to "rocks" and other suitable movements. *Kitty Of Coleraine* was another tune associated with the area. Miss Mulholland's choreography for this used a sort of contrapuntal beating to the melody. When I heard it first, I was too young to understand its sophistication and thought it a bit strange. Many years later, I heard a James MacCafferty choral arrangement of the song using a similar technique and thought how interesting it was that the song had provoked the same approach from the two different musicians.

Trotting To The Fair was danced by several young men, their girls clutching them round the waist from behind. One young man used to give his "trotting" all he'd got and his partner complained that it felt like dancing with a pneumatic drill.

THE OUL' LAMMAS FAIR IN 1900	
DULSE SELLER	Michael Gilfedder
YELLOW MAN SELLER	Valerie Canavan
COCKLES AND MUSSELS	Marlene Baillie
BALLOON WOMAN	Patricia Mulholland
MARY ANN	Sheelagh McDade
YOUNG LADIES:	Olive Melville, Patricia O'Neill, Margot Bell, Patricia Boden, Lynne Maxwell.
FARMERS	Clive Kingham, John Garvin
THE HERO	James Rooney
THE MASHERS	Dermott Brooks, Seamus Agnew, Brian Bunting
LORD AND LADY OF THE MANOR	Colum McBennett, Anne McManus
THEIR CHILDREN	Brenda Quinn, Joyce Ann Henry, Brendan O'Neill
THE NANNY	Frances Tumelty
URCHINS	Frances O'Harra, Sheelagh Gilligan, Geoffrey McNabb, Kieran Doherty.
ORGAN GRINDER	Reginald McClure
MONKEY	Edmund Henry
SOLDIER	Thomas Graham
KITTY OF COLERAINE	Stella O'Neill
BARNEY MacCLEARY	Kevin Campbell
TINKERS	Michelle Forster, Sharon Tansley, Catherine Gilmore
AUCTIONEER	Hugh Murray

Programme from the 1960s.

Stella O'Neill and Kevin Campbell as Kitty and Barney.

Dulse-seller Colum McBennet and rival, yellowman-seller Valerie Canavan.

Above: Hugh Murray was the first auctioneer in The Oul' Lammas Fair. *Below: Hugh still clowning around off stage.*

Tom Graham as the soldier and Sheelagh McDade as Mary Ann in The Oul' Lammas Fair.

The men's chorus dance St Patrick's Day.

The soldier-hero entered to *The Inniskilling Dragoon*.

Sculptor George McCann (married to Mercy Hunter) had served with the Inniskilling Fusiliers and his military training came in useful when a group of Mulholland dancers had to learn some drill for their part in a visiting opera company's production of *La Grande Duchesse*.

A highlight of this ballet was a comedy auction during which the auctioneer clowned about to the tune of the *Kilkenny Races*. Miss Mulholland's treatment of this popular set-dance tune and the antics of the auctioneer have meant that I've always had difficulty in taking it seriously. Which is not to say that if adjudicating, I've never awarded prizes to dancers who chose it for their set dance, just that they've had to be especially good to overcome my attitude.

In later versions, the men danced *Planxty Hugh O'Donnell* rather than *St Patrick's Day*.

In just eight years, Patricia Mulholland had taken her Irish Ballet from the experimental idea of producing a short piece for a concert to a regularly performed repertoire of seven ballets.

In the Arts Council report of 1959, the Drama Committee, which still included Alfred Arnold and Lillian R Hogg, commenting on The Irish Ballet's introduction of three new ballets, *The Black Rogue, The Mother Of Oisín* and *The Oul' Lammas Fair*, stated, 'Miss Mulholland's work with this group has been an unique development in the field of ballet and one of which Northern Ireland may feel justly proud.'

Miss Mulholland and cast on stage for bows at the end of a performance of The Oul' Lammas Fair.

Figure of Eight: 1961–68

Patricia Mulholland has done more than any other artist to reveal to Ulster and to Ireland the special quality and excitement of their heritage in dance and melody and myth. **Arts Council of Northern Ireland, 1965.**

The Opera House was a wonderful theatre to work in with its huge raked stage, though many of the dressing rooms left a lot to be desired. Since its modernisation (after bombing), the backstage facilities are excellent and the stage is now level. During the 1960s, the Northern Ireland Drama Festival in May always started with a performance of the Irish Ballet Company on the Monday night.

The Children Of Lir
First performed: Grand Opera House, Belfast, 1961.

The Children Of Lir is one of Ireland's best-known and best-loved legends. Perhaps it enjoys this popularity because of the three locations in which the story is set, including the North, West and Midlands of Ireland, and is therefore not limited to one locality. Perhaps it is one of the last links with pre-Christian Ireland, told and retold and adapted into a story with an acceptably Christian ending. Whatever the reason, this story of four children turned into swans by a jealous stepmother has an enduring appeal across the centuries and has been represented in various media.

The Moore's Melody *Silent, O Moyle* was a popular song in Victorian parlours; Redmond Friel, the Derry composer, wrote an orchestral piece, *The Children Of Lir*, in 1953, as indeed had Hamilton Harty; just a few years later, the poet Pádraic Colum wrote the libretto for a cantata on the theme to which he hoped James MacCafferty would put some music with his Little Gaelic Singers. Unfortunately, the work was never finished. Almost every school library has at least one version of the tale, some very loosely based.

The metamorphosis of humans into swans is not exclusive to Irish folklore. But throughout Ireland one can find statues, murals, jewellery and even bronze-effect lamp-bases executed on this theme.

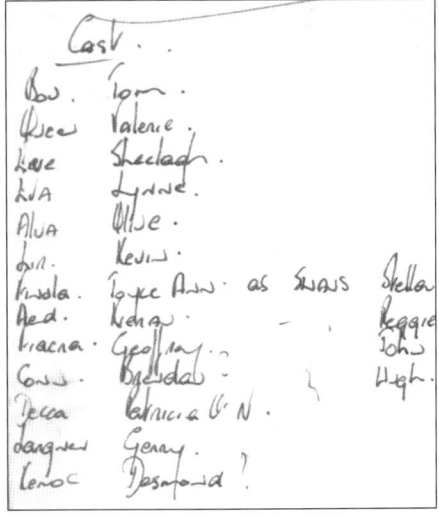
Miss Mulholland's first draft cast list for The Children Of Lir.

```
                    CHILDREN OF LIR


                              CAST
                       (in order of appearance)

        BOV THE RED, King of the DeDanaans  .   .   . Thomas Graham
        HIS QUEEN    .    .    .     .     .     .  . Valerie Canavan
        EVE     .    .    .    ⎧ Bov's     ⎫  .  . Sheelagh McDade
        EVA     .    .    .    ⎨ foster-   ⎬  .  .   . Olive Melville
        ALVA    .    .    .    ⎩ daughters ⎭  .  .   . Lynne Maxwell
        LIR     .    .    .    .    .     .    .   . Kevin Campbell
        BOV'S COURT  .    .    .    . Marlene Baillie, Patricia Bowden,
                                      Margot  Bell,   Patricia  O'Neill,
                                      Anne McManus, Seamus Agnew,
                                      Dermott Brooks, Clive Kinghan,
                                      James Rooney, Brendan Campbell.
        BOY SERVANT  .    .    .    .     .     .     .   . Sean O'Hare
        FINOLA  .    .    .    .    .     .     .  . Joyce Ann Henry
        AED     .    .    .    .    .     .     .  .   . Kieran Doherty
        FIACRA  .    .    .    .    .     .     .  . Geoffrey McNabb
        CONN    .    .    .    .    .     .     .  .  . Brendan O'Neill
        SERVANTS     .    .    .    . Frances Tomelty, Brenda Quinn,
                                      Clive Kinghan, Colum McBennett,
                                      James   Rooney,   Brian  Bunting,
                                      Seamus Agnew, Dermott Brooks,
                                      Sharon   Tansley,    P a t r i c i a
                                      Mulholland, Catherine Gilmore,
                                      Michelle  Forster,  S h e e l a g h
                                      Gilligan, Yvonne Canavan.
        BEARERS .    .    .    .    . Brendan Campbell, Seamus Agnew,
                                      Dermott Brooks, James Rooney,
                                      Clive Kinghan, Brian Bunting.
        CHILDREN     .    .    .    . Joyce Ann Henry, Kieran Doherty,
                                      Geoffrey McNabb, Brendan O'Neill.
        MANSERVANT   .    .    .    .     .     .     .  . Clive Kinghan
```

Programme with first Lir *cast, 1961.*

My first brush with *Clann Lir* was at the feet of my father's mother, a woman called Margaret Henry (née Keane) who was brought up in a place called Cross, on the Mullet peninsula in Mayo, just opposite Inish Gleoire. She told the story with her own local details. In the standard version, the spell is to be broken when the princess of the south marries the prince from the north and when the Christian bell will ring in Ireland. Grandma Henry's story had the enchantment ending at the sound of the consecration bell at Mass in Cross Abbey.

Certainly, Ireland, never mind Lir's children, was changed forever by the arrival of Christianity.

Patricia Mulholland applied her creative energy to the story in 1960. It has always held a special place in my heart, not just because I was cast as the first Fionnuala (and subsequently as the swan, Aodh) but because of the personal connection with Inish Gleoire – the island off the Mullet peninsula where the children were doomed to spend the last 300 years of their enchantment and where they finally found a resting place, embraced by Christianity.

An ancestor of mine, Darby Keane, bought the island from Bingham, the hated local landlord, with money made from raising sheep which he carried out from Cross on the mainland to the island in a curragh. This is no mean feat when you consider how thin a curragh's skin is and how often you see sharks in these waters! At the time, it was the only freehold land in the barony of Erris. Nobody lives there any more since all the small island's inhabitants were removed after a tragedy at sea. It is used only by fishermen today.

Four little graves, purported to be those of Lir's family, and arranged traditionally, Conn and Fiacra on either side of Fionnuala with Aodh at her feet, can be seen there near the ruined abbey founded by St Brendan.

Nor is the Lir legend the only magic associated with the island. There is a well, out of which it was forbidden to draw water while the men were at sea or a storm would be sure to blow up. The ground itself is said to have preservative properties; bodies buried there are said not to decompose in the normal manner.

The derivation of the name Inish Gleoire is unclear. Some say it is from *glor* meaning voice; and the Atlantic waves pounding on its shores certainly make a characteristic sound. Others say it is from *gluaire* meaning brightness and in a certain light, with ocean spray being flung up all round it, the island has a sort of halo, lending it a floating, magical effect. I incline to the brightness theory, myself.

Patricia Mulholland did a lot of painstaking research for her ballet *The Children Of Lir*, which included watching waves on Belfast Lough for hours at a time. She also studied swans on Belfast's Waterworks lake.

Her chorus of waves in the stormy Sea-of-Moyle scene was especially effective. This consisted of between sixteen and twenty girls in blue and green tunics.

They started in four or five rows on their knees, bent right over, forehead touching the floor, and raised and lowered their backs slightly, like the rise and fall of breathing. This was to the tune of *Silent, O Moyle*, a continuation of the accompaniment to the solo dance of Lir's heartbreak. Then the music changed to a special composition of David Curry's, which rose in a crescendo as the waves rose with it and drew back and swept forward, gathering to crash down on the swans as they sought shelter on a lone rock.

Special lighting effects by Henry Lynch-Robinson added to the spectacle and any ex-dancer of a certain age will remember how, as children, we loved to help

Patricia Mulholland, left, niece of Miss Mulholland, with Jim Maze and Catherine Gilmore.

Mr Maze, the percussionist, at rehearsals with his wind machine and drums, to provide the required gales and thunder.

In this ballet, as in all the others, the choice of music was neither random nor accidental. The first Lir was Kevin Campbell who was red-haired, and one of the tunes Aoife danced to was *The Red-haired Man's Wife. An Páistín Fionn* (The Little Fair-haired Child), was played for one of Fionnuala's solos – the first Fionnuala was blonde.

Lir 'told' his children the story of *The Minstrel Boy. Silent, O Moyle* preceded the storm.

Henry Lynch-Robinson's watercolour sketch for the lakeside scene in The Children Of Lir.

Aoife shows jealousy as children listen to Lir's story.

Sketch for servant's costume for The Children Of Lir *court scene.*

Above: A costume sketch for Bov's wife. Below: The finished dress worn by Valerie Canavan, with Kevin Campbell (left) and Tom Graham.

The company danced to *The Three Sea Captains* and *All The Way To Galway* as Lir and Eva, his first wife, changed before going on a journey. *The Lone Rock* was the appropriate theme for the ballet and was played as the swans gathered, one by one, after the storm.

One popular scene, certainly for those who danced in it, was at the lakeside before the swans left Lir. He and his men danced a hornpipe together while the swans did a single jig in a circle round the outside. On a large stage, like the Opera House or the Grove, it was wonderfully exhilarating to cover wide expanses round the outside of the men rattling off their heavy dance.

But there was at least one serendipitous matching of music to locale. After the drama of the storm and just before the little birds appeared to listen to the swans' singing by the lakeside, the four swans rushed out onto a bright stage to a tune called *The Silvermines*. A few extra notes changed this old reel into one with great driving force. Miss Mulholland was delighted to learn that the beach at Cross, just opposite Inis Gleoire, is composed of incredibly bright, silvery sand, and that the shore of the next bay is strewn with large, glittering silvery stones.

A special innovation in this work was "talking with the feet", an unaccompanied mime and footwork used in the court scenes. For example, in the relating of Aoife's wickedness to Bov and his courtiers, the rhythm of the step was supplied by the dancer hearing the words in his head. When Bov asked Aoife, ' My child, where are the children?' it was translated by one step forward on the right foot and close with the left, for 'my child.' Then, a double beat and step to the side and forward with the left, close with the right for the rest.

Lir's answer, 'Through her spells, she has changed them into four swans and they now swim on Lake Derryvarragh,' was communicated by a jump, landing with feet apart and hands in the air for 'through her spells.' Then a slow "drum", four fingers held up and swept down across the body, finishing with a slow turn. This was followed by a *Dance Of Rage* performed by the entire company, before Bov turned Aoife into a spirit of the air.

As the years wore on, the footwork changed somewhat, rather like a game of Chinese Whispers. Mind you, so did a lot of the more subtle movements. If the original cast of dancers had compared what they had learned with what the younger dancers were doing in the ballets, there would certainly have been discrepancies, despite the original choreography being written down and kept in notebooks.

The original costumes for the swans, who at first included three men, were made in a foam-rubber material which must have been very uncomfortable to dance in. This was substituted by chiffon.

Left: Sketch for courtier's costume. Right: Sketch for Bov's wife for the Dance Of Rage *scene.*

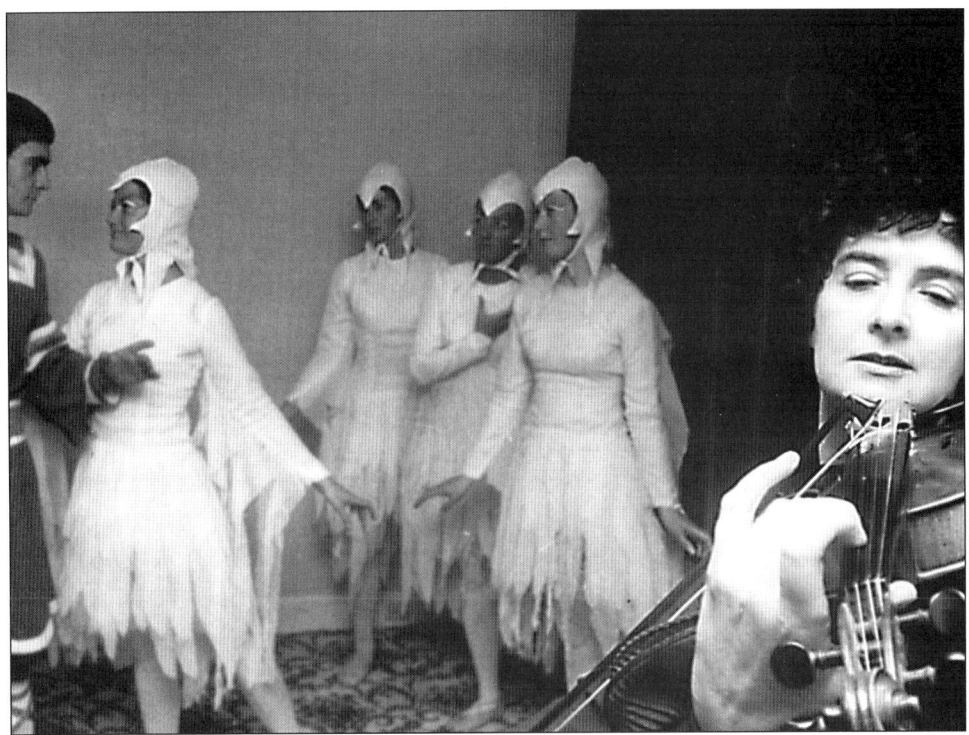

Ciarán Doherty, Catherine Gilmore, Frances O'Hara. Sharon Tansley and Sheelagh Gilligan, with Patricia Mulholland playing the violin at rehearsals for The Children Of Lir.

Mercy Hunter designed the swans' make-up also. Roma Tomelty remembers going to Mercy's flat in Botanic Avenue to learn how to apply it. She had lots of pictures of swans lying round the place and they simply worked at it for some time until it looked right.

It was around this time (1961) that flesh-coloured tights and pumps became the usual garb for the girls. It meant that one didn't have to change shoes when changing costume and also produced a tidier, more uniform effect than made-up legs and different coloured pumps. Prior to this it could happen (as it did to Audrey Clarke among others) that you'd raise your foot in a slip-jig step and discover that you'd forgotten to change out of green pumps into white ones.

Donna Revie, ex-Mulholland dancer and daughter of Carolyn MacMaster, produced an excerpt from the Lir story using classical ballet for the opening of the Waterfront Hall in Belfast in 1998. This homage to the Mulholland work reflected it in direction and even in costume.

Phil The Fluter's Ball
First performed: Grand Opera House, Belfast, 1961.

In addition to the well-known characters of the song, guests at the ball included *The Star Of The County Down, The Spanish Lady, Rory O'More, The Pride Of Petravore, Bridget O'Flynn* and *The Wild Colonial Boy.*

Henry Lynch-Robinson's preparatory sketch for Phil The Fluter's Ball.

Costumes were designed by Mercy as usual. The Misses Brady were originally outfitted as beautiful young women with *décolleté* dresses in pastel shades. But when the BBC decided to film this ballet in 1961, producer Alan Tongue felt that the "beautiful" in the "beautiful Miss Bradys with their private ass and cart" was ironic and so they danced then, and subsequently, in high-necked, black-beaded dresses with trains, and were made up to look much older than they were.

Left: Mercy Hunter's sketch for the Spanish Lady in The Fluter's Ball. *Right: Valerie Canavan, in finished dress, as the Spanish Lady.*

BBC TV studio, Belfast, at a recording of Phil The Fluter's Ball *in 1961. Della Feely, "daughter" of Mr and Mrs Denis Dogherty, has a good look at the Misses Brady, played by Margot Bell and Marlene Bailie.*

The one-act ballets that ended a performance were often an opportunity for dancers to "ad lib" or insert little extras of their own devising. If you weren't given to ad-libbing yourself then at least you soon became adept at surviving the ad-libs of others.

When Michelle Forster took the part of the widow Cafferty, she decided to wear, under her widow's weeds, bright red bloomers, which got plenty of airing during her high-stepping solo. Miss Mulholland never quite knew what was going to happen next. The widow's son was played at one point by my brother Phelim. One night, he picked up a cigarette-butt thrown down by the Wild Colonial Boy and puffed away until he was thumped by his "mother" – all unscripted but kept in thereafter. During this same period, Ciarán Hinds was one of the asses.

The men danced the set dance *Hurry The Jug* (at the beginning it was done by the entire male chorus but it dwindled down to five in the '80s, when the other men threw master Cafferty up in the air while they passed round the jug). The ladies "took the huff", but eventually softened as they were persuaded to dance with their partners to *Tabhair Domh Do Lámh* (Give Me Your Hand).

Towards the end of her life, Miss Mulholland had difficulty using her left hand. She got very tired after playing for any length of time; sometimes she could not actually feel what her left hand was doing. It was fortunate that one of her dancers, Iain Mackay (pupil and teacher of the Mackay school) was an accomplished violinist and could not only act the part of Phil's fiddler but could really 'twiddle on the fiddle-o' throughout the ballet until he had to dance *Hurry The Jug*, by which time Miss Mulholland's fingering was back in action.

The Variety Market (1960)
First performed: Grand Opera House, Belfast, April 1963.

Many Belfast people enjoy a visit to St George's Market on a Friday morning for fresh foods or maybe just a browse, but somehow it has never become the kind of tourist attraction that other markets are; perhaps its day is coming too. It is now entirely under cover, but up to twenty years ago a lot of the stalls were outside, providing a strong visual contrast to the Law Court next door (no less appropriate, when you think of it, than markets in front of grand cathedrals).

Now, as then, you could buy fish, fresh from Ardglass, and possibly find antique knives nearby with which to eat it. During the early '60s, it was not only a source of a huge variety of produce and products, new and second-hand, but was also a meeting place for "Teddy Boys", with their "drainpipe" trousers, winkle-picker shoes and "DA" hairstyles. This latter was a reference to the part of a duck's anatomy that the haircut at the back of the head resembled. Students from the art college used to visit the market to sketch the Teddy Boys and other local characters.

The ballet opened to the traditional tune *The Next Market Day*, with dealers preparing their stalls. Min Milligan (Lena Tomelty's mother) was of great assistance to Miss Mulholland in recalling old songs and singing them for her. One such was:

'Rosie, Rosie, pretty Rosie keeps a flower stall,

Fresh and fair, you'll find them there,

No matter when you call.'

Frances Tomelty and I were the first flower-sellers, a part that disappeared from later performances.

Then there were traditional mill songs with lines like 'Yous'd easy know a doffer when she comes into town . . .' and 'On Monday morning when she comes in, she hangs her hat on the highest pin.'

Another incorporated into the action was 'Our queen can burl her leg, burl her leg', sung for the May Queen, reflecting an old Belfast custom when gangs of little girls would tour neighbourhoods, dressed up in any finery they could lay their hands on, boasting about the attributes of their queen – all with a view to collecting money. One of Carmel McGovern's early roles was as part of Deirdre Tansley's retinue, and when it came to 'burling her leg', it was discovered that Carmel had forgotten to put on her bloomers, you can imagine the scolding that awaited her.

She was not the only May Queen follower to have difficulty with her bloomers. At an earlier time, when the ballets were still performed in the Opera House, Noreen McBride was dancing the same role. Her mother had made her costume including matching bloomers. Noreen needed to visit the lavatory. She couldn't find it and went on climbing stairs until she found one. This was one of the perks of appearing in this theatre – the exploring of all the nooks and crannies. But it was her first time to have to negotiate the layers of costume involved and by the time she left the ladies' toilet, she couldn't find her way back to the stage. It was coming near the time of her entry and she began to panic, still clutching her collecting tin tightly and fighting back the tears. Fortunately, scouts had been sent from the dressing rooms to find the missing child. Gerry O'Hare caught a glimpse of her and had to climb over seats and other barriers before lifting her up and carrying her down to the wings, just in time.

The same Gerry had several of the children convinced that he owned a lot of things in the building because, as he pointed out to them, his initials – GOH – were everywhere!

The climax of the ballet was reached when the "green" architects danced to *The Wearing Of The Green* and the "orange" art students to *Lillibullero*, thus provoking a riot.

Teddy Boys versus architects in The Variety Market: *Ed Henry, Michael Devlin, John Mooney, Henry Toner and Kevin Rafferty.*

The curtain closed on everyone going at it, hammer and tongs, and reopened a few moments later with the riot still in full spate. James Young incorporated this scene into one of his television shows in the 1969–70 series.

This ballet was firmly fixed in a particular era and dated quickly because of that. Despite some changes in costume and characters, it could never quite catch up and so was wisely presented as a period piece by adding the year 1960 to the title.

"Architectural students" relax at rehearsals for The Variety Market.

At one point, Miss Mulholland asked me to wear a black-and-white PVC dress from my own wardrobe, attempting to update a "beatnik" art student into a "mod", but, of course, Mercy heard about it and went mad. I refused to apologise when asked by Miss Mulholland, as it hadn't been my idea in the first place. I was never a likely candidate to genuflect in Mercy's direction at any time. I think Miss Mulholland was a little afraid of her.

An example of the frequent ad libbing mentioned earlier can be seen in the photo below. This was not in the original direction; nor indeed was the actual bodily harm inflicted by the "Mrs Mops" with their feather dusters during the riot! But the effect can be judged by the letter (*opposite*) from a child to Miss Mulholland after a performance in Antrim.

Teddy Boys Gerry O'Hare, Brian Bunting and Seamus Agnew study the sketches of art students Stella and Patricia O'Neill.

However, the unexpected act that must have taken her completely by surprise was in Limavady in the '70s. A group of us from Derry, who had left the company some time before, went to see the ballets in the Technical College and during the second interval my brother Edmund and Kevin Rafferty disappeared. We thought they'd come in late

Some unscripted "ad libbing" by Brian Bunting who kisses Patricia O'Neill in The Variety Market.

and had just sat down at the back of the hall but, lo and behold, when the Teddy Boys appeared, who was leading them but Ed and Kevin! Not only did they have the nerve to get up and take part in the performance but after the final curtain Ed actually brought Patricia Mulholland up on stage for her bow, as if he were still a principal.

> Throne Primary School,
> Newtownabby,
> Co. Antrim.
> 6th March, 1967.
>
> Dear Miss Mulholland,
> I would like to say thank you for inviting us to come to the Irish Ballet. Our class went on Friday night. We are P5. P6 and P7 went on Wednesday night. Our class enjoyed the ballet very much. We liked the dancing at the beginning and the battle in the story of Angus Og was great. We all laughed at the market, especially when the teddy boys came in and one of them tried to kiss one of the artists. We hope we will be able to come next year and we wish you and your dancers luck in the future
>
> Yours sincerely,
> Shirley Montgomery.
> P 5.

Letter of appreciation from a young Newtownabbey girl who enjoyed the antics of the Teddy Boys.

The Hound Of Culann
First performed: Grand Opera House, Belfast, May 1964.

The Hound Of Culann was Patricia Mulholland's second exploration of the Cúchulainn theme, this time taking the story right from how Setanta came to be called Culann's hound – *Cú Chulainn* – through to the hero's end on the field of battle. For some unaccountable reason, later programmes called the ballet *The Hound Of Cúchulainn* which was tautologous and inaccurate.

She used Mercy Hunter's scenario, which condensed and modified episodes from the *Táin Bó Chuailgne*, to fit the constraints of time and logistics. (The 1953 ballet had finished with celebrations after Cúchulainn's defeat of Ferdia.)

The ballet opened with a group of youngsters vying with each other to be the most accomplished at court, only to be beaten hands down by Setanta. The bright, joyful scene gave way to darkness and foreboding and the sudden attack of a great hound on the little boy. My own children were very impressed by this duel. The savagery of the hound was captured particularly well by Ciarán Hinds, who had danced as Setanta a few years earlier – now gone on to greater things.

Setanta (Roy O'Donaghue) begs Culann (Reggie McClure) for forgiveness and offers himself as a substitute hound in this poster for The Hound Of Culann.

Fianna with Red Branch Knights in The Hound Of Culann.

Critic Ray Rosenfield in 1968 recognised that the 'variety of mood and the flux of the drama tested the adaptability of the idiom', but she was satisfied that everything in the ballet 'was beautifully realised from Roy O'Donoghue as the braggart boy and Ciarán Hinds as the leaping hound to Ciarán Doherty dancing light as air or roaring against monsters or ghosts.'

THE HOUND OF CULANN

Devised to traditional music by Patricia Mulholland from a scenario by Mercy Hunter, based on the 7th century legend.

Settings and Lighting by Henry Lynch-Robinson.

Costumes designed by Mercy Hunter.

Properties by George McCann.

This ancient Irish story tells of the friendship of Cuchulainn of Ulster and Ferdiad of Connacht and the fatal quarrel between them which Medh, Queen of Connacht, contrived. It is unfolded in eight scenes of epic splendour, fantasy and colour.

Scene 1—How young Setanta (later Cuchulainn) vied with the youngsters at the Court of Conchubar, High King of Ulster and became their liege lord.

Scene 2—How Setanta killed the hound that guarded Culann's fort, and in remorse, himself took on the duty of watchdog and the name of Hound of Culann, or Cuchulainn.

Scene 3—How, years later, he wooed and won Emer at the fort of her father Fergall, in company with his friend Ferdiad of Connacht, but could not wed Emer before undergoing tests of courage.

Scene 4—How Cuchulainn and Ferdiad survived ordeals by ghosts and monsters.

Scene 5—How Cuchulainn celebrated his marriage with Emer; how at the feast the warriors fell into a magic sleep, in fulfilment of an ancient curse, how news came of the defeat of Ulster by the Queen of Connacht and how Cuchulainn, parted from Emer to do battle with the army of Connacht ("Emer's farewell to Cuchulainn" is an old name of the folk tune better known as "The Londonderry Air").

Scene 6—How the Queen of Connacht, after her army had been overcome by Cuchulainn, persuaded Ferdiad to fight him by promising her daughter's hand in marriage.

Scene 7—How Ferdiad and Cuchulainn fought at the ford, and how Cuchulainn killed his greatest friend.

Scene 8—How Cuchulainn alone fought once more the army of Queen Medh, and how he met death, still upright and inspired by a vision of his beloved.

CONCHUBAR, HIGH KING OF ULSTER : James Rooney
THE KING'S WARRIORS :
FERGUS (attendant to Conchubar) : Niall Boden
CONALL : Gerard O'Hare
CELTCHAR : Kevin Rafferty
AILLEL : Edmund Henry
BOYS OF THE KING'S MACRAD : Phelim Henry, Michael Devlin, John Mooney, Peter Toner, Geoffrey McLaughlin, John O'Hara
SETANTA (the boy Cuchulainn) : Roy O'Donoghue
THE HOUND OF CULANN : Ciaran Hinds
CULANN : Reginald McClure
EMER : Joyce Ann Henry
FIAL (sister of Emer) : Marlene Baillie
CUCHULAINN : Ciaran Doherty
FERDIAD : John Garvin
HANDMAIDENS TO EMER :
GRAINNE : Sheelagh Gilligan
CAIREEN : Patricia Mulholland
CEITHLIONN : Patricia O'Neill
FEDELN . Maire Bunting
CONCHENN : Frances O'Hara
DERVOGH : Jane McGuigan
MURGAN : Lynda Hamilton
ETAIN : Catherine Gilmore
CONNLA : Michelle Forster
BOANN : Sharon Tansley
GHOSTS : Patricia Gilligan, Lynda Tansley, Linda Connolly, Siobhan Graham, Anne Marie McLaughlin, Noreen McBride, Finola McLernon, Margaret Stewart, Maire Byrne, Jane O'Rawe
MONSTERS : Kevin Rafferty, Edmund Henry, Niall Boden, Henry Toner, Ciaran Hinds, Peter Sturdy
CLOTHRN : Catharine Gilmore
EITHNE (Queen of Conchubar) : Sharon Tansley
DERBRINN : Patricia Mulholland
EITHNE : Lynda Hamilton
MUGAIN : Sheelagh Gilligan
LOEGAIRE : Kevin Lawson
BRICRUL : Niall Boden
MEDH (Queen of Connacht) : Michelle Forster
FINDABAIR (Daughter to Medh) : Patricia O'Neill
A MESSENGER : Edmund Henry
CAOINERS : Lynda Hamilton, Frances O'Hara, Catharine Gilmore, Jane Mooney
THE WARRIORS OF CONNACHT : James Rooney, Edmund Henry, Kevin Rafferty, Reginald McClure, Henry Toner, Peter Sturdy, Kevin Lawson, Niall Boden, Ciaran Hinds, John Mooney
EUGAID (Captain of Connacht Warriors) : Gerard O'Hare

Culann *programme from 1968.*

Among the romantic airs accompanying the love interest, like *The Moon Behind The Hill* and *Believe Me, If All Those Endearing Young Charms*, was *O'Cahan's Lament* – also known as *Maidin I mBéarra*, *The Derry Air*, or *Emer's Farewell*. Whatever we like to call it, the air is indisputably a lament and was used to great effect in the scene where Cúchulainn had to leave Emer (because he was *faoi dheis* – under obligation – to go and fight). There was rarely a dry eye in the house at that parting.

Prior to this melancholic scene was the celebratory banquet during which the warriors were supposed to perform feats of athleticism. This was transmuted into short bursts of dancing from individual men, incorporating leaps and turns as the bystanders clapped in time to the music.

The protagonist danced the set dance *The Blackbird*, which was entirely appropriate for anyone who remembered the incident in *The Táin* where Cúchulainn is found

Patricia Gilligan as Emer.

whistling to a blackbird with the blackbird whistling back to him.

Maeve's offering of her daughter as a bribe to Ferdia to persuade him to fight Cúchulainn was carried out to the tune of *Fil, A Rún* (Return, My Love) – this would have had all sorts of resonances for anyone who knew the words of one version asking, as they do in it, someone not to betray his upbringing.

The fight at the ford was yet another example of how Patricia Mulholland could choreograph a fight scene just as well as a three-hand reel. Kevin Campbell and John Garvin were the first duelling heroes and provided drama of the first order. I always think of them when I pass the bronze statue of Cúchulainn and Ferdia in Ardee.

The hero's lament for his dead foster brother was represented by four keeners (from the Irish *caoineadh*, meaning lament) who covered Ferdia's body with a silk winding-sheet decorated with a Celtic design of Mercy's. The music was specially composed to give an impression of keening and the movements required a suppleness and balletic grace that was never so well-exemplified as by Catherine Gilmore who went on to play the part of Emer.

L-R: Maire Byrne as Finnabar (Irish form of Guinevere), Lynda Tansley as Maeve and Kevin Rafferty as Ferdia.

Some of the women's costumes in this ballet were particularly attractive. One of the choruses was dressed in asymmetric chiffon gowns, one shoulder exposed and one arm covered in a wide sleeve, in rainbow colours. They danced a reel to *The Foggy Dew* (the 'Angelus bell o'er the Liffey swell' version as distinct from the slow air). Emer's main costume was in purple silk with mediaeval sleeves and a belt of gold braid fastened by a sunburst-style clasp, from which were suspended gold ropes.

There were ghosts and monsters too, with mummy-like wrappings and papier-mâché heads (one of which was worn by Gerry O'Hare in Belfast's first psychedelic experience in the old McMordie Hall at Queen's. Clare Czonka, Gerry and I writhed and gyrated to Bach's *Toccata And Fugue In D Minor* while Paul O'Shea threw slices of bread at the audience).

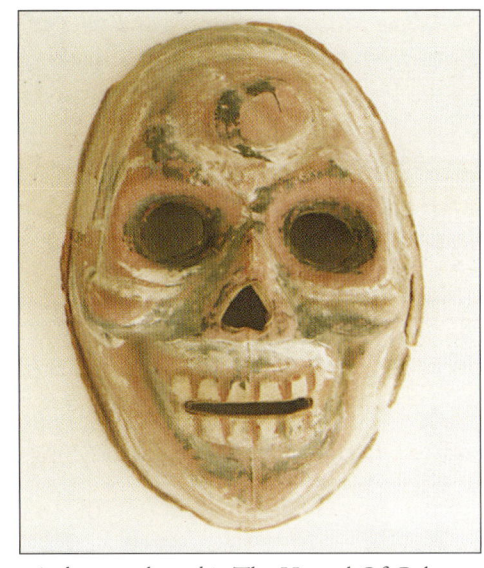

A ghost mask used in The Hound Of Culann.

Costume designer Mercy Hunter was head of Art at Victoria College in Belfast and a member of the Ulster Academy. And, of course, she was an artist above all, with a blithe disregard for the exigencies of couture. The trouble was, her sketches were impressionistic and their translation into actual garments was problematic, especially when it came to raising arms, for example, and a ballet company does a lot of raising arms. When a ballet was first produced, you were handed your sketch and got on with it. But this in itself allowed a fair amount of interpretation. One of Frances Tomelty's costumes in *The Hound* looked in the drawing as if the skirt were pleated. Mrs Tomelty went to great bother and expense to have the material professionally pleated, only to have Mercy blow a gasket at the dress rehearsal.

Eventually, for one ballet at least, all the costumes were made by one set of dressmakers, led by Mrs MacMaster (mother of dancer Carolyn), who measured and tailored and did a very good job of it.

The initial performance of *The Hound Of Culann* was at the Grand Opera House in Belfast; at that time it had a raked stage which enabled Brian Bunting to skid downstage very effectively in his pre-battle "psyching-up" of his Connacht warriors.

Mercy's costume sketch for a warrior in The Hound Of Culann.

While Miss Mulholland was always adamant that you should be able to use whatever space was available, big or small, there can be no doubt that the huge expanse of the Opera House stage suited full-company scenes, and especially battle scenes, better than a school or parochial hall. In particular, the last scene of this ballet, where the Connacht host defeat Cúchulainn, never really came off as well on smaller stages. The final moment was the realisation that the Ulster hero (curiously described as a god in one Ulster Museum exhibition) was dead though still on his feet – a scene depicted in bronze by Oliver Sheppard in the GPO in Dublin – and the pillar to which he was attached was usually counterbalanced by a member of the stage crew, hanging on like grim death while crouched in behind.

The props and scenery suffered a fair amount of damage from use in action and sometimes they just got lost in transit, so there was sometimes a need for repair or replacement as the letter below illustrates.

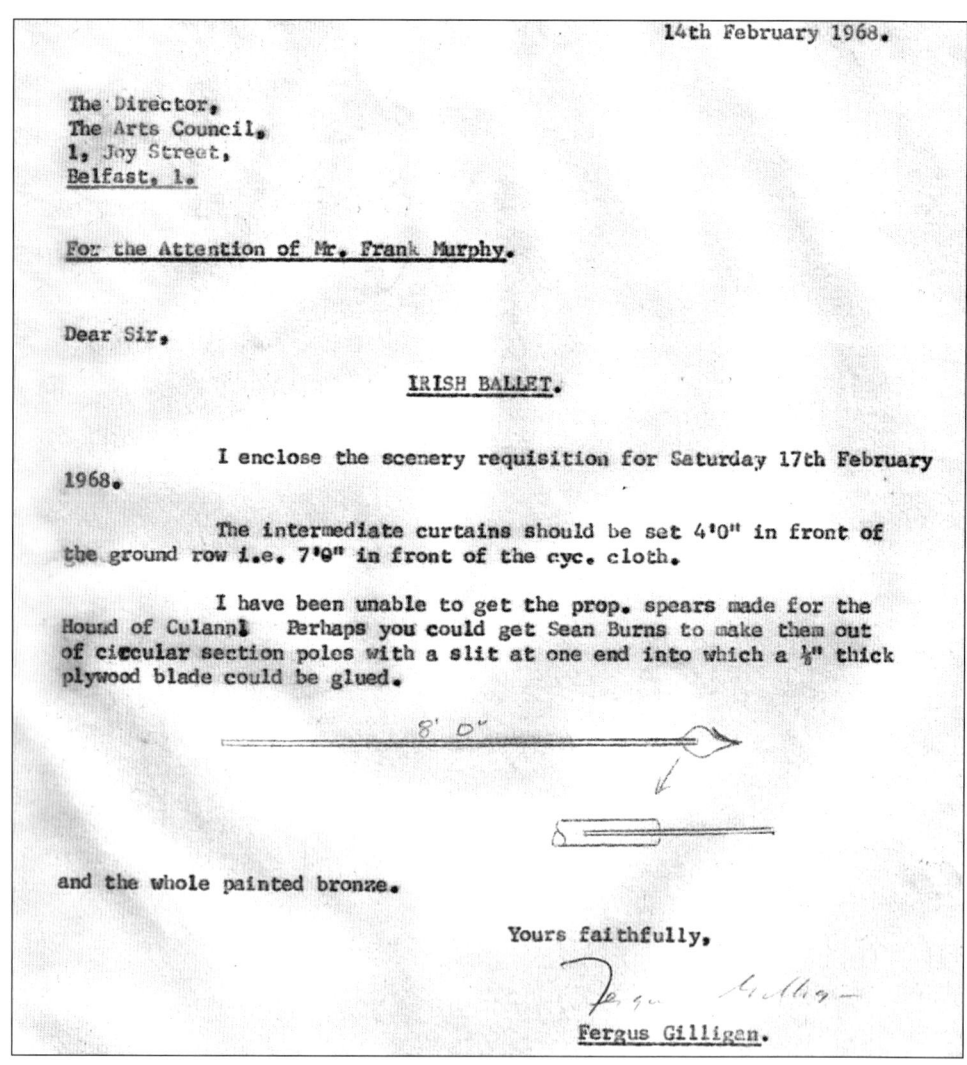

Letter from Fergus Gilligan to the Arts Council with an unusual request for new spears!

Telegram for Miss Mulholland from Michael Emmerson, the first director of the Belfast Festival at Queen's.

Celtic Anthology
First performed: Grand Opera House, Belfast, May 1965.

Celtic Anthology was a departure from the usual narrative ballets in that it was a display of largely traditional dances executed in Mulholland traditional style. It was almost a revelation of how the Mulholland style had developed. It was a fast-moving kaleidoscope, greatly helped in this instance by Mercy Hunter's colourful costumes. This 'bright, lyrical essay', as it was once described, arranged dancing episodes in a similar way to passages of music in a symphony, the dances blending into one another almost seamlessly. Geraldine Neeson, writing in the *Irish Times* in 1971 described the company as 'well-disciplined and sensitively aware of the rapid flow of rhythmic change in the divertissements of *Celtic Anthology*. Individual dancers were good but it was the fluid linking of dance to dance that was most impressive.'

   The curtain opened on most of the company: the girls in short, brightly coloured tunics (mine was kingfisher blue with an orange belt), men in kilts and colourful shirts, all arranged in "rings of four" for *The Three Tunes*.

Rehearsal of the opening dance for Celtic Anthology.

Once, in the Whitla Hall, the audience was composed mostly of delegates from a BMA conference and a number of them started to wolf-whistle when the girls appeared in their short tunics. Miss Mulholland brought everyone off the stage, 'until such time as the audience learned to behave.' At an earlier performance for the same group in 1962, the doctors seem to have been more circumspect, though I do remember one delegate asking me on the way in if we were going to do St Vitus' dance.

For *The Gates Of Derry,* the introductory colour theme was grey, followed by a couple in bright red doing a reel. *The Gap Of Dungloe* was dressed in lilac and purple.

The girls perform the Mountains Of Pomeroy.

The girls danced a sort of multiple three-hand reel to the lovely *Mountains Of Pomeroy*, in subtle autumnal shades of satin, dancing off the stage in a single line as the men passed them, also in single file, starting into *St Patrick's Day* – the music changing key and rhythm smoothly. One of the features of the men's set dance was their dancing without music, their feet beating out the percussive rhythm alone before the fiddle joined in again for the climax of the dance.

After this excitement, the pace changed again, this time to an elegant slip-jig duo.

The last episode in *Celtic Anthology* was a team dance called *Erin*. This was best appreciated seen from above for its representation of the symbols of the four provinces of Ireland. For the first performance in the Opera House, Miss Mulholland decided to try out the effect of dancers carrying torches for the finale. As I remember it, fellow dancer Geoffrey McNab and I were persuaded to fashion the torches out of polystyrene and batteries (polystyrene was then a very new material; we had to learn how to use a hot-line to cut it rather like cutting cheese with a wire), but the illumination provided was negligible and so it was never repeated.

Celtic Anthology was performed in the Gaiety Theatre in Dublin in 1966 for the RTÉ St Patrick's Day concert. It was a foreshadowing of another RTÉ entertainment; one with girls in short tunics, rows of dancers using unaccompanied beating, one tempo changing into another . . . *Riverdance*, of course.

The fact that there were echoes of earlier performances in this wonderful extravaganza did not escape the notice of many people in the North. For instance, Gerry McCrudden, in his letter to the *Belfast Telegraph*, pointed out that in the combination of David Curry's Irish Rhythms and Patricia Mulholland's Irish Ballet was an embryonic *Riverdance* from two great Northerners. He called David Curry 'the forgotten man of Irish music.'

ARTS COUNCIL OF NORTHERN IRELAND   1 Joy Street, Belfast 2
Telephone, Belfast 33051

Miss Pat Mulholland,
17 Newington Street,   Director, Mrs. S. E. Capper
BELFAST 15.   25 February 1966

Dear Pat,

I would like you to take this as emanating from the Arts Council and not from myself personally, because I just want to say how very thrilled we all were with three marvellous nights of dancing at the Grove Theatre earlier this week.

The presentation of twelve ballets in three nights is a major triumph of which any professional company would be proud, and it is an achievement for which we in the Arts Council have nothing but the deepest respect. I would be glad if you would congratulate, on our behalf, every single member of your company and those who worked so splendidly behind the scenes, your musicians and designers – in fact, the whole group of highly talented people with whom you have surrounded yourself and who have contributed so richly to the success of your company.

I have heard more praise for the Irish Ballet in the last week than I have for any of the other visiting companies which have played in the same theatre, and I would just like you to say to your company how very much we at the Arts Council appreciate their excellence.

Very sincerely,

Ken.

J. KENNETH JAMISON
Deputy Director

Letter from Ken Jamison, Deputy Director of the Arts Council who were still very much in support of Miss Mulholland at this stage in 1966.

Gerry Hobbs in a letter to the same paper mentioned 'the great delicacy of time and rhythm in Irish footwork . . . well-reflected in David Curry's orchestrations. Traditional céilí band purists did not favour his arrangements.' But there are many, myself included, who find the single-line approach of many traditional players boring in the extreme where everyone chaws away on the melody, no matter what instrument they play.

David Curry is another Ulster talent who has been hugely undervalued.

The Philanderer
First choreographed: Circa 1961 – first performed in costume in 1966.

The philanderer of the title was the only male in this team dance who "dallied" with each of four girls in turn before throwing them over. They eventually decide to act together and turn the tables on him. It was originally a team dance, a five-hand reel, but was given a special look when Mercy designed costumes in eighteenth-century style.

Like *Follow Me Down To Carlow*, this new work was useful in that it was short and light-hearted and perfect for, say, inclusion in a concert where something different from a traditional team was required. It was included in an RTÉ programme called *Serenade* in 1966, produced by Patricia Foy (biographer of Margot Fonteyn) when Tibor Paul conducted the RTÉ Symphony Orchestra playing music arranged by David Curry. The rehearsing on the hard studio floor made for very sore muscles, but there was worse discomfort to come, for on the way home from Dublin in the wee small hours, the car I was travelling in burst into flames after hitting a ramp. Fortunately, the car in front noticed that we had disappeared from the rear view mirror and Patricia O'Neill turned round and rescued us.

Shortly after their return in 1964 from Royan in France, the dancers were appearing at a concert in the War Memorial Hall in Waring Street and Kevin Campbell was unavailable, so Reggie McClure took his place in *The Philanderer*.

Brian Bunting, John Garvin and Gerry O'Hare give Paddie Bell a helping hand with her music at rehearsals for The Philanderer.

The girls decided to really gang up on him and actually danced off and left him alone on stage. Fortunately, he had got wind of their joke and had mentioned it to Miss Mulholland, so he rather turned the tables on the four jokers, as he carried it all off with great aplomb and to loud applause from the unsuspecting audience.

Patricia was anxious to dissociate Irish dancing from any stiffness or rigidity and she felt that skirts and waistcoats helped to convey a lighter touch and a more natural aspect than the usual dancing costume. Mulholland dancers often wore this sort of outfit when dancing at events less formal than concerts.

Audrey Clarke, Stella O'Neill, Lynne Maxwell, Margot Bell and Kevin Campbell before Mercy had designed special costumes for The Philanderer.

The Young Men And Women
First performed: Grove Theatre, Belfast, March 1967.

Much was made of the "op-art" costumes designed by Mercy Hunter for this ballet and indeed they were eye-catching, the black-and-white "bull's eye" and abstract designs setting them firmly in the mid-'60s. They were even more experimental than those of *Celtic Anthology* and reflected the progress of Patricia Mulholland's creativity.

However, one set of designs just did not – literally – come off; the leotard-like one-pieces that the girls were to wear in the "lovers" scene. Miss Mulholland had composed special music for this scene and her choreography was demanding, requiring suppleness as we bent right back in our lovers' arms. The one-piece was half-red and half-green and was designed to have straight-cut legs like an old-fashioned swimsuit. We were then to quickly put over it a circular skirt for the last scene. Needless to say, the straight cut made everyone's legs look about twelve inches long. I had got my grandmother to cut mine high on the hip, which looked marginally better, but it was decided to wear the skirt for both scenes.

The ballet started with a very animated line of couples, the young men and women of the title entering hand in hand and dressed in shades of grey and green. They were followed by a more sober group, the married ones.

Sheelagh Gilligan, Joyce Ann Henry and Margot Bell. Margot's hat represented the married state in The Young Men And Women.

A bright episode in the middle was provided by an *Irish Mazurka* danced by a girl in a tomato-soup-coloured dress. This dress had a wide rectangular neckline with narrow strips of contrasting colour set in, reminiscent of a Mondrian design, and it was virtually impossible to get to sit properly on the wearer. She had to dance between three kneeling suitors before choosing one.

The moods changed throughout, contrasting lights and colours complementing the dancing until the last scene which had a bacchanalian flavour and was danced in reel time. The work explored relationships, flirtations of the young, the more settled nature of married couples, the passion of physical love. It was really quite adventurous, and though the dances had originally been choreographed to order, Patricia Mulholland was able to tie them together in a complex, unquestionably artistic manner, to make a satisfying whole.

Sheelagh Gilligan, Margot Bell, Ciarán Doherty and Joyce Ann Henry dancing in Bedford Street, Belfast (by kind permission of the Belfast Telegraph).

Three Lovely Lassies In Banyon

First performed: Grove Theatre, Belfast, December 1968.

The abstract, in the shape of *Celtic Anthology* and *The Young Men And Women*, was to be left behind for a new ballet in 1968. This time, the principle behind the deceptively simple narrative was satire.

I was familiar enough with the song, though when I went to the Grove Theatre to see this ballet, I did not expect to have to touch up my make-up because I'd laughed so much my mascara ran.

Miss Mulholland's niece, Patricia O'Neill, represented the old regime of stiff, joyless dancing at its worst. She was a fine heavy dancer and her high level of competence was required in order to be able to satirise the kind of dancing that Miss Mulholland hated and had spent her whole life resisting.

The costumes were high-waisted gowns and frock coats, reminiscent of Jane Austen novels and evoked a genteel sort of ambience – a good foil for the antagonism between the dour representatives of the regimented style and the light-hearted "progressives".

This ballet did not last long in the repertoire, perhaps because it demanded huge energy and skilled dancing from most of the company throughout. Festival dancers do not, as a general rule, kick up their feet behind them doing the basic promenade step, so the cast disliked having to use this style.

Cue	Time	Action
		BANNION
1		CURTAIN AFTER TUNE PLAYED ONCE.
2	0.00	Music
	0.20	3 lassies
	1.00	
	1.20	Boy enters.
	2.20	4 dance together.
	3.10	2 lassies alone.
	3.35	2 lassies exit.
	2.40	Boy and girl return.
	5.10	Enter 4 more boys and girls.
	5.40	6 boys and girls dance.
	7.15	Exit 4, enter 8
3	8.55	End dance. BLACKOUT
		CHANGE STAGE.
4	0.00	Music.
	0.15	Enter 6 boys and girls.
	1.00	Enter father and mother.
	1.50	Girl dances.
	3.25	Mother dances.
	4.50	Dance ends.
	5.00	All dance.
	5.30	Dance ends.
	5.35	Shoes
	6.00	Petticoat.
	6.45	Shoemaker dances.
	7.00	Dyer dances.
	8.20	Brush man dances.
	9.05	Two girls get shoes and petticoat.
	9.30	6 girls dance.
	11.00	All dance
	11.35	Men dance.
	13.15	Boy carried.
	13.50	Dance ends.

Running order for Three Lovely Lassies In Banyon.

Sketches for (above) the mother's costume and (below) Kevin Rafferty's costume.

Edmund Henry's name on Sheelagh's design means not that he wore the same costume but that the same colours and materials were used in his outfit.

Patricia Mulholland and Kevin Rafferty in Three Lovely Lassies In Banyon.

Cast Off: 1971–91

Each presentation is an administrative and artistic achievement for which Patricia Mulholland must be seen as the key, co-ordinating figure.
Eulogy at Miss Mulholland's conferring.

During the 1950s, Patricia Mulholland had succeeded in developing a firmly based, though amateur, company. Having drawn inspiration originally from Irish legend and the songs and poetry of the locality, not to mention its music, she went on in the '60s to stage work that was more abstract yet still evidently grounded in its Irish roots. If the same circumstances had prevailed in her later career that had enabled the flowering of her talent, who knows what direction her Irish Ballet Company might have taken? However, fate stepped in to slowly stifle her artistic output.

Patricia Mulholland faced a problem, along with everyone else in Belfast, due to the political unrest of the early '70s. Nobody could feel sanguine about bringing young people across town, especially late at night, so the ballets were less frequently performed during this period. In turn, parents were reluctant to send their children out unnecessarily and potential audiences were discouraged by the unpromising climate that prevailed at the time.

Carmel McGovern believes the entire dancing school was hit quite hard by the Troubles. For instance, the Saturday rehearsal, which started with senior class and continued, for the most part, with the rehearsal of the ballets, had to end at 6.00 pm so that nobody was out at night. She remembers one afternoon, as she was just about to receive a scolding, a British soldier popped his head round the door and told everyone to get out because of a bomb scare. The practice at this time was close to Girdwood Barracks, off the Antrim Road. She could be said to have been saved by the bomb.

Another example of the direct effect of the Troubles happened when the company met down town, as usual, to get on the bus together to go to a performance outside Belfast. By some unfortunate chance, the percussionist's case was left on the pavement outside the Ulster Hall and was blown up as a suspect package by the security forces. Jim Maze had been the percussionist for many years, but this incident left him with less enthusiasm for the job.

Coming home late at night and being stopped at check-points could provide unforeseen excitement for all concerned. Taxis usually ferried groups of dancers from the same areas to their homes. But when Noreen McBride learned to drive, she used to take her group in her old Wolsey Hornet. Henry Toner, Reggie McClure and my brothers, Ed and Phelim, were in the car one night when they were stopped. This disparate sextet probably seemed strange enough to the soldiers to warrant seeing inside the boot. Their suspicions were not at all relieved by the discovery of wooden swords and shields so they insisted on seeing inside the cases. As tights, tunics, make-up etc were pulled out, the incident ended with everyone in stitches of laughter.

Public unrest affected all arts productions, including Mulholland performances – which continued, perhaps on a less regular basis and with less touring of the province.

The inspiration for the ballets changed too, just as it had in the previous decade. The great stories from ancient literature were not so prominent as before – *Deirdre* was the only one of this kind in the latter part of her career. Miss Mulholland had to cut her coat according to her cloth. The themes became less and less grand. The number of dancers in her classes decreased somewhat so the pool of possible performers for the ballets diminished. Many believe the magic had not just disappeared from her inspiration but also from the performances. However, the show did go on.

In 1971, there was an arts initiative called Ulster 71. As part of this, the Arts Council financed a book and record of Ulster dances, which inspired Patricia's next work.

Ulster Anthology
First sponsored by the Northern Ireland Arts Council, 1977.

The ballet *Ulster Anthology* used as its base the dances that had been presented in the book *Ulster Dances*. It was quite similar to *Celtic Anthology* but with an entirely Northern flavour. It consisted of a suite of dances that included *The Cutting Of The Turf, The Splashing Of The Churn, The Flax Flower* and a beautiful ensemble, *The Herring Fleet*, some of which can be seen as team dances at festivals. The Ulster Tartan, a blend of saffron and red, was a traditional plaid apparently commonly seen in the past, and the weaving of this was represented in one of the dances.

The costumes were cut out by Mrs MacMaster (Carolyn's mother) and Mrs King and then handed out in kit form. Noreen McBride remembers sewing her costume on an old Singer and thinking how convenient a machine with a zigzag stitch would be for edging all the seams.

The company at a dress rehearsal of Ulster Anthology.

Nearly thirty years later, this piece was resurrected for a dance show in Bangor – a very successful entertainment, showing Irish, Scottish and classical ballet dancing – called *The Shamrock And Thistle*; Carolyn Revie was the driving force behind this. Her daughter Donna produced the balletic part of the evening, with Grainne Gilmore and Margot Bell responsible for resurrecting the Ulster dances.

In 1965, the Arts Council had spent £17,000 in converting the Grove Cinema to the Grove Theatre. The building was not to everyone's satisfaction, but as Sam Hanna Bell remarked in his 1972 book *The Theatre In Ulster*, 'Some notable productions were staged there by visiting as well as local theatre companies. None, I think, equalled in beauty and delight the appearances of the Irish Ballet. Almost a decade later, that tribute still stands to these young artists and their gifted founder.'

Twenty-fifth Anniversary Celebration at Dunadry

In 1976, Sheelagh Gilligan and Frances O'Hara organised a twenty-fifth anniversary celebration of the Irish Ballet Company in the Dunadry Inn.

They put together a very interesting display of photographs and other memorabilia. Miss Mulholland played after dinner, and two of the dances performed that evening were *The Hills Of Pomeroy* and *St Patrick's Day*. This was shortly after the birth of my son James and I had squeezed myself into a tightly fitting shirt. Everything was fine until it came to the raising of the arms in *Pomeroy* – I could not get my hands past eye-level!

Sheelagh Gilligan and Frances O'Hara at the 25th anniversary party of the Patricia Mulholland Irish Ballet Company in 1976.

Miss Mulholland was presented with a glass sculpture by Brian Coleman, who had been principal in the first ballet, *The Dancer*. Restricted arm movements notwithstanding, all the guests had a whale of a time

Brian Coleman presents Miss Mulholland with a glass sculpture at the 1976 anniversary party.

Deirdre
First performed: Arts Theatre, Belfast, 1979.

The last Mulholland treatment of an Irish myth, that of Deirdre and Naoise, took place in 1979. A Scottish influence evident in *Ulster Anthology* was perhaps at work here, too, as the Deirdre story moves from Ulster to Alba (Scotland), reflecting the close historical ties of these two places.

> **Deirdre**
>
> Scene 1.. (White) Red. Purple. Black. Red.
> A) Cathbad (Druid) Conor (King) Fergus centre stage with Red Branch Knights Dance.
> 2. Entrance of Maidens in green from each side of stage. Dance.
> 3. R.B. Knights + Maidens very short dance together.
> 4. Short fanfare on entrance of Mother of Deirdre + Felim. Entrance down stage R. (Purple. Black. Yellow)
> * (R.B. Knights form diagonal lines to flank their entrance)
> 5. Mother is received by Conor, circles stage presenting her to company, passes her over to Fergus who repeats, then he goes to pass to Druid but her turns away. Druid down stage L.
> 6. Druid's Prophecy.
> 7. Two R.B. Knights run from centre up stage to kill Mother. Conor restrains them. offers marriage.
> 8. Mother goes to Conor kneels, moves centre stage dances.
> 9. General Dance, dance off.

Scenario of Deirdre *in Miss Mulholland's own hand, 1979.*

Her two principal dancers of that period, Carmel McGovern and Leslie Baird, were the inspiration behind this work. These two had been dancing with Miss Mulholland from a very young age and they became almost like surrogate children to her. Leslie celebrated his fourth birthday shortly after he started with Miss Mulholland, and she nearly went mad when she discovered just how young he was; she had thought he was about seven. Fortunately, she relented and allowed him to stay at the class.

Carmel had a shaky enough introduction to Miss Mulholland, too. Her mother had to fit in her interview before she herself went to work. So when they arrived at Newington Street, the Mulholland household was just beginning to stir. Mrs Mulholland opened the door and Patricia appeared at the head of the stairs in a red dressing gown. She barked down at them, 'I didn't think you'd come this early!' Nevertheless, they were ushered in, and after seeing Carmel do a basic step or two, she said, 'Okay, I'll take her – but don't cut her hair.'

On the first occasion that Carmel danced this role, Marjorie Gilligan, who had been wardrobe mistress for several years, left a rose in her dressing room.

A scene from Deirdre *in which Carmel McGovern and Leslie Baird, as Deirdre and Naoise, are protected by his brothers, Robert Hunter, left, and Martin McKinley.*

One critic, Charles Fitzgerald, after the premiere of the ballet, compared the Mulholland dance form to Tennyson's poetry, equating her interpretation of the Red Branch Knights' saga to the poet's treatment of the Arthurian legend. The same man was particularly impressed by one scene, where he felt the traditional Scots and Irish idioms were intermingled most successfully.

Choice of music was, as always, perfectly fitted to the action, whether in Mulholland's own compositions or melodies drawn from the traditional repertoire. For example, Eithne, mother of Deirdre, danced to the *Gartan Mother's Lullaby*, and a graceful ladies' ensemble dancing to *Planxty Irwin* contrasted well with the martial beginning of the ballet performed by the Red Branch Knights.

Patricia's ability to successfully choreograph battle scenes was evident again in this ballet; the contrast these provided with the romantic, lyrical dancing of the principals' *pas de deux* was remarkable.

Unfortunately, most of the Red Branch Knights were played by girls, a necessity at that point because there were fewer boys attending dancing class.

The final scene, in which the ill-fated couple are united forever in death, was conveyed tenderly by the dancing of the two trees that entwined over the lovers' grave.

The early performances of *Deirdre* were marred by overlong intervals slowing the action considerably; at one point, the intervals seemed as long as some of the scenes, but this problem was solved mainly by a fresh approach from a new stage manager, much to the improvement of the overall effect.

In 1983, BBC producer Alan Tongue recorded this work at Narrow Water Castle, making it the second (and last) Mulholland ballet to be televised.

Courtin' In The Kitchen
First performed: Arts Theatre, Belfast, 1980.

Courtin' was very much a product of its time and Miss Mulholland's take on the rock music scene. Rather like *The Variety Market*, it became quickly dated, so the year 1985 was later added to the title to identify it as a period piece set in a disco.

Individual dancers were given their head to some extent in this piece. Martin McKinley was memorable, his trendy haircut and modern dancing skill adding to the overall effect. Robbie Lightbody's tap routine and natural humour suited his character. Paddi Lamb's dramatic flair, along with that of her sisters, was a vital ingredient. Any onlooker was impressed by the enjoyment the dancers derived from the ballet. The ensemble dancing was a joy to watch, with its combination of Irish and disco steps.

As usual, the music was well-chosen and remarkably adapted to the modern idiom. For example, Captain Kelly and Miss Tulip (Robert Hunter and Caitriona Crilly) performed a dramatic and amusing tango to a stirring hornpipe.

Rathcol of the *Belfast Telegraph* – in March 1983 – wrote, 'In *Courtin'*, Paddi Lamb and Robbie Lightbody excelled, and Robert Hunter's captain, Caitriona Crilly's seductive Miss Tulip and Leslie Baird's absurdly amusing transvestite were all first rate.'

Love's Young Dream and *The Girl I Left Behind Me* appeared briefly, and several bright reel tunes lent themselves surprisingly well to the disco dances of the youngsters; it was really difficult to sit still while listening to the fiddle during these episodes. Indeed, the playing of these reels was possibly the most enjoyable and infectious playing to be heard from Miss Mulholland during the later period. However, it was fairly evident that the company was just a little less disciplined than she would have stood for in the past.

Leslie Baird was invited back to dance in this ballet after a considerable absence (this must have been popular with the rest of the cast). He was unsure about it, as he felt his talents were more suited to dramatic than comedic roles, but his fears were ill-founded and the ballet proved popular, especially with the younger generation.

The costumes were disco-style, for the most part, all glitter and lycra.

Mercy held less sway at this point than heretofore. Funding was dwindling away prior to being cut entirely, so the dancers designed and provided their own costumes for this work.

Paddi Lamb and Carmel McGovern are ready for action in Courtin' In The Kitchen.

The Midday Special
First performed: Arts Theatre, Belfast, 1983.

This was one of those "romps" that showed us to ourselves and made us laugh, as we could recognise all the characters. The humour was greatly helped by the personality of Paddi Lamb, who portrayed the "man robed in a little brief authority" in the role of the bus conductor. The joggers, road-sweepers, girls on horseback, and the lady with her dog, who was refused entry, were all acutely observed and well played. These characters and their dances were reminiscent of the much earlier *Follow Me Down To Carlow* without being copies. The end of the ballet – when the cast formed themselves into a bus, complete with wheels and rolled off – was perfect.

Interpretations

Interpretations represented a return to a suite of dances giving impressions of various scenes from country life, but it was also something of a departure for Patricia Mulholland, for this time she invited Niall McGahon (husband of her niece, Maeve) to sing *Eileen Óg, She Moved Through The Fair* and *Bantry Bay*. The dancers then interpreted the songs – hence the title. Niall's singing received generous praise from at least one critic, Charles Fitzgerald.

The ballet was not to everyone's taste, being rather slow moving. Nevertheless, it was a brave experiment on Patricia Mulholland's part, including, as it did, quite a balletic *pas de deux* in *She Moved Through The Fair*. One of the dances was performed by a graceful female team to *The Herring Fleet* (in a slow hornpipe tempo); they held up the edge of their skirt with one hand, giving an impression of a sail. This effective idea was suggested by Lena Tomelty, who was wardrobe mistress for a time.

Many years before, the idea of using singing accompaniment had been introduced by Desmond Turner, who used to sing along to *Follow Me Down To Carlow*. He had gathered together several members of the company to develop the idea of singing along with the dancing. But after the first practice, when the music had been handed out, it suddenly bit the dust; the emphasis at that time was to remain firmly on the dancing.

A Day At The Festival

The Festival was another piece in which Patricia Mulholland showed how she could encapsulate human emotions in a few steps – from the "feis mother" to the doting father who has no interest in dancing and prefers to read the paper but who is prepared to bribe the adjudicator in the face of his daughter's disappointment at not winning. She also used the adjudicator in this ballet to express her own credo that dance should be graceful above all, without any stiffness.

The End of an Era

By the end of the 1980s, Patricia Mulholland's artistic output, in terms of new, full-length ballets, was certainly on the wane. Nevertheless, the repertoire was always kept up to scratch, with around a dozen, say, up to performance level, running at any one time.

As Rathcol of the *Telegraph* put it, 'A capacity audience and immense enthusiasm was no more than the last night of the Patricia Mulholland Irish Ballet's season in the Arts Theatre deserved, when this talented company completed the formidable task of presenting thirteen ballets in six days.'

In forty years, she had choreographed and directed twenty-odd ballets. She taught the steps and mime to newcomers to the roles, directed the dramatic work, and was always on the lookout for suitable themes and music.

Some ideas would never make it as far as the stage but would still have demanded time and energy for discussion. For instance, Roma Tomelty and she explored the idea of a ballet based on Robert Emmet; there is a cornucopia of beautiful music associated with this character – think of Moore's melodies – and there is plenty of drama in his life and death. Roma had quite a body of research done for the project, which later found expression in her own play on the 1798 rising. Perhaps this theme was just too politically charged for Miss Mulholland.

The Irish Famine was a topic that the dancers themselves discussed with Patricia, but again, it came to nothing.

One of the last ballets composed by Miss Mulholland was *The Birthday Party*, which really consisted of children in party clothes (some of them Grainne Gilmore's children's dresses), doing party pieces and team dances, one of them *The Poacher*. In this piece, there is an extra boy and he dances with each girl in turn before handing them back to their partners. The last partner thinks he, too, will get his girl back, but the poacher dances off with his chosen one and the deserted boy can only chase after them, shaking his fist. This was not at all demanding for Miss Mulholland and deliberately chosen for that reason. In fact, the dance could be seen at festivals in the team-dance section. Her health was not good and she no longer had Arts Council funding, so the idea behind the ballet was basically to attract as big an audience with as little effort as possible. All the lovely little children had relations who would come to see them.

The Junior Company

Clare McKeever	Eamonn Largey	Claire McGuigan
Ciaran McKinney	Daire McGill	Catherine McKeever
Fiona Keave	Adrian Hickey	Fiona Neary
Rita Higgins	Paul Conlon	Sinead O'Connor
Aine Rosato	Pat McKinney	Fiona Trainor
Kerrie Scott	Una Carson	Colette White
Maurice Lunny	Michael Carson	Anna Wills
Ciara Trainor	Paul Harkin	Fiona Wills
Niamh Loughrey	Oonagh Mullan	Rory Wills
Ruth Hicks	Oonagh Blair	Suzanne Cairns
Orla Conlon	Gemma Frizzell	Jane McKeever
Terri Doherty	Roisin Sweeney	Helen Largey
Ruth Alton	Brenda Loughrey	Conor McClements
Aoile Brennan	Bronagh Watson	Philip McKee
Keava Freil	Bronagh Cullen	Clare Doherty
Rory Neary	Rachel Hession	Caoimhe McGill
Niall Carlin	Clare McFerran	Laura Magill
Catherin McKee	Clare O'Connell	Maria D'Agostino
Maeve Macdonald	Brigeen McKeague	Laura McCarthy
Helen McKeever	Bronagh Haren	Karen Doherty
Zara Birch	Aoibheann Lamb	Catherine Doherty
Orla Brennan	Roisin McKinney	Emma Jane Carlin
Paul Carson	Colette Archer	Kathleen Ferguson
Marcia Cassidy	Ciara Leonard	Joclyn Hughes
Fionniala Donnelly	Orla Leonard	Catriona Farrell
Laura Donelly	Danielle McAlindon	Jennifer Carlin
Una Donnelly	Suzanne McAlindon	Donna McLaughlin
Antia Harding	Claire McCusker	Marila Maginness
Emma Harkin	Fiona McKee	Kathryn Lahen
Timothy Harkin	Peter McKee	Blathnat Mullan

The Senior Company

Mary Blair	Carmel McGovern
Peter Brannigan	Neil McGuigan
Andrea Brown	Claire McElhinney
Olivia Buckley	Mandy McKee
Damien Corr	Alison McKinley
Jackie Cullen	Clare O'Connor
Karen Fulton	Rosemary O'Connor
Andrew Harding	Brian Reilly
Angela Harding	Lilias Reilly
Elizabeth Harding	Emma Shaw
Nicola Harkin	Kerry Sweeney
Cathy Hollywood	Gavin Thompson
Jane Hoy	Lynda Thompson
Siobhan Higgins	Niaomh White
Heloise Archer	Stephen Harding
Kirsky McKay	Darragh Morgan
Maeve Largey	Garth McKeever
Clare Donnelly	Marc Frizzell
Tracey Lamb	Paul McKerren
Sarah Loughran	Iain McKay
Elaine McCarthy	

Left: Junior Company of Mulholland dancers, 1990.
Above: Senior Company of Mulholland dancers, 1989.

The Patricia Mulholland
IRISH BALLET

Traditional music arranged and ballets devised and directed by	PATRICIA MULHOLLAND
Special music composed by	DAVID CURRY ALFRED ARNOLD JACK BLAIR
Costumes and backcloths	MERCY HUNTER
Wardrobe	CAROLYN REVIE YVONNE McKINLEY WINNIE BRIGGS MARJORIE KING
Make Up	GRAINNE GILMORE EILEEN O'CONNOR
Production Manager	BRENDAN CARSON
Stage Manager	DOUG REVIE
Stage Assistants	KENNETH THOMPSON BRIAN REILLY HARRY LARGEY
Musicians violin piano percussion	PATRICIA MULHOLLAND MARGOT BROWN MARGARET THOMPSON

There will be two intervals of 15 minutes in each programme.

Left: Programme showing that friends and relations of Miss Mulholland were rallying round; the technical staff were mostly ex-dancers or their spouses.

PATRICIA MULHOLLAND IRISH BALLET

Belfast Civic Arts Theatre
BOTANIC AVENUE

Tuesday, 20th February – Saturday, 24th February
Nightly at 7.45 p.m.

Tickets £3.50
(Children/Students/Senior Citizens £2.50)

Reductions for parties of 10 or more

Booking from Arts Theatre Box Office, Botanic Avenue
Monday – Friday 10.00 a.m. – 5.30 p.m.
Saturday 10 a.m. – 2.00 p.m.

The programme is as follows:

Tuesday
20th February, 1990
A Piper
Cuchulain
Courtin in the Kitchen

Wednesday
21st February, 1990
The Black Rogue
Mother of Oisín
The Festival

Thursday
22nd February, 1990
The Mid-Day Special
Children of Lir
Phil the Fluter's Ball

Friday
23rd February, 1990
Interpretations
Deidre
The Mid-Day Special

Saturday
24th February, 1990
The Birthday Party
The Dream of Angus Og
Phil the Fluter's Ball

Right: Programme from 1990 illustrating the range of Mulholland ballets still in the repertoire.

However, the lack of discipline in the dancers, noticeable before, was beginning to change the whole aura of the Patricia Mulholland Irish Ballet Company; the golden days were long gone. Re-jigging of dance routines led to repetition in places; perhaps this was to save Patricia from having to teach newcomers the roles. The dancers were getting away with things that would never have been overlooked when Miss Mulholland was youthful and in her full health. Mime was unintelligible at times: entrances and exits were untidy; some performers didn't seem to fully understand what was required of them. Arm movements in particular were becoming quite careless, some being compared to the changing of light bulbs! And Patricia's playing was a pale shadow of what it had been. Sometimes it was painfully sad to listen to, making the audience very uncomfortable.

In spite of these problems, in 1988–89 and 1990, the Patricia Mulholland Irish Ballet Company staged thirteen to fourteen different ballets in the Arts Theatre in one week, attracting good houses. Yet, a decade earlier, the Arts Council had already withdrawn steadily dwindling funding from the venture. Rumour has it that they had been trying to do this for several years but that she had a champion in Frank Murphy, who fought her corner well. But in the end, even Frank could not defend some of her more impossible demands and she was cast adrift.

Some Arts Council personnel continued to give technical assistance, such as Brendan Carson, who stayed on as production manager in a voluntary capacity, and Noel Mallon, who had been the stage electrician for many years. Few, if any, of the dancers would have realised the huge effort required from the crew to stage the ballets, especially when touring, so the loyalty and energy of technical experts were vital.

Noel had been asked to come and work for the ballets by Henry Lynch-Robinson in 1960. He started in a part-time capacity, never signed a contract and was there until the end. Initially, it meant long hours and hard work. If, say, there was a show in Castlederg, the day started with a very long journey (no motorway then), and the crew would have to leave early in the morning to be there in time to build an extension to the stage etc. Some halls wouldn't have had a fuse-box in the wings, so the electricians would have had to run a long cable from, say, the canteen.

Noel worked with other touring companies of all sorts and worked backstage at several of singer James Johnston's concerts. He has a great store of memories, including one about a visit of the ballets to Ballycastle in the early 1960s when the electricity went out and lighting was provided by Tilley lamps. This venue required crew and dancers alike to go outside to cross to the other side of the stage and, in the dark, Jimmy Robeson fell and broke his arm! Jimmy was a well-known figure to anyone who attended the Friday night concerts in the Ulster Hall, where he was a commissionaire.

Another anecdote is from the Grove Theatre. Henry Lynch-Robinson (erstwhile scenery and lighting designer) was back home on holiday from Ghana and came to visit the ballets. He had brought Mercy Hunter a pair of earrings as a present. These were for pierced ears and Mercy didn't have pierced ears – until then. Henry's Ghanaian friend performed the necessary operation there and then, in the bar!

Noel also recalls that Lord Wakehurst, then Governor of Northern Ireland, was a big fan of Miss Mulholland's. He used to come unannounced to performances, travelling in a Rolls Royce with no number plates. The crew used to tease young policemen about this, saying, 'Look – that car has no licence plate. Are you not going to tackle the driver?' The rookies would be halfway to remonstrating when the boys would relent and save their blushes.

Brendan Carson's first link with the company was an indirect one – he was taught maths by Kevin Campbell.

His introduction to Henry Lynch-Robinson was an inauspicious one. In the early '60s, he was helping his father with a show in the King George VI Memorial Hall, where his father was caretaker. Henry sent him for a certain kind of light bulb. When he duly reported back with what he'd been sent for, Henry rewarded him with the princely sum of sixpence (approximately two and a half pence in today's money).

His first official work for the Arts Council was with actor Max Adrian. This Portora old boy was Dr Pangloss in Leonard Bernstein's *Candide* in Boston in 1956. (I was very impressed by his Jacques in *As You Like It* in Stratford in 1962.) But good old Northern Ireland was not interested; his tour was cancelled after one week at the Arts Theatre.

Brendan continued to work on various Arts Council productions and eventually became stage manager for the ballets when Fergus Gilligan left.

He was responsible for publicity and, with others, arranged the link-up between Norman Maen and UTV in 1981 to surprise Miss Mulholland on the occasion of the thirtieth anniversary of the founding of the ballets. Beforehand, Patricia was querulous, complaining that she had to get her hair done and asking why she had to go to the studio etc. But, of course, she was delighted afterwards and amazed at the phone calls and good wishes that came flooding in.

When the Arts Council stopped funding the Patricia Mulholland Irish Ballet Company (in an unnecessarily arbitrary way, in the view of many, though anyone who ever worked with her knew how autocratic and downright difficult at times she could be), Brendan Carson became a true friend to the company. There were other technical staff, like Noel, who helped out with staging the ballets in the Arts Theatre, but Brendan's voluntary contribution to the venture was indispensable.

Outwardly, Patricia was quite flippant about the withdrawal of funding and, truth to tell, she was not quite as dependent on their financial help as she might once have been. But those close to her believe that she felt the blow more than she allowed people to see. She could not possibly have kept coming up with new work in the same way as she had done in the past. Her health (including her diminishing control of the fiddle), possibly even her age, and the changing nature of the composition of her classes all conspired against the sort of work that could continue to attract official funding from the Arts Council. However, such was the esteem in which she was held that loyal supporters rallied round and kept the company afloat for a decade.

When Eileen O'Connor heard the news, she organised a sponsored "dancethon". Eileen's daughters were keen and capable dancers; Kathy now has her own school of dancing and has followed in the footsteps of Patricia Mulholland in producing Irish Ballets.

In spring 1991, Margot Brown organised a surprise anniversary party for Miss Mulholland in the Landsdowne Court Hotel in Belfast. Poor Patricia was led into a darkened room, suspecting nothing, and suddenly all the guests jumped out. She recovered graciously and enjoyed meeting all the old friends who attended.

Grainne Gilmore and Sister Mary Turley (a dancer in another life) involved themselves in working to ensure that Patricia Mulholland was presented with the Flax Trust Ireland 1991 Award for the greatest contribution to reverence for cultural difference in Northern Ireland. A second source of consolation was the Flax Trust Bursary, an entirely separate award, which is given to a group deemed to have encouraged cross-community links.

Caitriona Crilly, Robert Hunter, Kevin Rafferty, Paddi Lamb, Patricia O'Neill, John Mooney and Lillias Reilly re-enact the battle from Angus Óg *at the 40th anniversary of the Patricia Mulholland Irish Ballet Company held in Belfast in 1991.*

Bantry Bay
First and last performance: Golden Threads Theatre, Belfast, 1991.

This was the last ballet ever to be produced by Patricia Mulholland. There had been no Arts Council funding for several years, so there was not the same professional approach to design and costume. Nor were there many boys available, as they just did not come to Irish dancing class in the numbers that they had in the past.

Miss Mulholland did not spare herself when it came to her contribution to the new work. First, she chose an abstract theme so that the small number of male dancers was of no account. Secondly, she composed three new reels and some slip-jig tunes. And thirdly, she even went to the extreme of handing over some of her favourite outfits to the wardrobe department.

Mrs King from Bangor, who can always be found in the front row at Bangor Festival, made all the costumes.

Miss Mulholland, Kevin Campbell, John and Valerie Garvin, and Jo Tomelty, watching dancers rather ruefully at the 1991 anniversary.

Water had always been an inspiration for Patricia, from her enjoying the feeling of rain on her face to the power she could see in the waves of the ocean. The ballet evoked different emotions, suggested by images as diverse as the danger of a maelstrom, portrayed by Kathy O'Connor in the set dance *The Whirlpool*, and the sentimentality of the song *The Meeting Of The Waters*. This last was sung by Dr Sean Donnelly.

There were about sixteen of a cast in the ballet, mostly girls, and it was performed only once – in the Golden Threads Theatre on Belfast's Crumlin Road.

Patricia Mulholland's later years were bedevilled by ill health, but she kept going, working right up to just months before she died at the age of seventy-seven. She simply did not have the energy she once had and, sadly, lost the ability to cope with a demanding career.

Despite her own determination and the help from all her well-wishers, an era had ended.

Sidestep – Mulholland Dancers on Tour

None, I think, equalled in beauty and delight the appearances of the Irish Ballet . . . that tribute still stands to these young artists and their gifted founder.
Sam Hanna Bell

From the mid-1940s, when they started to make a name for themselves, Patricia Mulholland's dancers were much in demand to perform outside Ireland. These invitations continued right up until the end of Patricia's life and, for the most part, came from international festivals. International travel in the '40s and '50s was not the commonplace activity that it is now, and one can only imagine the excitement that these invitations created. The dancers already had plenty of experience of being away together as a group, at All-Ireland and Ulster Championships, and their enjoyment of these events was equalled, if not outshone, by the fun they were to have abroad. The element of competition was removed, of course, leaving the way open for a more relaxed time. One of their first visits was to Wales, to the Eisteddfod.

And their travels were to extend beyond the shores of the United Kingdom. For instance, they went to Denmark and Sweden and met people there from all walks of life, including the Swedish royal family. Yvonne Hood recalls a folk ballet they saw here. Might it be possible that this was a seed that would produce such a harvest?

Princess Margaret greets (L-R): Bridie Begley, Maureen McCann, Yvonne Hood, Patricia King and Sheila Fitzpatrick in Edinburgh in 1948.

Group members at the 1950 Eisteddfod. Front row, L-R: Brian Coleman, Patricia Mulholland, Madeleine Mackey, Leonard McGrath. Back row: Bridie Begley, Brian Lilly, Patricia King, Yvonne Hood and Norman Maternaghan.

One of the international festivals they attended was in Edinburgh in 1948.

Norman Maternaghan had to travel to Edinburgh a day later than the rest of the company. His parents left him to the airport. While his father was in some trepidation, his mother was quite enthusiastic about his flight, as he was himself, and thrust a handful of white fivers into his fist for his journey. There was some mix-up, for nobody met him as planned on the other side and he was forced to take the unusual step of taking a taxi (apparently he's been taking them ever since) and arrived in just enough time to change for a performance.

Mulholland dancers enjoying the company of some locals in Venice in 1949.

The dancers also attended a festival in Venice in 1949, which they all enjoyed enormously. In fact, Norman had such a wonderful time that he could never bear to go back in case it would not live up to his expectation.

Patricia's teams also danced in Pamplona and Majorca.

The Festival of Britain in 1951 has been mentioned before – an occasion when Patricia brought a team of Guides to dance in London. They subsequently appeared on the Pathé newsreel in cinemas all over the UK.

Mulholland dancers appeared in the Albert Hall in London several times at Folk Dance and Song festivals during the '50s and '60s.

At one such event in 1962, a Macedonian team and the Mulholland dancers were voted the most popular visitors to the event. Shortly after their return from London, I remember a rehearsal in the Scout Hall on the Antrim Road when some of the men grabbed snooker cues from the table and did an impromptu performance of a Belgian Stick dance that they'd seen in London. Shortly afterwards, there was an earthquake in Macedonia, and Kevin Campbell recalls how the dancers took a more personal interest in the tragedy because of the friends they'd made there.

Dancing in the Albert Hall, London, 1962.

The critic AV Coton wrote in the *Daily Telegraph* of one appearance in the Albert Hall that the Mulholland dancers, '. . . showed some delicate country dances in a unique idiom. Here the balance and the footwork were quite magical in effect, and while the men seemed to be treading velvet, the girls stepped only on air throughout.' He went on to state that the Irish dances were probably the finest of the entire folk canon of the British Isles.

Miss Mulholland and some of her dancers sampling perfume in London, 1952.

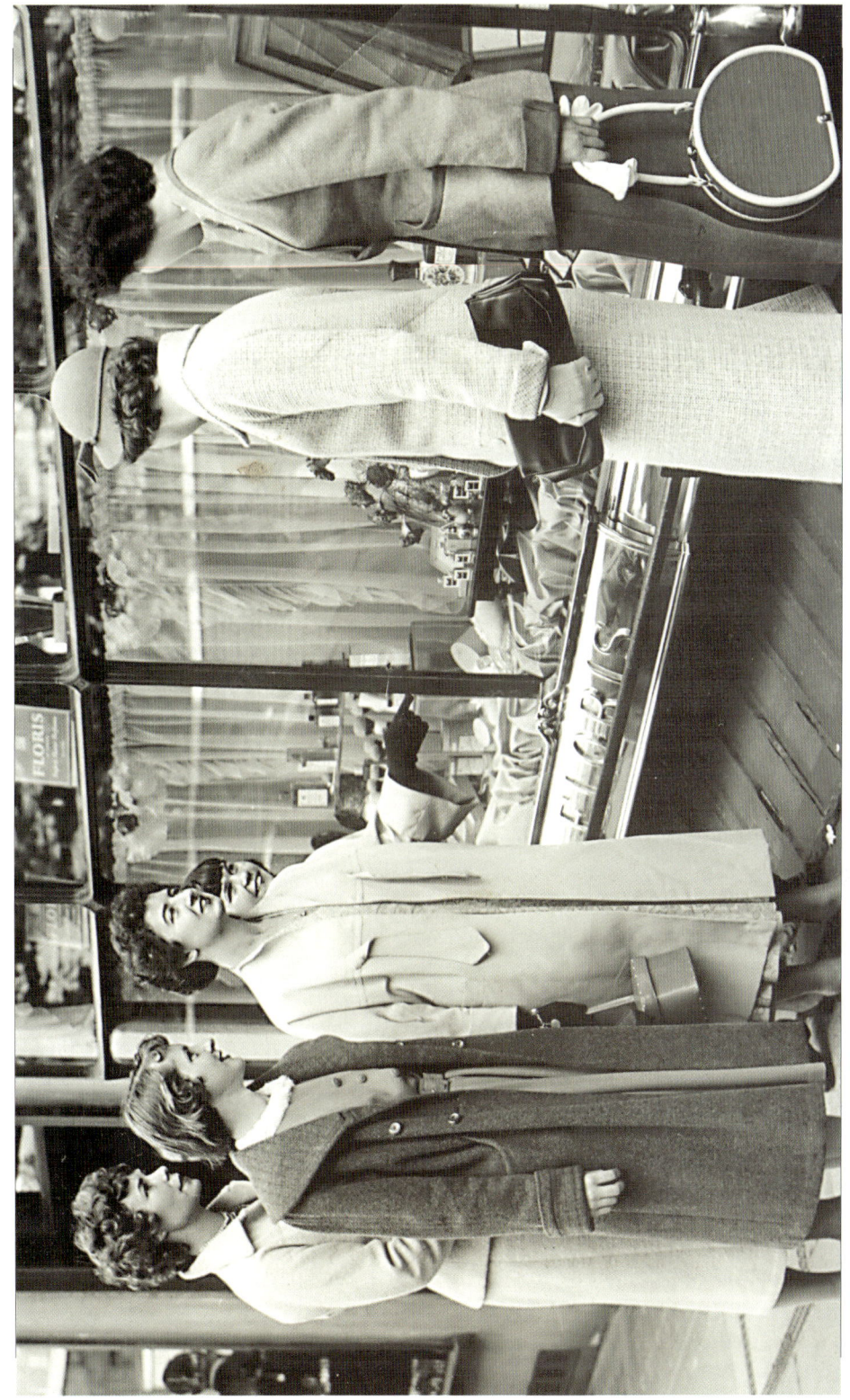
Miss Mulholland and some of her dancers window-shopping in London.

In 1957, two Mulholland dancers, Patricia King and Audrey Clarke, went to Russia. Patricia King had been to Belfast Royal Academy, where she'd been particularly strong in art and at games. Her Aunt Ruth encouraged her to join the Guides and it was as a Guide that she was introduced to Irish dancing and Patricia Mulholland. Once she discovered that she was good at dancing, she became quite committed to it. She was part of the team who danced for Princess Margaret on several occasions and was also part of the Guide team who had such a good time at the Festival of Britain.

Patricia became an inspired and inspiring teacher of art at Sullivan Upper, where she took over from George McCann (Mercy Hunter's husband). There seems to be an invisible thread connecting all the actors in this episode, for Patricia's then fiancé, James Hawthorne, had, as a student, taught Audrey Clarke at Methody. He was at Art College at the same time as Norman Maternaghan, Patricia's leading man in *Cúchulainn*.

Audrey Clarke also learned her first basic steps in Irish dancing from Guide leaders, but her first trip outside Northern Ireland as a dancing Guide was with the team trained by Patricia Mulholland for a conference in Oxford. They stayed in Burnham (a stately home near Beaconsfield), had their own butler and met such dignitaries as Lady Baden-Powell.

However, their biggest audience and most enthusiastic reception was a result of Audrey's singing talent. She was a member of the Belfast Girl Singers, who were invited to an international cultural display in Russia in 1957. This group had often included some folk dancing in their performances before this. Audrey and her friend Patricia were very keen to go. Mind you, Patricia's fiancé accompanied them, disguised, as he put it, as a Belfast Girl Singer. However, their dancing teacher disapproved. She denied them the use of the Mulholland costume and they had to use the one they'd worn in their Guides team instead. This costume was blue.

Russia, being Communist and atheist, was anathema to a Catholic as devout as Patricia Mulholland. She was fervent and pious, very conservative when it came to Church regulations, and would not have dreamed of disobeying them or doing anything that smacked of unorthodoxy. For instance, the dancers were performing out of doors one cold Ash Wednesday in Dublin. She insisted that her niece must not eat meat on this day of abstinence but take the only alternative, which, in this case, was an egg dish. The result was that the niece was sick and finished even hungrier than she'd started.

One day in her home during a thunderstorm, she surprised me by reaching for her rosary beads and clutching them until the thunder and lightning passed over.

The Cold War was very much a part of the political scene then. The rivalry between the West and the Soviet bloc meant that you couldn't just hop on a plane to Moscow or vice versa without letting the relevant authorities know your intentions. Audrey and Patricia had their names entered in police files before they left.

The Folk Festival that Audrey and Patricia were attending was the first since the closing of the Iron Curtain and there was huge excitement in the country on this account. There were dancers and musicians representing many areas – even China and India – travelling to the festival.

John Beckett, the lute player, got on the train at Ostend and travelled with them the rest of the way. The journey took a week and was not a comfortable one.

Patricia King in Cúchulainn, *1953.*

L-R: Kay Simpson (MD, Belfast Girl Singers), Audrey Clarke and Patricia King admire the view from their train in Russia.

They sat on hard wooden seats, three facing three, and Jimmy recalls that Audrey and Patricia looked different from the Russians on the train, not just because of their clothes, but also because they sat up straight, whereas the others slumped in their seats. There seemed to be one style of dress for all the women: a cotton frock with puff sleeves. They wore ankle socks with low-heeled black shoes. Local women gave no impression of being interested in their appearance.

Patricia and Audrey with two translators and an unusual Russian hat!

Crowds met the dancers at every station . . . . . . and on every street.

There was no buffet car, so they bought what they could at stations and picnicked on the train. Patricia's and Audrey's training in the Guides (perhaps it was an innate gift) meant that they managed to stay clean and tidy despite the privations, even when the water ran out. But not everyone in their party met the challenge with the same success.

At every station, there were crowds waiting for them – even in the middle of the night. Patricia and Audrey felt that the journey had been worth the effort for this alone. At one point, they had to change trains because the tracks were a different gauge.

In Moscow, they were ferried about in lorries, and again the spectators came out in their thousands.

Audrey's recollection of the halls they performed in is that they were all wonderful. At the first concert, there were impressive displays by Ukrainian dancers, including the women who moved around smoothly as if on castors, and Jimmy wondered to himself if two girls doing a two-hand reel or slip-jig would be able to hold their own there.

He needn't have worried, for they were mobbed by the young men in the audience. Indeed, after every performance, they received four or five curtain calls and flowers were thrown on stage. Jimmy then began to wonder if his ring would stay on Patricia's finger, so much adulation came her way.

When they were travelling round Moscow, they were given Irish tricolours to carry at first. Then Jimmy pointed out that this might not be too popular at home in some quarters, so they made up some kind of Ulster flag to wave.

Patricia, left (incidentally showing engagement ring), translator and Audrey, with armfuls of flowers.

They went to a gymnastics display in the Lenin Stadium and saw Khrushchev from a distance.

There they saw, for the first time, the kind of mass pattern-making that we take for granted now at Olympic Games ceremonies or the like, where people carry differently coloured cards and hold them up at the appropriate time to make designs.

Mass pattern displays inside the Lenin Stadium, Moscow.

Patricia and Audrey perform while, in the background, a McPeake piper accompanies them and smokes one cigarette at least that Khrushchev didn't get!

The McPeakes, who were also part of the Belfast contingent, played for the dancing and they actually met the Russian leader Khrushchev who, they complained, showed a fondness for their cigarettes.

A highlight of the visit was seeing the famous ballerina Ulanova dancing the role of Juliet in the Bolshoi Theatre.

They were away for a month and tasted vodka and champagne for the first time – drinking both from mugs!

Russia was still a totalitarian regime at this time and the populace was obviously deprived of what outsiders took for granted, like a choice in toiletries. Audrey remembers the ubiquitous smell of the government soap.

Jimmy recalled how a group of lady pharmacists came up to them to ask if they might talk to them. One thing they were keen to know about was modern art – they wanted to know if the visitors had seen Picasso's work, for instance, and what it was like. In communist Russia, modern art was considered a symptom of the decadence of life in the West. As a student, for example, Kirill Sokolov (later a popular artist in the Soviet Union) was reported to the authorities simply because of his interest in Picasso.

Patricia, as she was a teacher of art, was well-qualified to answer their questions. In fact, during the successful run of *Cúchulainn*, she was studying for her final teaching diploma at the Belfast College of Art, which led one local paper to use the headline, 'From the Easel to the Footlights.'

Patricia outside the Bolshoi Theatre.

When they came home, they had to report to the RUC station at Castlereagh because they'd been behind the Iron Curtain. However, they were able to convince the authorities that they posed no threat to local security and their names were erased from the files.

Whether Patricia Mulholland liked it or not, her brand of Irish dancing had been seen and appreciated in Communist Russia.

When we were going to different places here in Ireland, we normally travelled on a bus or train. But for some reason we all went to Termonfeckin (outside Drogheda) in a convoy of separate cars. Frances Tomelty and I accompanied Gerry O'Hare and his brother Seán in their car. We were behind Stella O'Neill and her party, and the whole way down, we could not help but admire Stella's hand signals – she was not simply graceful while dancing but even when signalling to other motorists, especially when slowing down, when her gesture resembled the action of a swan's wing.

Audrey and Patricia at the Kremlin.

Trips to national and international festivals continued throughout the '50s and '60s, staging excerpts from ballets as well as team dances, and the dancers had plenty of free time to enjoy themselves between exhibitions. One such was to Royan in Charente Maritime in France.

Entry ticket to the gala in Royan, France.

Marching in Royan, Charente Maritime, France.

Bernie Gallagher, Fionnuala Flanagan and Michael Slevin at the RTÉ recording of
The Midnight Court *at Jerpoint Abbey in Kilkenny in 1966.*

In 1966, RTÉ made a film of the Brian Merriman epic poem *Cúirt An Mheán Oíche* (*The Midnight Court*), produced by Louis Lentin, on location in Jerpoint Abbey in Kilkenny. It starred Fionnuala Flanagan, Bernadette Gallagher, Derry Power and Eoin Ó Súilleabháin, among others. Patricia Mulholland was invited to choreograph, and her dancers also provided the mob for the crowd scenes.

Local residents visiting Jerpoint Abbey during a break from rehearsal.

Those who know this eighteenth-century broad satire will be aware of its bawdy nature. We all went along to Newington Street before work started on the dancing to hear a synopsis of the poem and it was perhaps just as well that very few of the dancers, or Miss Mulholland herself, had any more than a *cúpla focail*. For instance, there was a cue for us all to laugh at a description of a young woman's notorious behaviour all over the countryside:

Ach bheirim don phláigh í lá mar chínn í
Leagha láimh le Gárus sínte,
Caite ar an ród'is gan orlach fúithi
Ag gramaisc na móna ar bhóithre Dhubhrois.

This is translated by Patrick C Power (*The Midnight Court*, 1971):

'But a plague upon her! I used to see her by day
Near to Garas Mills stretched and laid
Thrown on the road and with nothing beneath
With the turf-cutting mob from Dooras boreens.'

The word *móin* means turf in Irish. We could all recognise *móna* – from *Bord na Móna* briquettes etc – and would laugh away, but we had no real idea of the intricacies, or indeed, indelicacy of the charges brought against the accused in the court of the title.

One senior member of the company thought he was impressing us with his expert knowledge of Irish when he exhorted us to be ready to laugh when Eoin Ó Súilleabháin said, '. . . *na móna.*' Brian Bunting, who had more Irish than any of the rest of us, mischievously asked him, 'Is that just after he says, "*Fornocht do chonnac thú, a áille go háille, Is do dhallas mo shúil ar eagla go stanfainn.*"?'

'Yes,' he said, 'that's right.'

Fornocht . . . etc is the first verse of *Diúltú* – a poem by Pádraic Pearse. (Joan Denise Moriarty was commissioned to produce a ballet for the 1979 Pearse centenary and chose this poem as its theme.)

Musicians Pilib O'Laoghaire, James Mullen and Edward O'Farrell enjoy a joke with the RTÉ floor manager during the recording at Jerpoint Abbey.

A little learning is a dangerous thing. On one occasion, we were guests of the Royal Scottish Dancing Society, and one of their members, fully accoutred, showed us his *scian dubh* and informed us gravely that *scian* meant black and *dubh* meant knife. It's actually the other way round.

The location shooting for this film, Jerpoint Abbey in Kilkenny, was very isolated and most meals were taken in nearby Thomastown.

On the first day, my friend Suzy McGuigan and I were walking over the bridge there when a man leaned out of a passing car and asked us, 'Say, there, do you want to be in pictures?' We were already in one!

We worked all night, from seven in the evening until five in the morning, and an abiding and dramatic memory of that time is coming home in a bus through the misty plains at sunrise.

Several of us were boarding in a house in Kilkenny (you had to be up early to be sure of the bathroom), where every wall, door and table were covered with holy pictures, statues and what used to be called "pious ejaculations". The one on our bedroom door (there were three of us sharing) read *Jesus, Mary and Joseph 300 days*. It was reminiscent of a TV show called *Me Mammy*, which starred Milo O'Shea; perhaps its designer had boarded there too! What our Protestant colleagues thought of it all, they were too discreet to say.

Patricia Mulholland (Miss Mulholland's niece), Catherine Gilmore, Margot Bell, Brian Bunting, Marlene Bailie and Kevin Campbell, strolling through Kilkenny, 1966.

The nights were quite cold. It was late August and early September and there were no toilet facilities (Jerpoint being a ruin), so in answering a call of nature, in the almost absolute darkness, one had to risk nettle stings and tripping over colleagues similarly engaged. We realised then for the first time that being on location is not all a bed of roses.

The men had to wear wigs, and two of them, John Garvin and Brian Bunting, caused quite a stir when they drove into Dublin, in full costume and wig, to book seats for the new film, *Dr Zhivago*, for a number of us. When we went to see this, it was surprising how aware we'd become of the technicalities of filming, even in such a short time, especially in our observation of crowd scenes. One bright spark pointed out that the mob singing outside the restaurant (where Julie Christie shoots Rod Steiger) were all going 'la-la.'

Miss Mulholland's niece – also called Patricia Mulholland – had to act as a stand in for Fionnuala Flanagan in one scene and it was fascinating to watch how she metamorphosed into the actress.

Other scenes were shot in Montrose Studios, Dublin, and there was a party at the end in Groom's Hotel in Parnell Street at which the spirit of Merriman seemed to have taken over Michael Slevin, the film's co-director. At one point, he pulled down, or pretended to pull down, the zip on Miss Mulholland's dress at which juncture she left, understandably enough. Perhaps we all seemed rather naïve Northerners to the "arty-farty" personnel who were involved in this film and so they took a perverted delight in shocking us. But, truth to tell, we *were* quite shocked a lot of the time by the language and the behaviour of some of them. Miss Mulholland took us all out for a meal in The Fleet when official business was over, and it could be said that she'd been driven to drink, for I believe it was on this occasion that she first tasted an alcoholic drink.

While in Dublin, we were all staying in a hotel in Westland Row. One night, the entire company was in Kevin Campbell's room for a chat and the manageress woke Miss Mulholland to complain that there were girls in one of the men's rooms! There were, indeed, about seventeen of us. What made Miss Mulholland angry was not our behaviour (these were innocent days even after a fortnight with the *Midnight Court* crowd) but the fact that it was the first night in a very long time that she had fallen asleep without having to resort to a sleeping pill. Throughout her life, she was a poor sleeper. Audrey Clarke remembers that she sometimes used to use this time to work out new choreography.

On another occasion, after dancing at a concert in the Gaiety Theatre in Dublin, about ten of us decided to stay overnight in the flat of the aforementioned Suzy McGuigan, who was working in the city by then. Her landlady took not at all kindly to this rather unrealistic arrangement and threw us all out – including Suzy and her sister Jane. Fortunately, Suzy had a friend living close by without the encumbrance of a resident landlord and so we all trooped round to his place. We "snuck" in as quietly as we could, not wanting to antagonise anyone else, only to discover in the morning that the place was empty!

Shortly after our adventures with eighteenth-century Irish poetry, we were on our travels again, this time to the Isle of Man.

Mulholland dancers at the Viking Festival of Peel in the Isle of Man, 1967. Back row, L-R: Linda Connolly, Niall Boden, Frances O'Hara, Edmund Henry, Frances Tomelty, Ciarán Doherty, Michelle Forster, Kevin Campbell, Sharon Tansley, Reggie McClure. Front row: Marlene Bailie, Kevin Rafferty, Joyce Ann Henry, John Garvin, Sheelagh Gilligan, Brian Bunting, Patricia Mulholland, Kevin Lawson, Catherine Gilmore, Gerry O'Hare and Ursula Quinn.

Patricia Mulholland and Margot Bell fraternising with three "Vikings" at the Isle of Man Festival accompanied by Sharon Tansley, Michelle Forster, Catherine Gilmore, Sheelagh Gilligan, Carolyn Revie, Marlene Bailie and Linda Connolly.

On our first sojourn in the Isle of Man, I remember a lovely morning in Peel when Frances Tomelty and I rose early, went out and hired ponies and trotted about through leafy boreens. Afterwards, on our way to the bus for Douglas, Frances posted some kippers to her father – he was partial to this Manx delicacy. Our energy back then seems boundless now; we spent the afternoon rowing round the bay (where we met fellow dancer Gerry O'Hare on the little island there – he was returning to his roots as it were, for his father was from Douglas) before returning to Peel for the evening performance.

The casino also provided a lot of amusement for some.

In 1968, the Viking Festival of Peel invited the Mulholland dancers to return and perform as they had done in 1967, to the enjoyment of all concerned. This festival commemorates the Vikings' arrival in Peel. It's an odd concept, celebrating being robbed, killed and enslaved by invaders, but a seemingly popular one. Stockades, representing the Manx villages, were set up on the beach at Peel. The dancers were

General Stuart's Reel	Lord McLay's Reel
Golden Pheasant	Fergus McIver
Cauld Kail in Aberdeen	Letham Ladies
Laird of Milton's Daughter	Muirland Willie
Maxwell's Rant	Bonnie Brux
Garry Strathspey	Hamilton Rant
Peggy's Wedding	**JACKIE JOHNSTONE**
JACKIE JOHNSTONE	Miss Mary Douglas
Duke and Duchess of Edinburgh	Silver Tassie
Middleton Medley	Cadgers in the Canongate
Bonnie Anne	Shoulder to Shoulder
Robertson Rant	Neidpath Castle
Strathspey, Reel and Reel of Tulloch	Todlem Hame

Programme for a céilí in Leeds showing Scottish dances.

in a specially marked stockade, ready to appear and dance after the "pillaging", but a group of invaders got carried away with their enthusiasm for the fight and attacked the stockade that contained Miss Mulholland and her company. If you've never seen a violin bow raised in anger, then you can hardly imagine what a good weapon it makes, for Miss Mulholland fended off her attackers with gusto. The event was actually quite frightening, but it showed a side of the woman that no one could have imagined.

On the first visit, the dancers performed team dances, but in 1968 they chose an excerpt from *Angus Óg*.

One year, we all went to Leeds to a festival of the Royal Society of Scottish Dancing. We could not believe the indefatigable enthusiasm for Scottish dancing exhibited by the members of the society. Not only did they dance all afternoon and watch exhibitions, but they also finished off each evening with a céilí and then repaired to various members' homes and listened to Jimmy Shand records. Scottish dancing can look so graceful you'd think it would be less demanding than Irish, but if you're accustomed to using a different set of muscles, it can be remarkably taxing. We stayed at a college of education residence; it was very relaxing to be able to use the swimming pool in the evenings.

Volunteers from the society ferried us round the dales and to and from official venues. One of the drivers who picked us up at the station drove a racy little sports car – there was a scramble to see which of the men would be chauffeured by its attractive blonde driver. She caused a sensation early in the proceedings, innocently making light chat by announcing that her father had spent time in Ireland – oh yes, he'd been in the Black and Tans!

Dancers receive an enthusiastic greeting at Cork train station en route to the Cork International Festival.

Mulholland dancers appeared at Cork International Festival more than once as invited guests to entertain the visiting competitors. Renowned musician and chairman of the festival Aloys Fleischman was anxious to demonstrate the best of Irish dancing at this prestigious event.

On several occasions throughout her career, Miss Mulholland had been asked to bring dancers to the USA. But every time an invitation arrived, either the dates didn't suit or her health prevented her making the arrangements. However, Mulholland dancers did make it to America – eventually.

Three of her principals, Kathy O'Connor, Carmel McGovern and Leslie Baird, danced in New York in 1992. They performed various examples of the Mulholland style.

Sadly, that was two months after Miss Mulholland's death.

Carmel McGovern in Irish dancing costume in the New York Hyatt Hotel, 1992.

Recall and Awards

I'd give up the dancing rather than the music . . . People used to say to me to teach, but I wouldn't have taught music for anything. I loved it too much.
Patricia Mulholland

I remember Miss Mulholland vividly.
She had a lovely face, dark curly hair and lively blue eyes with dark lashes. Her voice was always quite hoarse; as she talked to you, she had a characteristic way of leaning her head on her hand, index finger curved against her chin. She kept her fingernails short, of course, but usually polished with clear varnish, and always wore a loose wristwatch, marcasite for special occasions, which she rattled into place with a flick of the wrist. She was very partial to dramatic green-tweed capes, usually decorated with a large Tara Brooch, and was never without a gold Celtic cross on a chain round her neck. Her shoes were always comfortable-looking.

But what was she really like? What made her tick? When I think of her, I first hear her ready laugh and her voice calling over the sound of the fiddle and dancing feet. I think of all the fun I had in her company, even after leaving the dancing.

For instance, there was always a warm welcome to the Rosemary Street Festival for the visitor, whether adjudicator or spectator. Before my first attempt at judging the dancing, I was naturally unsure about whether I could actually discharge my duties as required. (In fact my hands shook along with the mark sheets when I got up to speak at first.) The fact that Miss Mulholland had asked me to try it was the only reason I was there. But she was most reassuring. 'Anyway,' she said, 'even if you do it all wrong, it won't matter, for we're all friends here.' Encouraged by this

Patricia Mulholland at a photo call.

Miss Mulholland caught in pensive mood.

disclaimer, I took to the adjudicating like a duck to water and all was going well until we arrived at a competition in which none of the prize-winners was a Mulholland dancer. As I passed Margot and her, to hand out the medals, she commented loud enough for everyone to hear, 'And not one of them mine!'

Apart from this momentary aberration, I always found the atmosphere at this festival warm and friendly. There was a fair bit of hidden "carry on", too: if a competitor who was plumper than the average dancer arrived on stage, chances were the choice of music would be something like *The Bag Of Potatoes* or *The Belfast Ham.*

Barry and Clive Kinghan, who'd been in the 1953 *Cúchulainn*, would often come along, as did Gerry Hobbs, the Comhdháil adjudicator. (Gerry privately "adjudicates" some competitions, with a prepared sheet, from his seat in the audience.) No matter what the circumstances of leaving had been, most people, with very few exceptions, came back eventually, whether as assistants, spectators, adjudicators or simply as visitors. One could always be sure to meet old friends at this event and Patricia loved to greet them.

Some years there would be a céilí on the last night and we'd all enjoy the exercise. During one *Haymaker's Jig*, Kevin Rafferty danced from start to finish, completely out of time and with his toes turned in. Other times, the competitors would devise and perform a revue and satirise the adjudicator. Ed Henry, Ciarán Hinds, Kevin Rafferty and Linda Tansley sent up George Leonard once, with devastating accuracy. Mr Leonard either was, or pretended to be, bewildered by their portrayal, but I, for one, remember him criticising the width of the elastic on a dancer's shoes! Dominic Graham, at one year's entertainment, did a marvellously exaggerated Mulholland slip-jig. During all of these occasions, the spectators would be nearly helpless with laughter and Miss Mulholland would take it all in good part.

There were always willing helpers at this event, too, making and serving meals (Yvonne Hood's scones were invariably delicious and Grainne Gilmore's offerings always something special). Margaret Thompson, Carolyn Revie and Bronagh Hinds were among those who also helped with calling competitors' numbers etc. What can only be described as a family atmosphere always prevailed.

After you had adjudicated at her festival, Patricia always wrote a letter of thanks – this was never simply by rote. She would take the time and trouble to appreciate certain aspects of the festival and compliment you on your contribution to its success. She was always generous, too, in her remuneration of adjudicators.

After performances of the ballets, Miss Mulholland was always surrounded by old friends dying to have a chat. I remember at one of these events, one of my boys was "lepping" off the stage, obviously inspired by what he'd seen, and I was vainly trying to stop him. Her reaction was to say, 'Imagine, I would have him if you lived here!'

However, there were also some fraught moments. I can remember the time she put the phone down in mid-conversation when I told her I couldn't attend a rehearsal. I remember having to bring her in all my costumes because of the *possibility* of my going to Aden to join my father for Christmas. (As it turned out, I didn't go: unfortunately, the High Commissioner's daughter was killed just before my proposed visit, so my trip was cancelled.)

Ciarán Hinds, left, and friends: Linda Tansley, Peter Sturdy, Patricia Gilligan and Anne Marie McLaughlin.

I remember disputes about tight trousers and an embargo on dancers going to Belfast's first skating rink, a whole furore about hair dye, whispered conversations downstairs in Newington Street about who said what at whose party, and a general over-zealous acting *in loco parentis* for people who were, many of them, over twenty-one.

However, I believe Patricia Mulholland was an exceptional woman.

She was the product of a background that was rigidly Catholic and fairly poor. Given this background and the circumstances of her early childhood, it is all the more remarkable that she contributed so much to the cultural life of Northern Ireland. She is an outstanding figure in the field of Irish dancing, particularly cross-community Irish dancing, and should be more widely recognised as such, particularly in her own country.

If we look at her formative years, we must be impressed by her sense of dedication. That music was important in the Mulholland household is obvious; the father had a good tenor voice and the children were sent to classes and instruments bought for them. The fashion of the time dictated that home entertainment was important in providing "good pastime". Singing, playing instruments, reciting poetry, were the ways many families passed their leisure time in the days before television took over the world. So it was from this sort of background in music that Patricia Mulholland was to emerge, rather than from a more bohemian life that one might suppose. Nor was she imbued with Irish culture in the way that, say, her teacher Peadar O'Rafferty was.

I remember how much enjoyment she derived from watching Cardiff Singer of the Year on television. Her influences and tastes seem to have been formed in an almost Victorian mould. Both Mulholland sisters showed an aptitude for music and so their lessons were to be more than just an enjoyable hobby; they would use this ability to provide a livelihood. Indeed, it was entirely through her own effort that she became so proficient a violinist, practising so diligently as to worry her mother.

It is perhaps no wonder that she showed little interest in Irish music at first. Her sister Stella was the Irish expert, as it were. She needed to play for her dancers and was building up a repertoire to suit her occupation. But Patricia was going to be a concert violinist and she was devoting all her energies to that end.

Now, there is a huge difference between playing a musical instrument alone and performing in front of an audience. Some people are perfectly competent instrumentalists in a private capacity; just don't ask them to play in company. (I have a cousin who, when his parents had visitors, would only play his melodeon in the hall, and a nephew who plays the piano beautifully as long as nobody's watching.)

Some are marvellous *répétiteurs*, accompanying soloists expertly at rehearsal but not doing nearly so well on stage. It's quite difficult to believe that Miss Mulholland really suffered from nerves. She could get up on any stage, in front of any kind of audience, and play exquisitely for her dancers without showing the remotest sign of nervousness. If, for some reason, you had to dance without her accompaniment, you felt the lack of it. Her presence and her playing provided huge support. Gerry O'Hare, who danced for Sheila Hughes before he became a Mulholland dancer, loved Seán Maguire's accompaniment and once told the famous fiddler that it was worth extra marks if he was playing for you at a competition. The same went for Miss Mulholland's playing. Curiously enough,

Seán Maguire, too, had played in orchestras before being completely dedicated to Irish music.

But then, accompanying is a different discipline from performing solo. An accompanist performs, of course, but he/she is not the main focus of attention. It is indisputable that many virtuoso performers have grave difficulties with their ability to overcome stage fright, to the extent that they have to seek psychological help.

I believe that there were certain influences at work on Patricia Mulholland in developing her attitude to life. One was the feeling of insecurity caused by changes in family circumstances. Another, a compounding of the first, was the fact that she was obliged to change her career due to circumstances beyond her control.

She herself, when describing taking over Stella's classes, underplayed it, as if it were the most natural thing in the world to change horses in mid-stream. At one level, it was an obvious line of action; Mrs Mulholland was angry when, against her wishes, Stella went off to get married.

Patricia was twenty-one when Stella got married on 29 June 1936, at 9.00am Mass in St Joseph's. Neither mother nor sister attended.

Stella comes across as having a lot more spirit than Patricia at this time. She'd been bringing home the bacon for several years and did not wait for Minnie's approval, probably knowing that it would not come. It seems rather odd that Patricia sided with her mother rather than her sister at this time, but she must have been in some conflict about it. There was absolutely no reason to disapprove of Stella's choice of husband. You might have thought that the Mulholland household would have welcomed a capable man with open arms (Frank, the only son, was just seventeen then). But Minnie and Patricia disapproved. Their own head of the household had seen his influence being steadily diminished. Why would they want another man on the scene?

Patricia was beginning to move in the sort of society that would never have opened up for her parents and even played in John Crowther's orchestra. John was quite a famous musician in his day in Belfast and wrote songs that were popular in the 1930s.

ORCHESTRA

Miss B. Turley (Leader). Miss F. Harrison. Miss C. Murphy.
„ E. Alexander. „ R. Irvine. „ E. O'Callaghan.
„ K. Cousins. Mrs. D. John. „ B. O'Callaghan.
„ E. Doak. Miss D. M'Crea. Mr. G. O'Neill.
„ D. Daunt. Mr. F. M'Crea. Miss M. Robertson.
„ N. Dolan. Miss P. M'Cleery. „ P. Scott.
Mr. D. Darcy. „ I. M'Donald. Mr. T. Stitt.
„ J. Donnan. „ M. M'Saveny. „ P. Sythes.
Miss D. Forster. „ W. Marsden. „ S. Taylor.
„ J. Forster. „ C. Matthews. „ W. Wilson.
„ C. Green. „ E. Mawhinney. Miss M. Wilson.
Mr. J. Green. „ M. Mercer. „ E. Wilson.
„ S. Gregg. „ P. Mulholland. Mr. J. Wylie.
Miss C. Harper.

Patricia Mulholland's name (bottom of middle row) in John Crowther's orchestra list.

She was starting to appear on concert programmes. Perhaps Mrs Mulholland was impressed by the new sorts of people her daughter was meeting. Patricia readily admitted that there had been a time when she looked down her nose at Irish music and that she saw the classical repertoire as socially more acceptable.

But who else was going to take Stella's classes? Were the pupils just to be let go? Of course not; good daughter Patricia could step in and fill the breach. And she did. But it can't have been done with any degree of equanimity at the time.

All her preparation up to this point had been towards an entirely different goal. She had had a dream and had been pursuing it single-mindedly. All right, things might change around her, but she was focussed; she was going to be a violinist. Then fate stepped in and drove her in another direction. Did she feel that becoming a dancing teacher was going to be only a postponement of her chosen career? Maybe she thought she'd go along with her mother's wishes for a while until an opportunity presented itself for returning to her first love. Of course, after a very short time she discovered that she had a real bent for the new career and the old dream faded away. But there was a pattern already established in her life – just as she became used to one set of circumstances, they would change.

Might it be possible that the Mulholland nervousness was a virtue being made of necessity? She undertook the teaching of Stella's classes because she was obliged to, but did she wonder about the road not taken? Did she chase away any doubts about her change of career by telling herself that she'd never have made it as a soloist anyway? Did she exaggerate the importance of the nerves because it reinforced the rightness of her choice? As she became established and successful as a teacher and choreographer, any doubts must have faded, but the stage fright by then had become part of the Mulholland legend, which she believed herself.

On the other hand, might taking Stella's place have presented her with a golden opportunity to rest from the labours required for entering an extremely demanding profession? And rather than admitting that she no longer wanted to rise to the challenge, did it suit her to say that she could have been a "contender" if only she hadn't suffered from nerves?

I believe that the seeds of her insecurity were sown in the upheavals of her early childhood. Just as the family was becoming used to one place, they'd have to move to another. It was not the moving in itself that was the problem, but the fact that Minnie and William disagreed about these changes and their antagonism filtered through to the young Patricia. And the seeds were then watered with the rain of snobbery.

Minnie was anxious to improve the lot of her family; this is not a bad thing in itself. She felt that if they could move up the social ladder, then they would not face the insecurity that was so much a part of their life with William. She could be amusing, if somewhat given to gossip, and she could never have been described as any sort of a shrinking violet. Did William begin to feel uncomfortable at home in an unequal battle – one wife, two daughters versus him and his son? Was Patricia caught in the middle, trying to be loyal to both? Mr Mulholland was still alive and fairly well until 1956, yet very few dancers visiting Newington Street ever saw him much – if at all. He was there but seemingly invisible.

Patricia Mulholland with her beloved violin.

It is possible that she inherited her musicality and artistry from her father. It's also possible that she developed a mindset under her mother's influence, a tendency to a fixedness of perception that, without a partner to leaven it, became an autocratic rigidity. It's all too easy a criticism, though perhaps no less valid, to suggest that she became a stereotypically narrow-minded spinster in some ways.

A niece called at the house one day after school just to pop in and visit. Patricia opened the door and sent her off with a threepenny bit. There seems to have been very little cordiality in Mulholland family relationships. And yet, her relations with her dancers could be close as any mother and child.

Patricia could have very fixed ideas about people with regard, for example, to relationships between them. She would have in mind a match for individuals who weren't remotely interested in each other and then take umbrage when things didn't turn out how she wanted. She disapproved of chosen spouses, when it was really none of her business, and could be icily cool, even to the point of breaking off relations with a perceived offender. She and her mother stopped all contact with various members of their family at one time or another, in one case the breach not being healed for ten years! How she squared this with a devout practice of religion is hard to fathom. Her religion played its part in the incident when her dancers went to Russia. In blind adherence to Catholic thinking of the time, she refused to allow two of her best dancers to wear their Mulholland costume behind the Iron Curtain; she didn't even have to consider it for a minute, and yet she would push her Protestant dancers out to Church on a Sunday morning with more energy than their parents probably would.

One morning, just after Internment (August 1971), she was on her way to Mass as usual and stopped to talk to a neighbour. This woman's son was serving a sentence in Long Kesh, but in a previous life he'd been a Mulholland dancer. Patricia had heard about riots in the prison on the wireless (loyalists were in charge of the republicans' food at the time – you can imagine the scenario) and asked warmly about the prisoner. His mother said that she hadn't had any word yet and Patricia told her she'd include him in her prayers at Mass. When she met this man after he'd "done his whack", she took his hand and slapped his wrist as you would a bold child.

But I suppose we are all, to some extent, a mixture of ambivalent ideas. She was a web of contradictions.

She was an obedient daughter to her mother and to her Church, seemingly unquestioningly so. Perhaps the feeling of being restrained rendered her more rebellious, consciously or subconsciously, in other circumstances. The minute she was told she couldn't do something, like, for example, play for dancers where the *Queen* might be played, then the blood seemed to rush to her head and the divil take the hindmost.

She would take it into her head that a certain individual was the right person to help her out with her teaching, maybe even to inherit her classes, and then would be disappointed or even displeased because that person had other ambitions. She would never have discussed these possibilities with the dancer concerned but would decide in her own mind that this was a good idea and then be amazed because he/she had no inkling about Patricia's plans – and no interest. She asked one dancer, a schoolteacher, one day out of the blue, 'What time can you be here on Monday?' The young woman answered that what with after-school duties it would probably be about four-thirty. 'Oh, you'd be no good, then. You couldn't take over the classes.' A few others were "approached" in this way.

And yet she could be generous to a fault, more loath to spend money on herself than on other people.

In fact, when you think about it, she didn't really have much time devoted to herself. She was certainly not self-indulgent in any way. You can't imagine her kicking off her shoes, pouring herself a large gin and tonic and sinking into an easy chair.

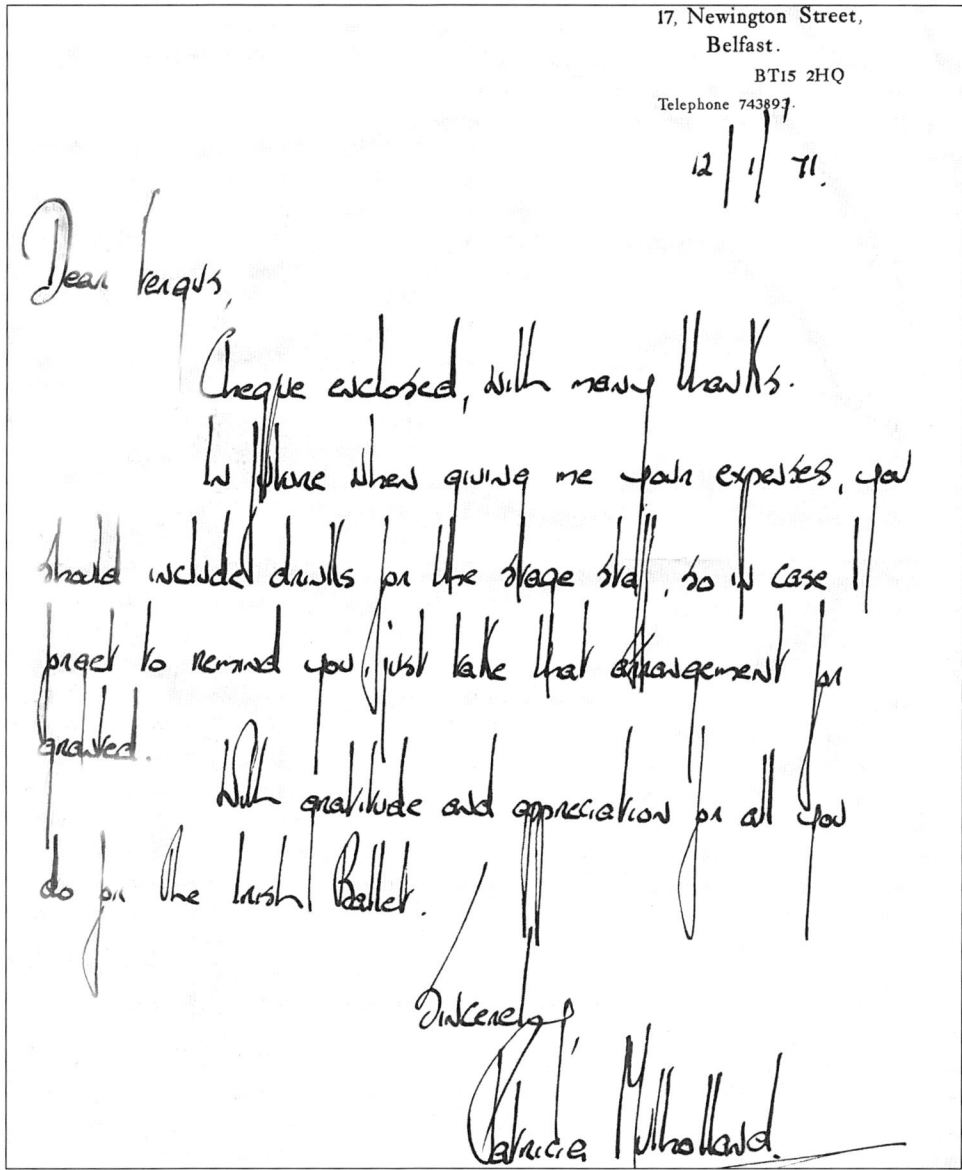

Letter from Miss Mulholland to Fergus Gilligan, reminding him to buy drinks for the stage crew, 1971.

She was an obedient daughter who worked hard to achieve results. She focussed on her career and gave abundantly of herself to her creation, the Irish Ballet Company. In her younger days, she had suffered chronically from dysmenorrhoea, she was prone to chest infections (might this have been a direct result of dust being kicked up from dancers' feet in dingy rehearsal rooms?), she had a thyroid operation, and then had two bouts of fighting cancer, one of which claimed her life.

She did not moan about her health or, indeed, about other trials and tribulations. She was flippant about her expulsion from the Irish Commission when it happened. Likewise, when the Arts Council funding dwindled and stopped, she was not, outwardly at any rate, disturbed by it.

Once, when she was burgled, she lay, pretending to be asleep, while the burglar made off with the family silver – which suggests a fair amount of sang-froid. However, just after this event, she asked Leslie Baird to stay with her for a day or two for protection. He was glad to provide her with reassurance, but no matter how loyal, I doubt if he would have been anything other than reluctant to prolong the close contact.

She had always been very attached to her mother, and during the latter's last years, spent what was left of herself in looking after her. Anyone who has any experience of senile dementia knows how demanding it is for the carer. She indulged her whims and often had to snatch sleep, stretched across her mother's bed, as and when Minnie's wakefulness allowed. I marvel at her steadfastness in this.

Marjorie Gilligan, Lena Tomelty and Sheelagh Gilligan in Donegal with the Irish Ballets, 1972.

During the last few days of her mother's life, Lena Tomelty and Marjorie Gilligan kept vigil with her. Mrs Tomelty gave her a cosy dressing gown for the wakeful nights.

When Minnie died in 1977, it didn't mean that Patricia experienced a period of relief and new-found leisure time to indulge herself. No, it was during this year that cancer first attacked her. She met this challenge with true grit. I remember her coming to Bangor Festival immediately after a treatment and you'd have thought she was just coming from the hairdresser's. I'm told she used to walk up the stairs in the hospital, rather than take the lift, when she was attending various clinics.

Patricia Mulholland was indeed an innovative and inspirational teacher. She taught us to dance, building on our first, faltering steps of the light double-jig, to reach the stage where we could tackle anything from interpreting myth and song in her unique blend of Irish, contemporary and balletic dance, to providing a *corps de ballet* for visiting opera and ballet groups.

Her demonstration of steps was particularly clear. She had no idiosyncrasies of movement to "muddy" your view of what you had to learn, so it was easy to pick up steps from her. Her teaching of mime or gesture was equally easy to follow.

We imbibed, too, almost without noticing, a love for all that is best in Irish traditional music; we took for granted her expert playing of wonderful airs, only rarely equalled in either variety or quality since her passing.

As dancers, either in class or in the ballets, we picked up by example, without any need for sermons, that we were all equal in diversity. We might have come from different districts or gone to different schools, but we were one when it came to being Mulholland dancers.

Patricia Mulholland was an attractive woman, both in mien and in manner. Her musical ability and artistry in choreography are legendary, so it is perhaps not so surprising that a person so blessed with some gifts should have been deficient in others.

Although she had sufficient business acumen to make the fullest use of her proven record as a good teacher – her classes were expensive by comparison with others – she has often been accused of lacking business sense when it came to her ballet company. She would not take advice in this sphere. Several well-wishers offered their expertise, but Patricia was reluctant to take steps that would have changed her company utterly – and possibly wrested control from her. If you think of the huge expenses that are necessary for any professional ballet company, no matter how small, and the uncertainty that surrounds any undertaking of this kind, perhaps she was more perspicacious than many thought. This reluctance to launch into a professional company may go some way to explain why her fame is limited to a relatively small sphere of influence. Few people under a certain age, outside the world of Irish dancing and even inside festival dancing, have heard of her – or if they have, do not realise the extent of her work.

She was single-minded, capable of overcoming personal discomfort and even severe ill health for the sake of her company's performance – yet was often not good at dealing with people. She was so absorbed by her dream and dedicated to her work that she found it hard to see that not everyone was imbued with the same determination. Her company was amateur, after all. One young boy was looking forward to a school trip to Paris and mentioned it to Patricia. She told him that if he went, he'd miss the big part that she had for him in her new ballet. He withdrew from the holiday only to find that the big part was one of a chorus of little birds.

She expected others to work just as hard as she did, without any commensurate payment. Most people who had any long-term dealings with her eventually had a fight of one kind or another. And yet, even after the cooling of relations, she was capable of gracious gestures. For example, Marjorie Gilligan and she had often joked about her Tara china tea set, and even though there had been a distinct break between them for many years, the tea set was delivered to Marjorie according to the terms of Patricia's will.

She could be impressed by some to the point that she was slightly afraid of them, and yet she could overlook some of her pupils who were most loyal. I have seen her introduce a few of her dancers to visiting dignitaries while ignoring those she deemed just a little less important on the social scale. Yet these same "unimportant" people had families who used to book whole rows of seats for her performances. This unfortunate, snobbish shortsightedness made sometimes for unnecessary offence.

Clare McRandal in her costume for the chorus of little birds.

Her selective criticism could be quite puzzling: why would one dancer get away with cutting her hair and another wouldn't? (Patricia expected girls to keep their hair long for the ballets.) Why would one be reprimanded publicly for imperfect table manners and another wouldn't? Unfortunately, the answer is to be found in her uneven attitude to people because of their social standing. To be fair, she did not allow snobbery to influence her decisions when it came to selecting personnel for roles in ballets or places in team dances. Background was important, but could be disregarded when set against dancing ability. Sometimes you felt that in pointing out someone else's faults, she was demonstrating just how au fait with polite behaviour she was herself.

She could rarely bring herself to praise the work of ex-pupils as enthusiastically as one might have expected. She just did not seem to feel comfortable enough in her own skin to acknowledge that there's room for everyone, and they all can have their day in the sun. For instance, one of her most accomplished dancers, Norman Maen, talks about how he met and chatted to another of his mentors, Jack Cole, some time after he had made it to the top of his profession. Cole pointed out that his influence was no longer detectable in Norman's work, in the way that it had been initially, that he had developed his own approach and so on. Norman would have loved to have had this sort of discussion with Miss Mulholland, but it never happened.

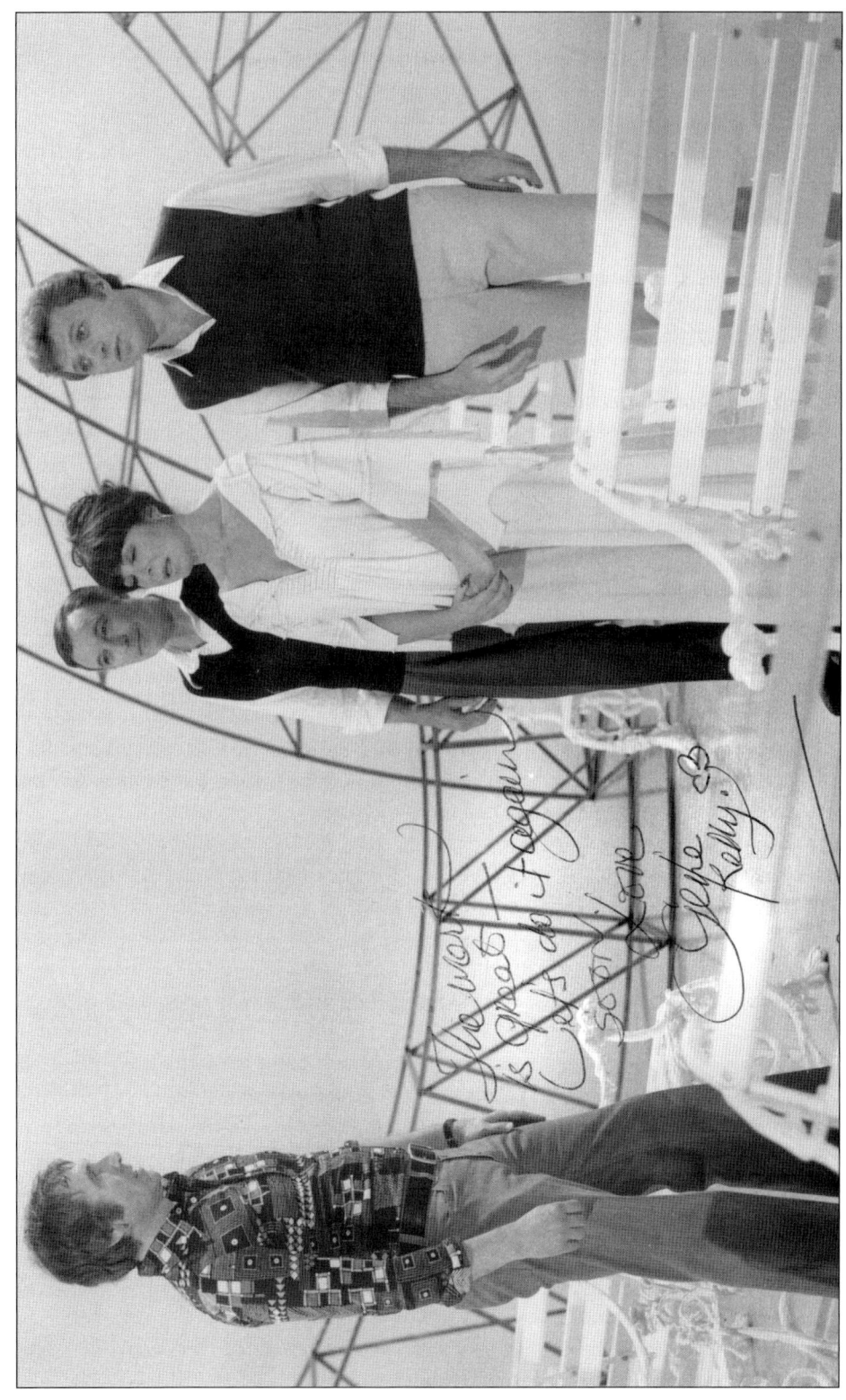

Norman Maternaghan/Maen directing Gene Kelly, Eydie Gormé and Steve Lawrence in Hollywood.

It is invidious to highlight these shortcomings, but they go some way to illustrating the complexity of the woman's character. In my view, this suggests that her achievements were all the more remarkable.

It was, perhaps, the tension between these two facets of her personality – the dogmatism versus the insecurity – that fuelled her artistic drive. Would she have striven so hard to develop her own brand of Irish dancing if she'd been more comfortable? If she'd just been satisfied with merely making a living from the profession that she found herself engaged in, would Irish Ballet ever have seen the light of day?

The energy that she had invested in becoming a proficient violinist and in considering a career as a solo musician was not to be dissipated, rather channelled into her choreography. That artistic drive coupled with an occasional rebellious streak enabled her to break new ground.

Several of her protégés went on to have successful careers in the world of dance, on the stage and in films. But even those of us who took a completely different direction for our chosen career cannot deny her influence. There are few, if any, ex-Mulholland dancers who do not have a love for Irish music at its best. A lot of us have had a lifelong interest in dance and the artistic side of things, which makes life more interesting and provides a respite from the more mundane. We became individuals who are more cultured as a result of our early exposure to the best in Irish culture.

In addition, most important of all, the friendships that were forged in Newington Street have withstood the test of time, friendships that would never had started at all if it weren't for Miss Mulholland's dancing class.

Jimmy Hawthorne's wife Patricia King met Anne O'Hara at the dancing. One, a Protestant from Doagh, the other, a Catholic from the Antrim Road in Belfast, they were the closest of friends throughout their lives, sadly dying within a short time of each other.

If Patricia Mulholland were to be remembered for nothing other than the friendships that were forged at her classes and in her ballet company, it would be a valuable legacy indeed. Those of us who were lucky enough to come under her influence were immeasurably enriched by the experience.

The goodwill that greeted me in the pursuit of this project in virtually every encounter reassured me that it was worthwhile. People wanted to talk about her, were eager to recollect their experiences, and all felt the better for having known her.

Where would I place Patricia Mulholland in the pantheon of notable Irish artists? I find myself in a quandary, not because I don't believe she deserves a place – I do firmly – but because I have stated more than once that I think her musicality was of the utmost importance, in fact the base rock on which her marvellous choreography was built. Yet can I point to any recording that illustrates this? Not really. The few official recordings of her playing – the 1950s record of jigs and reels (featuring *The Mason's Apron, The Holly Tree* and *Off To Puck Fair*) and the 1971 record of Ulster dances (*The Flax Flower, The Herring Fleet, The Cutting Of The Turf, The Splashing Of The Churn* and *Ulster Tartan*) – give no impression of her very real virtuosity, particularly as they do not include the kind of music that was the best vehicle for this, namely, her wistful airs, which were so emotive. And by the time her fans had video cameras and could record the ballets, her best playing was long since gone. But even in the later days, there was an occasional glimpse of genius. I remember being at a performance of the ballets in Derry in the early 1980s and one young member of the audience was very impressed by her playing. He could appreciate her virtuosity even then. He is now a professional orchestral conductor, Paul Murphy, currently with Birmingham City Ballet.

She was fanatically anxious to prevent anyone recording her playing at festivals or performances of the ballets (none but a chosen few was honoured with this privilege) and she would not be prevailed upon to make recordings of her music, though several did try; Frances O'Hara, for example, was one who asked her to lay down some tracks for posterity, but to no avail. So the people who actually heard her play in the good old days are steadily dwindling in number. But those not in that group don't just have to take our word for it. The fact that Ralph Vaughan Williams was interested enough to go and hear her is surely a fine endorsement.

At one of the many festivals to which Mulholland dancers were invited, Douglas Kennedy (President of the English National Folk Dance Society) introduced Patricia to Ralph Vaughan Williams. Much to her delight, the composer recalled how he had met Patricia before and that in fact he'd made a point of going to hear her play whenever he could. One has only to hear any version of *The Lark Ascending* to imagine how Ralph Vaughan Williams would have enjoyed Miss Mulholland's virtuosity. Her repertoire of folk music would also have been of great interest to him.

Her musical compositions stand on their own, her several slip-jigs and the set dances mentioned earlier.

When it comes to exploring influences that produced the choreographer Patricia Mulholland, this is no easy task either. She must, of course, have initially been influenced by her own teacher, Peadar O'Rafferty, and indeed her sister Stella. However, the greatest input into the making of her steps came, in my view, from the music itself. If we remember a description of her sitting down to choreograph, playing the fiddle while moving her feet, it tells us all. She did not often think of how other people performed a step, or what the fashion was, but went to the music first and then brought her experience and "vocabulary" of steps to it.

Which is not to say that she could not reflect changing fashion or that she could not choreograph to order. One might say that all of the choreography of the ballets was used to suggest certain moods or emotions. The ability to suit steps to individuals was the secret of her successful set dances.

The first time I saw the "hectic" beating of modern heavy dancing was in the feet of a girl who came to Miss Mulholland as an already established dancer. Linda McElwee had learned her Irish dancing in England and went on to have her own school of very polished dancers. But Miss Mulholland used to criticise her style at first: 'far too many beats,' etc. However, after Linda left, the Mulholland set dances began to change – more trebles were used per bar; it became much more complicated and demanding. Patricia could not resist swapping *The Blackbird* for her revamped *Rodney's Glory* in her ballet, *The Hound Of Culann*. Now it just so happened that among her pupils she now had dedicated enthusiasts: the Revies, Nicola Brown, Linda Tansley. They were not afraid of hard work and learned the new set dances a few bars at a time.

Perhaps the new-style heavy dancing had to wait for those capable of doing it, for I don't think my contemporaries, or those who followed immediately after, would have practised enough to cope with the new regime. (In fact, practising at all was not high on the agenda for most of us. There were a few exceptions, of course.) The new set dances simply cannot be danced without long practice, time and dedication. Peadar O'Rafferty proclaimed in the '60s that modern solo dancing was much more difficult than it had been in his day. It's rather like improvements in athletics, I suppose, where records are made to be broken.

But I can't point to the work of specific ballet companies or art movements that found their way into Patricia Mulholland's dancing in the way I can look at *Riverdance* and say, 'Oh, isn't that like the men in *St Patrick's Day*!' or 'Isn't that like talking with the feet in *Lir*!' It is true that she had seen short examples of European folk ballet on the continent. She was certainly aware of classical ballet and rightly supposed that Irish dance could be just as valid a medium for balletic expression. Nevertheless, I can't say that she went to see certain dancers or studied certain techniques in the way that I might if making a critique of modern dance experts, although, funnily enough, the reverse is true.

The Mulholland style and the Patricia Mulholland Irish Ballet sprang fully formed, as it were, from the mind of Patricia Mulholland, rather like Athena fully armed from the head of Zeus. Its development can be traced more easily than its influences.

The basic influence is, of course, Irish music (and in the case of the ballets, Irish legend). In this aspect, she might be compared with a composer who takes the folk tunes of his native land and uses them as the basis for a classical treatment. In an interview for the *Belfast Newsletter* in March 1991, just a year before her death, in which she was described by Steven Moore as an 'enigmatic music lover', she said, tellingly, 'Music is my life. I'd give up the dancing rather than the music. I always loved the music. People used to say to me to teach, but I wouldn't have taught music for anything. I loved it too much.'

She can also be compared with choreographer Joan Denise Moriarty. Miss Moriarty and she are very similar in that they selflessly pursued their own vision, continually hampered (especially at the end) by worries about funding. But the Cork woman's creation was in the established classical ballet mode; Miss Mulholland's was grounded in her own version of the local folk dance.

There is no question that she was an important figure in general dancing terms. Choreographers like Frederick Ashton knew her work and consulted her on occasion. (He, too, choreographed to an individual dancer's strengths.)

A public relations memo from the Arts Council in the '60s pointed out that: 'Patricia Mulholland and her company were once sought out by the great Massine to teach him the fundamentals of the Irish style, and companies as noted as the Netherlands National Ballet and the Ballet Rambert have paid Patricia Mulholland the compliment of serious study.'

Companies like Ballet Rambert and London Contemporary Dance visited her rehearsals when they were in Belfast (no doubt a little surprised to find some of the *corps de ballet* playing snooker at one end of the room – a Scout hall the rest of the week – and dancers eating bags of chips at the break).

> Believe I am most grateful for all you have done for the 'Irish Ballet' — I know it can be a most frustrating business, and sometimes, indeed very often I feel like twishing it all, and then I get a remark like this one, said to me last sat. by the leading male dancer of the Ballet Rambert, & I quote "some day I dream of going back to Scotland (he's a Scot) & doing for my Country what you are doing for Ireland". He & B. Neiby (televis Rambert) seemed most

Letter from Miss Mulholland to Fergus Gilligan, quoting compliments received from a dancer in the prestigious Ballet Rambert in England.

An incident from the 1960s illustrates just what an impression was made on professional dancers. Ger Van Leeuwen, the official photographer with Dutch Theatre Ballet was gathering Irish material for his book on the theatre and went to a Mulholland rehearsal to take photos. He told his own company, who were visiting Belfast at the time, about what he'd seen and they were intrigued enough to go and have a look. Two members of the Dutch group, Marten Molema and Joop Stokcis, had some difficulty in finding the Mulholland dancers but persevered and eventually found them performing at the War Memorial Hall in Waring Street. They expressed surprise at the professional standard of the dancing they found and actually learned a few traditional steps from Miss Mulholland before they left.

London Festival Ballet director Norman McDowell chats to Joyce Ann Henry, Marlene Bailie and Margot Bell on the Grove Theatre stage in 1967 (courtesy of the Irish News).

Within the confines of Northern Ireland, she was considered too temperamental to attract continuing serious funding from the Arts Council. The initial enthusiasm this body had exhibited waned as time went on and personnel changed. She had fewer champions to fight her corner.

Her company of dancers was not the same either; some of the individual dancers had great ability and technique but the ballets simply weren't the same. There were not enough boys to stage the work as intended. Her own weakening health, not to mention the passage of time, was taking its toll. She did not have the same grip on her dancers as before. Nor was she remotely interested in a more commercial approach when it came to her Irish Ballets if it entailed relinquishing her autonomy. A good business manager might have made a huge difference to her career and that of her company's. But by the time she might have been prepared to submit to such a consideration, the ballets did not have the commercial potential they might once have had. The moment had passed.

Then she was too avant garde, not to mention too Northern, to attract funding or even interest from the Irish arts machine, bar a few television appearances. (The Republic, of course, had its own doyenne of dance in Joan Denise Moriarty, who struggled throughout her career, finally having the rug pulled from under her just as her company was beginning to really attract international attention.)

Several people have suggested that the fact that she was a woman was a grave disadvantage and that her work as a choreographer would probably have been taken more seriously if she had been a man. It's difficult to prove this proposition, but there's every likelihood that her sex was no help. Legislation to deal with discrimination on grounds of sex is a comparatively recent innovation. While there's no suggestion that Patricia Mulholland ever felt this herself, the thinking of past times certainly tended to put men before women in every field. (My own mother thought that men should be paid more than women! Her mother, on the other hand, went to join the suffragette movement – apparently, they had an office in High Street in Belfast.)

Patricia Mulholland was simply far ahead of her time, and it is sad to think that her unique gifts escape the attention they merit.

Her dancers reflected the community from which they came. The Patricia Mulholland Irish Ballet Company was absolutely a product of Northern Ireland. But you cannot pin down the ballets and say, 'Obviously Ulster-Scots,' or even, 'Obviously Belfast or County Antrim.' There is a universality about the ballets and that is the best part of her achievement. Sure, it was definitely Irish dancing used as the basic medium, but the resultant works of art went beyond the local.

Did Patricia Mulholland make a contribution to Irish culture? Certainly – a significant one. From her first ballet *The Dancer* to her last *The Whirlpool,* she moulded the basic clay of traditional dance into a more universally acceptable art form. Audiences at *The Dancer* in the Ulster Hall in 1951 responded immediately and continued to do so to all the other ballets for the next forty years.

These works (with the exception of *Ulster Anthology*) have not been performed since her death, but they are not entirely lost to posterity; all the choreography was written down – Miss Mulholland had her own notation system – and these notes are in the possession of her family. There is a treasure trove waiting for someone to delve into.

While Patricia Mulholland's name may not be as celebrated as it should be, she was nonetheless appreciated by many more than her own dancers and audiences of her ballets.

International Women's Year, 1975, was the year that Queen's University conferred an honorary degree on Patricia Mulholland. She was admitted to the degree of Master of Arts in recognition of her contribution to the community. The encomium read out at her conferring listed all the institutes and organisations for which she had lectured, also the places to which she had been invited to bring teams of dancers, to name just a few: the Royal Albert Hall and Festival Hall in London, Oxford, Stratford-on-Avon, Italy, France, Spain, Sweden, Denmark, Isle of Man, Llangollen and Pitlochry.

It continued: 'Her eminence as an outstanding authority on the purest forms of Irish dancing is acknowledged and respected. Yet she has felt free to depart from the strict canons to evolve a folk ballet of national character and unique charm. Many of the ballets are based on Irish legends, others on traditional Irish folk and popular songs. Some of the ballets are intensely dramatic; others are gay, colourful, witty and entertaining. The substructure of the traditional dance form is always evident but it has been extended into a new context of freer movement and mime.

'She has also revived many little-known Irish dance-tunes in the minor key, which have since reached much wider audiences in arrangements by David Curry.

'All this activity has been made possible by a very remarkable personality that has attracted the enthusiasm of many talented and skilled people. The company has toured extensively in Northern Ireland under Arts Council auspices. It seldom numbers less (sic) than fifty people and each presentation is an administrative and artistic achievement for which Patricia Mulholland must be seen as the key, co-ordinating figure.'

Miss Mulholland showing her mother her Master's scroll in 1975. Sadly, by that time, it is unlikely that Minnie was capable of appreciating it.

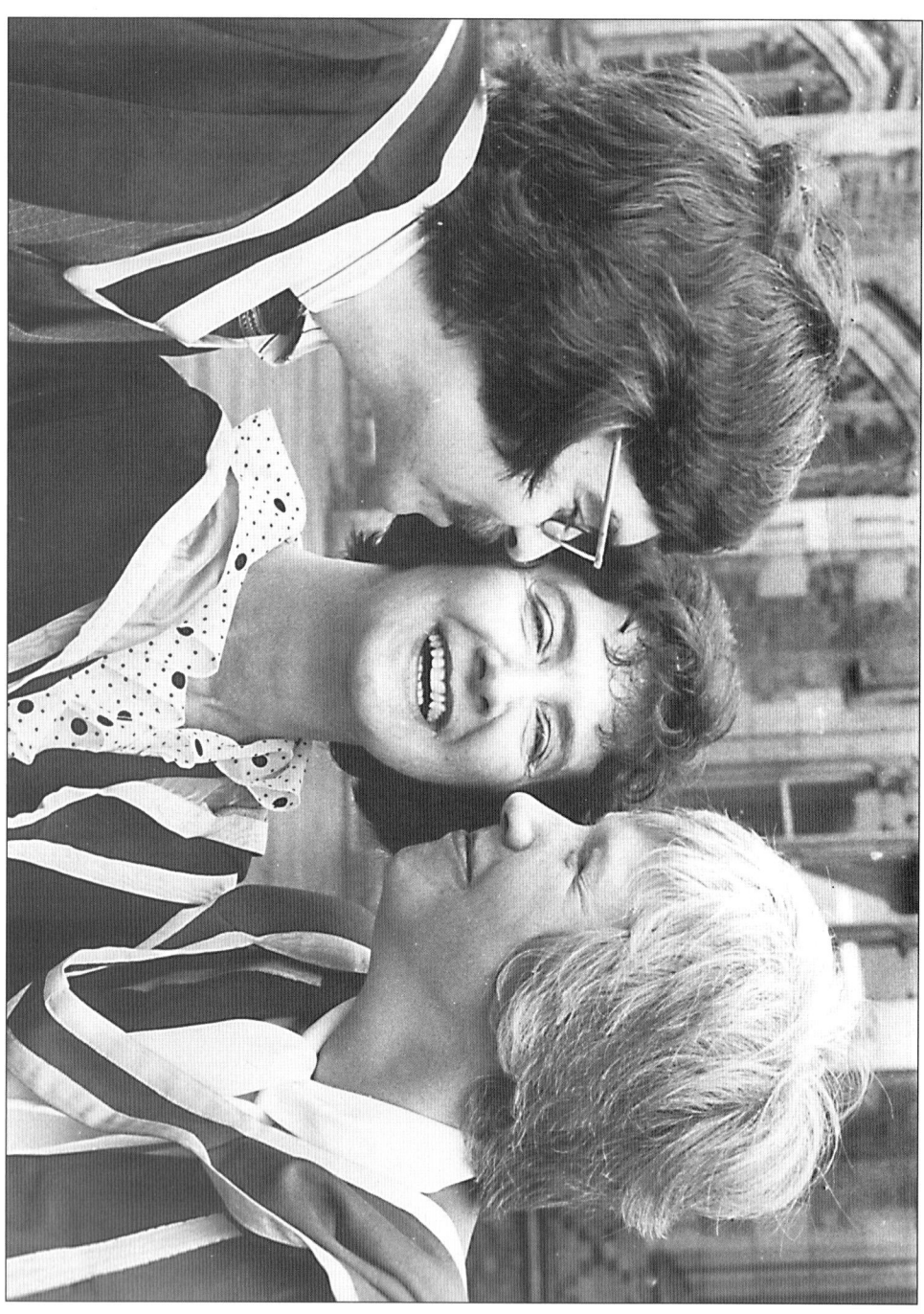

Henry Toner and Sheelagh Gilligan share graduation day with their dancing teacher in 1975.

Sr Mary Turley, Miss Mulholland and guests, Jo and Lena Tomelty at the Flax Trust Award ceremony in 1991.

The following decade saw Patricia Mulholland accepting an MBE for her services to dance. After receiving her medal at Buckingham Palace in 1984, she was taken to lunch at Claridges by Grainne Gilmore.

The last, and in the eyes of some, most prestigious award conferred on Miss Mulholland was the Flax Trust Award, which she received in 1991, shortly before she died. The trophy itself is a piece of bog-oak sculpted in hexagonal columns like the Giant's Causeway. It is awarded to people who have contributed to cross-community understanding.

The mission statement of the Flax Trust says that it is for 'the reduction and, if possible, the elimination of community tensions and religious prejudices engendered by the economic depression of the area.'

Miss Mulholland had worked to this end all her life. The lasting friendships of the members of her company, across all shades of religion (and none), are as much a testament to her good influence as the Flax Trust Award.

The list of other recipients of this award is impressive and includes Senator George Mitchell, General John de Chastelain, Jim Sheridan, Tom Foley, Mary McAleese, John Hume, Al Gore and Bill Clinton.

In addition to receiving this award, Miss Mulholland's company was presented with the Enrichment Through Respect for Cultural Difference bursary award. Both awards were presented to her at a gala evening in the Golden Threads Theatre, when those present were entertained to one of the last performances of the Patricia Mulholland Irish Ballet Company, which included the premiere of her last ballet *Bantry Bay*.

Patricia Mulholland died on 29 July 1992. On her memorial card were quoted lines of WB Yeats from *The Fiddler Of Dooney*:

'And the merry love the fiddle
And the merry love to dance.'

Nicholas Brady's *Ode On St Cecilia's Day* was also quoted:

'And every graceful note to Heaven
Repays the melody it lent.'

St Cecilia is, of course, the patron saint of music.

Hook and Chain – Festival Dancing

[Irish dancing] is probably the finest of the entire folk canon of the British Isles.
A V Coton, Daily Telegraph

The largest part of Patricia Mulholland's legacy is the treasure that she leaves in the memories of those who knew her. But a more tangible heritage is the successful growth of festival dancing.

When she started her teaching career, all Irish dancers competed together at both festivals and feiseanna. When she was expelled from the Irish Dancing Commission, festivals benefited greatly from being the only competitive platform for her dancers.

In a system lacking formal examinations, competition is important as a means of improving standards and shaping technique.

It is a common practice in Ireland for children to be sent to music, elocution or dancing lessons and for them then to perform on stage in competitions either as soloists or members of school teams. Although your first festival can be a bit bewildering for parents as much as performers, you soon become accustomed to the system. Grainne Agnew at her first outing faced the wrong way and performed into the wings. But she soon got the hang of it – believe me.

Leslie Baird was recalled *twice* by George Leonard in his first competition, the only recall out of 120 competitors, and his grandmother approached the adjudicator saying, 'If you just tell him what he's doing wrong, I'm sure he'll be able to fix it.'

There is a long tradition of this practice going back into the mists of time. But the institution of the festival competition in its present form can be traced to just over a hundred years ago.

Towards the end of the nineteenth century, competitions were springing up in many places in Britain for bands, choirs and other ensembles. This spirit was much in evidence in Ireland also, as Dublin's Feis Cheoil (now Siemens Feis Cheoil) was the first in the island, followed by Derry in 1899. At the start of the twentieth century, under the influence of folklorists and historians such as FJ Biggar, several areas associated with Irish culture started their own local feiseanna, eg Feis na nGleann was founded in 1904 in Glenariff and included competitions in Irish language, traditional music and dance, and contests in athletics and hurling.

Belfast and Coleraine Festivals were established in 1908, in Portadown and Dungannon in 1922, Carrickfergus in 1923, and Larne and Ballymena in 1925.

Some English festivals were started by famous individual artists, eg the Leith Hill Musical Festival in England was begun by Ralph Vaughan Williams in 1905. It was around this time that several people – among them Henry Wood (of Proms fame) – felt that an association of these festivals would be a good idea. But it was not until 1921 that the British Federation of Festivals was founded by a group of famous artists, Edward Elgar, Adrian Boult and Gustav Holst among them. Nowadays, about one million amateur performers in music, song and dance take part in festivals across the UK, Ireland and the Channel Islands.

However, the introduction of Irish dancing, under the title "folk-dancing", to several festivals here, dates only to 1927. As Éamon Ó Gallchobhair points out in his essay The Cultural Value of Festival and Feis (in Aloys Fleischman's book, *Music In Ireland*), referring to festivals, '. . . for financial reasons mainly, folkdance competitions have been provided.' Ulster was fortunate in that Peadar O'Rafferty was largely instrumental in getting it off to a good start. In July of 1927, for example, only two years after its foundation, Larne Feis committee decided to introduce Irish dancing to its programme and held a public meeting to test the water.

Contemporary newspaper reports describe how Peadar O'Rafferty was invited to address the meeting and was enthusiastically received, to the extent that the entire audience learned an Irish dance step then and there. He arranged to start a class the following Saturday, promising that he would bring along two of his dancers who also played the piano and violin. (Might these have been Stella and Patricia Mulholland? Later, Sharon Tansley's mother remembers being taught by Stella, with Patricia accompanying her, in the old King's Arms in Larne.) This was the start of Irish dancing in Larne, a town that has produced great dancers and devotees of Irish dancing ever since.

Two years later, in 1929, the first Northern Irish Dancing Festival was held in the Ulster Hall in Belfast. (Feis Béal Feirste did not start until 1932.) This was adjudicated by Dennis Cuffe. Dinny, as he was called, combined his dancing class with Kitty Murtagh's to allow his pupil, Maggie O'Kane, and Kitty's pupil, George Leonard, to dance couples together. They were never beaten.

Joint first prize-winners in the heavy jig at the '29 festival were Elsie Kerr and Frank Mulholland (Patricia's brother.) Second in the *Fairy Reel* was Miss Mulholland's team and, to quote the *Whig*'s description of the intermediate step-dancing (jig or reel), 'In this section, the beautiful, rhythmic dancing was enhanced by the beauty of the dress worn by Patricia Mulholland, who won first place, wearing a delightfully embroidered green dress and cloak.'

Larne Festival in 1930. Betty Lewis, on left, went on to win an All-Ireland title twelve years later.

The Honourable The Irish Society dance team, prize-winners at Coleraine Festival, 1935.

Ballymena Festival included Irish dancing from this time, as did Dungannon (1931). And Mulholland teams and those of the BFDS, the Lambeg FDS and Scouts and Guides were regularly mentioned in dispatches at these venues.

Dancers competed at both feiseanna and festivals. The Londonderry Feis (as distinct from Feis Dhoire) had Irish dancing competitions in the '30s and '40s, though not in more recent years. The Honourable The Irish Society School had prizewinning teams entered in Coleraine Festivals at this time.

Portadown Musical Festival's folk dancing section in 1933 had to arrange an extra session due to the record numbers of entries – this took place in the Boys Brigade Hall. All Irish dancers, up to about 1949 or thereabouts, would have been members of the same club, so to speak, and would have viewed the All-Ireland and Ulster Championships as the ultimate in competitions. That is not the case today.

Festival dancers and feis dancers never compete at the same venues now. Festival dancing is a completely different institution, with its own competitions and traditions. Before Mulholland dancers' departure from the Coimisiún, they would have participated in both types of competition. After their excommunication they followed one road only, that of festivals.

In 1951, Maureen McCann was approached by Major Affleck of Bangor Festival (founded in 1947) to organise the Irish dancing section there. She also started festival dancing in Newtownards and was largely responsible for its introduction to Holywood in 1954. Secretary of this festival is now Claire McElhinney, who teaches in the town and who once taught dancing on the Shankill Road in Belfast.

Maureen's father was Paddy McCann, a famous local footballer who played for Belfast Celtic and Glentoran. She learned dancing with Miss Mulholland, first in Bangor, but must have shown promise for she was asked to go along to Newington Street for extra lessons.

When she left school, the nuns there asked her to take over their dancing classes and

Below and right: Mulholland dancers perform St Patrick's Day *in 1983. L-R: Nicola Brown, John McCollum, Ida Lewis, Robert Hunter, Kathy O'Connor, Damien Corr, Deirdre Hawthorne, Leslie Baird, Lillias Reilly, Robbie Lightbody, Donna Revie and Dominic Corr (by kind permission of the Belfast Telegraph).*

this experience was to stand her in good stead when Miss Mulholland needed an assistant from time to time.

Being a generous and mild-mannered woman, she was saddened by the Mulholland split from the Gaelic League; however, she believes it was caused by jealousy rather than any infraction of rules. At the same time, she was delighted to be part of the teams who went to international festivals all over Europe and felt that a letter of thanks should have been sent to Dublin for freeing them for these trips abroad.

Maureen had a friend in the Red Cross who asked her to bring a group of dancers to an anniversary concert in London. She brought eight dancers (three of them Red Cross volunteers whom she trained in eight weeks) to the Albert Hall, where they danced to great acclaim. A Bangor factory made costumes for the dancers. On this occasion and on several others, in the course of her dancing and teaching, she was encouraged by people like Lady Londonderry and Princess Margaret, whom she described as a very down-to-earth, no-nonsense sort of person.

Maureen **arranged many concerts for the Catholic Church building fund. But it was at Bangor Festival that most of us would have met her first,** helping us to get ready for going on stage with infinite patience and kindness. She also helped at Belfast, particularly at the Gold Medal competition when, up to recently, she would have added the marks of the three adjudicators and kept at least one of them supplied with sweets.

In the '50s and '60s, several dancing teachers from the Commission tradition, like Patricia Mulholland and Maureen McCann, would have already been recognised teachers, though then operating at festivals rather than feiseanna. Adjudicators were from a Commission background, too. Senior pupils who wanted to teach dancing would simply have set up on their own and gradually built up their schools. In some cases, a prospective teacher would have been "guaranteed" by his/her own mentor as having the right credentials. However, as time went on, this was felt to be too casual. A group of teachers got together and decided that a recognised qualification would be a good idea.

It was also possible at this time to see Commission dancers, say, from Donegal or Tyrone, competing at festivals, although festival dancers could not reciprocate by competing in their feiseanna, so several teachers pooled their ideas for drawing up a more formal arrangement.

In 1972, the Festival Dancing Teachers' Association (FDTA) was founded. This group draws up its own rules and examines prospective dancing teachers. This examination takes the form of observing the candidate teaching a class. There is no written exam, but a candidate could be asked to take a class of eleven-year-olds, say, or a senior team dance, or to teach a set dance.

There is no prescribed list of set dances – a dancer is free to compose and choreograph as he/she sees fit and to take his chances with the adjudicator. Nor is there any rule about costume. However, there may be soon, as a few individuals have appeared recently wearing wigs – a practice that will be devoutly discouraged by the vast majority of the festival dancing world.

There are approximately thirty different schools, mainly in County Antrim, but also in Greater Belfast and its environs which belong to the FDTA.

The association runs its own Ulster Championships every Easter. A requirement of entry to this competition is to have danced and been placed, from first to eighth, in one or all of four festivals: Ballymena, Glenravel, Carrickfergus or Newcastle.

There is quite a range of styles of dancing within the group, from the obviously Mulholland-inspired O'Connor school and highly individualistic Graham school, to the approach of some of the Antrim dancers, whose style would not be too out of place at a Commission event.

Dominic Graham dancers. Dominic has schools throughout Northern Ireland.

It is fascinating to see several different styles of dancing in one competition, particularly in the case of the set dances where a dancer might even have prepared a piece set to specially composed music, completely outside the traditional repertoire.

However, not all festival dance teachers belong to the FDTA, and their pupils would limit their appearances, from choice, to Portadown, Bangor and their own class festivals.

One of the bigger competitions open to all festival dancers, whether FDTA or not, is the Northern Ireland Championships, held in May in Newtownards (up to very recently, this had always been in Bangor). This started in the year 1958, when the junior champions were Irene McCann and Brian Bunting, the intermediate champions Grainne Agnew and Dermot Brooks, and the seniors were Kevin Campbell and Bridie Kemp.

First winners of the Northern Ireland Championship with the Mayor of Bangor, 1958.

In June every year, what used to be a festival confined to those whom Patricia Mulholland wished to invite continues with a Gold Medal competition at its close. Like the Northern Ireland and Ulster Championships, there are three adjudicators and the prize is awarded on a points system, the prize being a genuine gold medal; a silver medal is awarded at a December competition.

Tír-na-nÓg school has a similar silver-medal event in October.

In 1996, the seventy-fifth anniversary of its founding, the British Federation of Festivals held a "Festival of Festivals" in the University of Warwick. Three hundred and three entries were chosen to represent the different festivals around the British Isles. In his introductory remarks in the programme of this event, the president of the federation, Sir Claus Moser, said, 'To be nominated for the Festival of Festivals denotes work of an exceptional standard.' There were three entries from festival dancing: a team from the O'Reilly school representing Bangor, a team of Irene McCann's representing Holywood, and soloist Iain Mackay representing Ballymena. Curiously, the Portadown dancers were not nominated from their own home town.

Holywood's committee, in view of the historic nature of the occasion, held a special competition with a panel of adjudicators to decide who would represent them in

England, and the McCann dancers won their place in this way. It is an unfortunate fact that some personnel connected with the running of festivals have, or had, what can only be considered a bigoted view of Irish dancing, without having any qualms, however, about accepting the lucrative entries from that quarter. Portstewart, too, was reluctant to allow an adjudicator even to nominate a certain team for consideration for the English festival. Happily, things are changing as the old regime gives way to the new.

The McCann team won a gold medal, one of only eight from among the 303 entries.

They performed *Treasures Of Ireland*, a pictorial team dance that illustrates various well-known ancient Irish artefacts such as the Ardagh Chalice.

Some of Irene McCann's dancers from Portadown.

Irene McCann has been teaching dancing for four decades now. She started off in Portadown Town Hall but has taken classes in several venues, including the Garvaghy Road. She is an ex-pupil of Yvonne Hood, which in itself is a recommendation.

Yvonne is another person who came to Irish dancing by accident but who turned out to be a star. Her family was from Islandmagee, where the family operated the ferry; her father was a sea captain.

She had a weak chest as a child and was convalescing in hospital, where she became friendly with a girl who did Irish dancing and who showed her a few steps. She picked up this dancing quickly and enthusiastically. And when her mother casually mentioned this to her doctor, he suggested that it might have a therapeutic effect. This was how Yvonne came to be sent first to Gladys Carmichael, who had been a pupil of Miss Mulholland's. After a while, she and her sister went to Miss Mulholland herself in the old Laharna Hotel in Larne, and there they joined Betty and Peggy Lewis, Marjorie Andrews and Maisie Gurley, among others.

It had been love-at-first-sight for Yvonne and Irish dancing; she became a champion and then a teacher. If her dancers reflected anything of her style, then there can be no doubt that Yvonne was a graceful dancer. I personally remember the elegant Loretto Breen in her cream costume with its blue-lined cape, doing rocks that nobody at the time could emulate. The Turleys were also expert pupils of Yvonne. Recently, I saw an old programme of Portadown Festival; it belonged to Valerie Canavan and her mother had marked the prize-winners on it. Imagine my delight to discover that I had been recalled in a slip-jig competition that was won by Loretto Breen – I've been basking in reflected glory ever since.

Yvonne helped Miss Mulholland with her teaching right up to the end. Indeed, several dancers have admitted that they would choose to go to Yvonne for help if they had forgotten something rather than Miss Mulholland. Her daughter Alison, a principal in the ballets, now teaches Irish dancing in Bangor.

So while Miss Mulholland cannot accurately be said to have started festival dancing, she can certainly be said to have been an essential part of its development and to have influenced it, both directly and indirectly. It is unlikely that it could have prospered in the way it has if there had not been a ready-made corps of entrants in her own pupils, and in turn, in their schools. Her dancers have continued the festival tradition since its earliest days, whether as competitors, teachers, adjudicators or administrators.

She was also essential to several festivals in that she was official accompanist at Bangor, Holywood, Portadown and Portstewart for a while. While non-Mulholland dancers might not have taken the same comfort from her presence as her own pupils did, they cannot deny that she provided a cornucopia of music to dance to, playing with great feeling, especially for the set dances.

The first time I adjudicated at Bangor – a time when she wasn't playing due to ill health – I almost dreaded what was in store; however, my fears were allayed when Jane Stewart took her place. While someone else's playing could never replace Miss Mulholland's, the old tunes played in non-traditional fiddle style still bring you back to yesteryear. Iain Mackay is now an experienced and entertaining accompanist at festivals, having been an excellent dancer to boot.

Iain Mackay and his mother Hilda are in the back row on the left.

I have enjoyed the keyboard skills and also the company of Rose Murray at different venues. It was with her that I first heard dancers asking for a set dance at such-and-such a speed, where she sets her electronic metronome at what they consider the optimum tempo for their performance. This practice ensures that they can't complain that the music is too fast/slow and avoids the waving up and down of hands during an introduction. At first sight, it seems terribly modern and mechanical, but I suppose it's no more so than the mention of 'length' on ancient manuscripts at the start of a tune, conveying the length of string in a pendulum that would provide the correct tempo – an early model of metronome.

Gertie Brady accompanied Miss Mulholland on the piano at festivals and the ballets for many years. Margot Brown took over from her in the early '70s and stayed with her right to the end. She's still to be found at the piano at Bangor, Holywood and Belfast. In my early days at the adjudicating, I found her help indispensable, especially during set dances that were outside the traditional, expected repertoire. For instance, during one period, somebody came up with the theme from the television series *The Thorn Birds* as a suitable theme for a set dance, called variously *Father Ralph, Megan's Song* or *The Thorn Birds*. I asked Margot to let me know, discreetly if possible, when the end of the right foot of the set was coming up, if I didn't need to see any more, because, of course, I was unfamiliar with this arrangement. Margot was more than helpful. As the end of the set approached, she removed her foot from the piano pedal and stretched out her leg. I got the message.

There are several obvious differences between festival- and feis-dancing which would strike the visitor straightaway. Some of the least attractive aspects of feis-going are thankfully missing from festivals and will remain unseen at them – I hope. For example, what I call the "Beauty Pageant Babies" are nowhere to be found – those very young dancers who are tanned and made-up like their older sisters and who hug their fellow prize-winners and cry when they discover they've won a competition. (Rumour has it that the Commission rules are to be changed soon so that junior dancers will no longer be unsuitably decorated thus.) Nor will you see dancers relaxing between competitions, wearing revealing practice outfits.

But perhaps the biggest contrast in senior festival dancing, other than appearance, is the almost total absence of antagonism or animosity. A colleague from school, who is more familiar with the feis side of things and who is no mean choreographer herself, accompanied me to a festival and was amazed to find such a relaxed and friendly atmosphere. The senior dancers all know each other; and while there is rivalry between schools and individuals, it is friendly rivalry and makes for a more relaxed and well-intentioned entertainment. Feis dancers might say, in their defence, that there is more to lose at their functions and more to gain, seeing that the vast majority of the professional Irish dance shows employ Coimisiún dancers. Nevertheless, the actual standard of dancing at both is similarly high. Gerry Hobbs, adjudicator for An Comhdháil, is of the opinion that there is no difference in standard between the two, though the styles may be dissimilar. He believes that in the '50s and early '60s, most festival dancers were well behind their feis counterparts in technique but that this disparity is no longer distinguishable.

Schools of Festival Dancing in Northern Ireland

Aislinn* (Denise Catney) – Belfast
Anderson – Portadown
Bangor* (Alison Graham) – Bangor
Ballynafeigh (Gertie Mulligan) – Belfast
Breslin – Newtownards
Castletown (Elaine Taggart) – Antrim
Dempsey – Larne
Dunlop – Ballymoney
Glenarn* (Michelle Oaks, née Forster) – Larne
Glenravel – Glenravel
Graham – Belfast, Newcastle, Ballymoney, Portrush
Hosik – Newtownards, Donaghadee
Knockagh (Joan and Shauna Caldwell) – Carrickfergus
Lough Giel (Marie Houston and sister Colette) – Loughgiel
McCann – Portadown
McElhinney* – Holywood
McGuinness – Limavady
Mackay* – Ballyclare and Templepatrick
O'Connor* – Belfast
O'Connor* – Banbridge
Ollar – Coleraine
Porter – Portaferry
Reilly* – Holywood
Royal Tara (McCalmont) – Carrickfergus
St Comgall's – Bangor
Seven Towers – Ballymena
Tír-na-nÓg* (Jackie White) – Belfast
Edwina Wright – Limavady

* Taught personally by Patricia Mulholland

Festival Dancing Venues in Northern Ireland

Ballymena	Holywood
Ballymoney	Larne
Belfast (Belvoir)	Limavady
Carryduff	Newcastle
Coleraine	Newtownards
Glenravel	Portadown
Greenisland (formerly Carrickfergus)	Portstewart

It is no exaggeration to claim that the vibrant state of festival dancing can be attributed largely to the efforts of Patricia Mulholland, for it was her pupils who performed in numbers at festivals and some now have classes of their own. Many teachers of festival dancing have been taught by Mulholland pupils in their turn, and so the legacy lives on.

Mulholland ballets have not been seen since 1991, but the fact that Kathy O'Connor has begun to continue the tradition is to be applauded. The Patricia Mulholland Irish Ballet Company has a direct descendant in Trim The Velvet. Its founder, Kathy O'Connor, has followed in her mentor's footsteps in not only teaching Irish dancing but also in choreographing and directing folk ballets – two, so far.

Kathy's mother, Eileen, danced in the first *Cúchulainn* in the Empire Theatre. She enjoyed this experience, but her dancing career was cut short when she was sent to boarding school in Kilkeel. (In January 1959, some of the girls in the company stayed overnight in the school when the ballets were being performed there.) It is no surprise that her daughters went to Miss Mulholland, for not only was there the earlier connection with Patricia, but it was convenient, too, because the family lived on the Antrim Road.

Kathy was always an enthusiastic dancer and learned avidly as a pupil of Miss Mulholland. She just loved going to dancing, taking to it like a duck to water. Not only did she attend her own class, but she loved to watch the dancers in older age groups. She would also have been a keen spectator at festivals, staying on after her own competitions.

Just as in the case of other talented and industrious dancers, she inspired new compositions from her teacher. Two set dances, *The Whirlpool* and *The Spinning Wheel*, were directly based on her ability and style.

Kathy's first role in the ballets was as a wave in *The Children Of Lir*. She went on to dance most of the principal parts and was cast as Sava in what would have been the last *Mother Of Oisín*, but she was disappointed that it never got beyond the rehearsal stage. The cancer that had first attacked Miss Mulholland in 1977 returned and this meant that major undertakings had to be postponed. However, Patricia rallied one last time and her final Irish Ballet was *Bantry Bay*, based largely on the set-dance music composed for Kathy but with the addition of other pieces with a watery theme, such as *The Meeting Of The Waters*. This venture was largely funded by Miss Mulholland herself. Kathy recalls, ruefully, that one costume was made from a flowing green dress of Patricia's own that she donated to be cut up and remodelled.

Kathy became a friend of Miss Mulholland's as much as one of her dancers and she used to drop in to visit her often and simply have a chat. This habit started early in their acquaintance and continued up to the end of Patricia's life.

It was a direct request from Patricia Mulholland that started Kathy on her teaching career. She was a first-year student at Jordanstown at the time, still keen enough to go along to dancing class and even help with the teaching. Miss Mulholland asked her to go to Cregagh Estate in Belfast one Saturday to start an Irish dancing class. There was no history of Irish dancing in the area. Kathy believes that it all started simply as a Saturday afternoon activity for young girls at a time when Belfast was still riven by inter-community strife. Miss Mulholland made sure that she remembered the basic dances for beginners, like the light double-jig and single-reels and supplied her with tapes of suitable music.

The girls who began dancing with Kathy then are, remarkably, still with her today. None of them had any connection with Irish dancing at all, and they were, every one of them, from the local community. The class continued in Cregagh for a while, but political unrest unfortunately made a move inevitable. An Irish dancing class composed entirely of Protestant youngsters had drawn attention to itself, and a newspaper was about to publish an article on this remarkable phenomenon, as some would see it, when Kathy was advised to stop the publication.

The O'Connor school moved to Belvoir. Kathy had applied to the Catholic St Bernard's new parochial hall for the use of a practice room. This application was refused. The Church of Ireland rector of Belvoir voluntarily offered her the use of his hall. (They say your own's the worst.)

The class has grown, so much so that Kathy teaches five days a week, taking off only Friday and Sunday. However, while the school was still in its infancy, their teacher had the opportunity to devote more time to them than she could now and she used to do little bits out of the ballets as well as the more usual repertoire of Irish dances.

Fond memories of dancing with Miss Mulholland and of the ballets were still very much with her. As her dancers matured, there were fewer challenges for them as they won competitions. So it was quite a natural development that Kathy should arrive at the point where she would choreograph an Irish Ballet.

There was no sudden flash of inspiration. Kathy says she always knew somehow that she would one day do something along the lines of a ballet. The notion had always been simmering away at the back of her mind and her dancers threw themselves into the new project with enthusiasm. In fact, the main problem was to come up with a story that did not require a company of men. Unfortunately, Kathy has no male dancers. Nowadays, if boys are keen on Irish dancing and turn out to be talented, they tend to join Coimisiún schools with the prospect of dancing professionally. So far, at any rate, there don't seem to be any young men in the Belvoir area interested in developing Irish dancing as a hobby.

Margot Brown's Aunt Clara found them the story of *The Fairy Thorn*. The next step was to find suitable music. Kathy says herself that music for accompaniment is a very big headache. She has to use recordings.

Although she would be the first to admit that Trim The Velvet's offerings are not on the scale of Mulholland ballets, and while she would be reluctant to compare herself with Patricia Mulholland, there can be no doubt of the source of her inspiration, which is instantly recognisable. She has stepped up to the mark and deserves great credit for even attempting to build on the tradition. *The Fairy Thorn* is her first entry into a "Celtic Twilight". Magic and menace are the themes and the overall effect is successful. The individual dancers are always impressive. The ending is sad and the emotion is heightened by the use of a solo violin which inevitably reminds the listener of Miss Mulholland.

The first performances of this work were in the studio theatre of the Waterfront Hall in Belfast. A contrasting piece was also performed. *Lannigan's Ball,* a colourful, light-hearted "romp" showing us dances of various nationalities, makes use of Kathy's pupils of different nationalities, including even an Egyptian belly-dance. The piece is based on the traditional team dance *Lannigan's Ball*, which is impressive when it is done well. Kathy's dancers exhibit great energy and vitality. Kathy claims that this ballet nearly composed itself. It is technically the first O'Connor Irish Ballet.

The O'Connor dancers do not limit their appearances to Northern Ireland; they are keen visitors to folk festivals in Scotland and France, for example.

There are two O'Connor sisters currently engaged in teaching Irish dancing. Clare has started a school in Banbridge – pioneering festival dancing in that area.

The two schools have similar costumes. Kathy's dancers wear a black costume trimmed with green; Clare's are the same, but trimmed with gold. Both wear a broad lace collar and have gold braid down the middle of the bodice, echoing the Mulholland costume.

This latter has now sadly disappeared. It could be seen for a while on the dancers of the Cavehill school. The Reilly dancers' new velvet costume is very similar to the Mulholland one, only the embroidery being different.

After Miss Mulholland's death, her school continued under this name, Cavehill. Margot Brown continued to teach, choreograph and accompany, as she had done for Patricia. She had started to accompany Miss Mulholland at the first performance of *An Bailé Gaelach* at the new theatre in Gaoth Dobhair, County Donegal, in 1972.

Yvonne McKinley has also helped with the teaching for many years

But as time has gone on, Margot has become Kathy's assistant and is happy to relinquish responsibility. So what remained of the Mulholland school has become subsumed into the O'Connor school.

However, reminders of the Mulholland costume can be seen, not only on the O'Connor dancers, but also on Claire McElhinney's dancers (blue with gold braid) and on Lillias Reilly's (green with gold braid).

This choice is quite deliberate – a tribute to their dancing teacher, whose like we will not see again.

A group of O'Connor dancers in Belvoir Theatre, Belfast, 2005.

Stiúrthóir : Patricia Mulholland
Bainisteoir Stáitse: Fergus Ó Giollagáin

1. Rincí éagsúla ó na Rinnceoirí

II. AN ROGAIRE DUBH

Mír 1. Sráidbhaile.

Ag rinnce daofa, cluin lucht an tsráidbhaile ceol nach sasuigheann iad. Ceol ó phíobaire agus é ag seinm "An Rogaire Dubh." Bíonn siad uilig ag magadh faoi ach amháin an cailín atá i ngrá leis. Cuireann athair an chailín an tóir air. Tig cailleach isteach le gandal. Goideann an píobaire an gandal agus marbhuigheann é.

Mír 2. Teach an Phíobaire.

Tá a mháthair mí-shásta leis. Tugann sé an gandal di. Tig an púca isteach agus cuireann an píobaire té gheasa.

Mír 3. Gleann na Sí.

Titeann an píobaire i ngrá le bean sí. Tig spiorad an ghandail aríst le píobá úra chuige.

Mír 4. Caoineann an chailleach a gandal. Iarann sé maitheamhnas uirthi. Bheir an púca a sheanphíoba arais don phíobaire agus tá a chuid ceoil níos fearr ná a bhí ariamh.

PRÍOMH-AISTEOIRÍ

Píobaire   -   -   -   -   Edmund Henry
A Chailín   -   -   -   -   Sharon Tansley
A hAthair   -   -   -   -   Séamus Rooney
An Chailleach -   -   -   -   Jane O'Rawe
An Gandal   -   -   -   -   Michael Newman
Máthair an Phíobaire   -   Síle Giollagáin
An Púca   -   -   -   Nóra Nic Giolla Bhríde
An Bhean Sí   -   -   -   Pádraicín Giollagáin

III. CUCHULAINN

An sean-scéal fá Chuchulainn gaisgíoch Chuige Uladh agus a chara Ferdia as Connacht. An dóigh ar éirigh le Meabha Banríon Chonnacht bruighinn a thógáil idir an bheirt charaid.

Mír 1. Cúirt Chonchubhar Mhic Neasa, Ard-Rí Uladh agus an gasúr Setanta ag imirt leis an aos óg.
Mír 2. Nar mharuigh Setanta an cú a bhí ag Culainn
Mír 3. Tír-ann Cúchulainn i ngrá le Eimer.
Mír 4. Cúchulainn agus Ferdia.
Mír 5. Pósadh Chúchulainn agus Eimer. Fágann Cúchulainn an féasta le troid in eadán arm Banríon Chonnacht.
Mír 6. Geallann an Bhanríon Meabha a níon le pósadh do Fherdia ach é an bhuaidh a fháil ar Chuchulainn.
Mír 7. Troideann an bheirt agus marbhuigheann Cúchulainn an cara is fearr a bhí age.
Mír 8 Cuchulainn ag troid ina aonar arm Chonnacht Bás Chuchulainn.

NA PRÍOMH-AISTEOIRÍ

Conchubhar Mac Neasa   -   -   Seán Ó Maonaigh
Setanta   -   -   -   -   Vincent Haigley
Culainn   -   -   -   -   Reginald McClure
An Cú   -   -   -   -   Peter Sturdy
Cuchulainn   -   -   -   -   Mac Uí Ghiollagáin
Ferdia,   -   -   -   -   Caoimhín Ó Raifterí
Eimer   -   -   -   -   Pádraicín Ní Ghiollagáin
             agus an comhluacht go h-iomlán.

IV. SIAMSA "PHIL THE FLUTER"
Siamsa grinn, scléip agus ceoil.

ÉIGSE ULADH
Dé Sathairn 15ú Aibreán
Leiriú ó na hAisteoirí ar chuid de scéaltaí Sheosaimh Mhic Grianna

Programme from the new theatre, Gaoth Dobhair, Donegal, 1972.

200

Leslie Baird is an experienced choreographer and producer of entertainments based on Irish dance.

Jackie White has begun to venture into this territory also, telling stories through dance.

Dominic Graham, while not a Mulholland pupil (he danced with Jean Tennant), has been a fan of Patricia's ever since meeting her at one Bangor Festival. His conversation with her there was the spark that kindled his own approach to Irish dancing. He has innovative ideas which have already caught the eye of television producers.

So I hope that the Mulholland inheritance will not be simply a thriving festival dancing scene (though that in itself is a good thing), but that it will continue to manifest itself in choreographers who are not afraid to experiment with new ideas while basing their work on truly Irish traditional dance and music.

Patricia Mulholland was far ahead of her time. It is perhaps only now that her approach to Irish dancing can be fully appreciated by anyone generally interested in Irish dance as well as those who were directly involved.

Commercially successful Irish dance productions have widened the audience for the art form and indeed, in my view, widened the outlook of the mainstream Irish dancing machine.

Ireland is a very different place now from what it was in 1949 – a more receptive place, I hope, and a more appreciative one for the exceptional talent of one of its daughters.

This book is an attempt to record the remarkable achievements of Patricia Mulholland so that her work can be appreciated by people other than those who actually knew her and to point out that she leaves a living legacy, not simply a dusty archive. Her spirit lives on in festival dancing. Long may it continue.

Bibliography

Bell, Sam Hanna, *The Theatre In Ulster*, Gill and MacMillan, 1972.

Blaney, Roger, *Presbyterians And The Irish Language*, Ulster Historical Foundation and the Ultach Trust, 1996.

Breathnách, Breandán, *Ceol Rince Na hÉireann, Cuid 1, 2 Agus 3*, An Gúm, 1985.

Campbell, JJ, *Legends Of Ireland*, Gill and MacMillan.

CEMA, Committee Annual Reports and Minutes, Public Records Office, Belfast.

Cullinane, John, *Aspects Of The History Of Irish Dancing* and *Further Aspects Of The History Of Irish Dancing*.

Fleischman, Aloys, ed, *Music In Ireland*, Cork University Press, 1952.

Fleischman, Ruth, *Joan Denise Moriarty: Founder Of Irish National Ballet*, Mercier Press, 1998.

Green, Alice Stopford, *The Old Irish World*, MacMillan and Co, 1912.

Hardiman, James, *Irish Minstrelsy, 1 And 2*, Irish University Press, 1971.

Hatton and Molloy, *Songs Of Ireland (Moore's Melodies)*, Boosey and Co.

Joyce, PW, *Old Irish Folk Music And Songs*, Longmans, Green and Co, 1909.

Kinsella, T, and Ó Tuama, S, eds, *An Duanaire: Poems Of The Dispossessed*, Dolmen Press, 1981.

Kinsella, Thomas, trans, *The Táin*, Oxford University Press in association with Dolmen Press, 1969.

Murray, Hugh, *Traditional Dance Forms With Special Reference To Irish Dance*, Linenhall Library, Belfast.

Ó Snodaigh, Pádraig, *Hidden Ulster: Protestants And The Irish Language*, Lagan Press, 1995.

O'Connor, Ulick, *All The Olympians*, Henry Holt, 1984.

Sutcliffe, Rosemary, The *High Deeds Of Finn MacCool*, Puffin.

The Petrie Collection Of The Ancient Music Of Ireland, University Press, Dublin, 1885.

Ulster Dances, Northern Ireland Arts Council, 1971.